For Annabel Sanderson, because you are awesome.
— Isabel Thomas

For my Sunshine Coast sisters, who opened my soul to the forest and the sea.
— Sara Gillingham

Dear Reader,

I've always been fascinated by wildlife, and after studying evolutionary biology, animal behavior and genetics in college, I thought myself quite the expert! Then, in my twenties, I left Europe for the first time. In South America, I got a hug from a giant anteater and watched a coati steal my snacks. In Australia, I saw cassowaries sashay along the roadside and heard the eerie clicking of snapping shrimp in a mangrove forest. In Southeast Asia, I caught the eyes of a slow loris in the glow of a flashlight and spotted stick insects the size of my arm. I realized I had barely begun to discover Earth's biodiversity, and set out to learn as much as I could.

Since then, I have written books about animals and microbes, plants and people—but this is the first book in which I've attempted to tackle the entire tree of life. An evolutionary "tree of life" models how certain groups of species are most likely to be related to one another, using the best evidence available at the time. Just like my adventures in the natural world, there is always something new to discover, and there is no such thing as a definitive universal tree of life. The tree of life we've used to organize the information in this book is based on two recent sources, which are listed below.

The tree of life continues to evolve. Perhaps you'll discover some of the secrets that still lie hidden in its extraordinary boughs and branches.

Isabel Thomas
–

The bacterial and archaean branches of our tree are based on: L. A. Hug, B. J. Baker, K. Anantharaman et al., "A new view of the tree of life," *Nature Microbiology*, vol. 1 (2016), article 16048.
The eukaryote branches of our tree are based on: F. Burki, A. J. Roger, M. W. Brown and A. G. B. Simpson, "The New Tree of Eukaryotes," *Trends in Ecology & Evolution*, vol. 35, issue 1 (2020), pp. 43–55.

As this book went to press, new scientific names for certain groups of prokaryotes (bacteria and archaea) were announced by the International Committee on Systematics of Prokaryotes (ICSP). The new names for groups included in this book are listed below, to help readers cross-reference new research.

- Acidobacteria will be known as **Acidobacteriota**
- Actinobacteria will be known as **Actinomycetota**
- Firmicutes will be known as **Bacillota**
- Bacteroidetes will be known as **Bacteroidota**
- Deinococcus-Thermus will be known as **Deinococcota**
- Dictoglomi will be known as **Dictyoglomota**
- Fusobacteria will be known as **Fusobacteriota**
- Gemmatimonadetes will be known as **Gemmatimonadota**
- Thaumarcheaota will be known as **Nitrososphaerota**
- Proteobacteria will be known as **Pseudomonadota**
- Spirochetes will be known as **Spirochaetota**
- Crenarchaeota will be known as **Thermoproteota**

For more information, see
https://doi.org/10.1099/ijsem.0.005056

A note about measurements:
Science uses the metric system of weights and measures (e.g. kilograms and meters). In the US, imperial measurements (e.g. miles and feet) are used in everyday life, so in most cases we have included both units in this book when describing the size of living things. The very smallest living things are described using metric measurements only, because there are no simple equivalents in the imperial system.

FULL OF LIFE

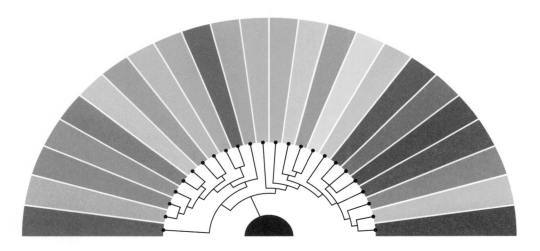

EXPLORING EARTH'S BIODIVERSITY

Words by ISABEL THOMAS   Pictures by SARA GILLINGHAM

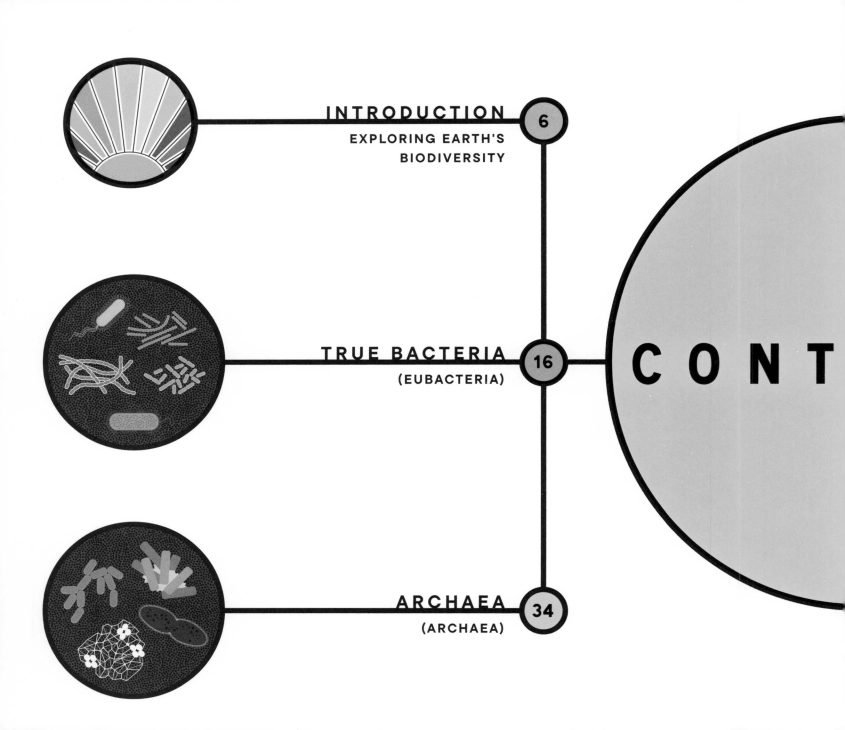

CONT

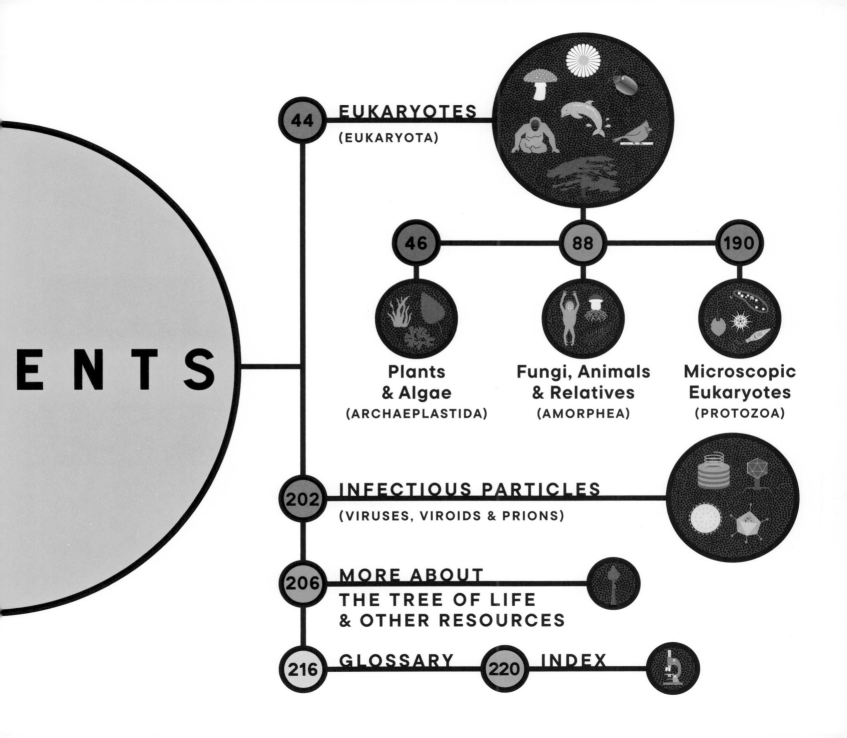

EXPLORING EARTH'S BIODIVERSITY

FROM THE TINIEST GERM TO THE BIGGEST BLUE WHALE, EVERY LIVING CREATURE IS PART OF THE SAME FAMILY TREE—EARTH'S TREE OF LIFE.

Earth is teeming, bustling, bursting with life. Fantastic creatures make their homes in every part of the planet, from the highest mountains to the deepest oceans. From scorched deserts to cold, dark caves. From fiery volcanoes to the folds of skin in your belly button.

Around 30,000 years ago, Stone Age people decorated caves with drawings of the living things they spotted: lions, bears, bison, deer, trees, water lilies, mammoths, and mushrooms. Ever since then, humans have been gathering knowledge about Earth's living things and passing it on through stories, songs, and paintings, in medical manuals and museum collections. The list has grown, and grown, and grown.

Each unique type of living thing—such as a sunflower, a lion, or a human—is known as a **species**. Today's computer databases include names for at least 2 million living species.

The largest species we've discovered so far is a humongous fungus that has been growing for at least 2,400 years. It spreads so far underground it could cover more than 1,665 football fields. The smallest species is a microbe called Nanoarchaeum, so miniscule that 2,500 could be lined up across the period at the end of this sentence. Nanoarchaeum can only be seen with a powerful microscope.

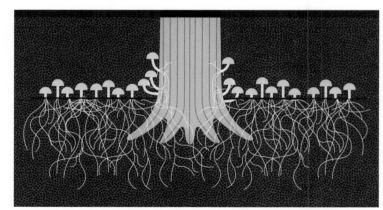

A honey fungus is Earth's largest living thing

KEEPING TRACK

Two million species is a giant list. If you named one species every second, it would take you 23 days to work through them all! The number is also changing constantly as new species appear and others die out and become **extinct**. So how do scientists keep track of the extraordinary, staggering, mind-boggling variety of life known as Earth's **biodiversity**?

At first, scientists interested in nature worked rather like the Stone Age artists did, making pictures of the plants and animals they saw around them. In fact, we can think of those ancient cave artists as the world's first **naturalists**, or natural history experts.

Gradually people began to record names and descriptions of plants, animals, and fungi. Creatures were collected from every corner of the world and sorted into groups based on the way they looked and behaved. This is known as **classification**. It was an important step toward better understanding life on Earth.

Naturalists also became interested in the fossils of creatures that used to live on Earth but are now extinct. A few hundred years ago, naturalists began to realize that some of these extinct creatures were the ancestors of today's living things. Based on all the evidence they had collected, scientists developed the theory of **evolution**, explaining that every living thing on Earth is part of one giant family tree: the tree of life on Earth.

THE TREE OF LIFE

A tree of life is a bit like a family tree that shows how you are related to your brother or sister, parents, grandparents, and all your other relatives. A tree of life shows how different species are related to one another.

Think of each of the world's 2 million living species as a leaf on the tree of life. We can trace back along the twigs, branches, and boughs to find its ancestors. All the species on the same stem, twig, or branch of the tree share at least one ancestor, known as their "**common ancestor**." If we keep going, we can trace right back to the root of the tree—the common ancestor of all life on Earth.

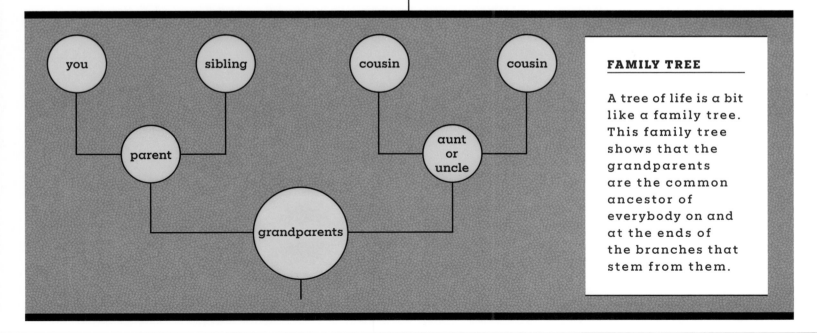

FAMILY TREE

A tree of life is a bit like a family tree. This family tree shows that the grandparents are the common ancestor of everybody on and at the ends of the branches that stem from them.

DRAWING A TREE OF LIFE

At first, trees of life were drawn by guessing how closely species were related by using clues from their bodies. For example, creatures with dry, scaly skin, such as snakes, lizards, and crocodiles, were put in a group called reptiles. Characteristics like scaly skin are inherited (passed on from parent to child), so scientists reasoned that the more similar two creatures looked, the more common ancestors they shared—and the more likely they were to belong on the same branch of the tree of life.

As scientists developed new technology, they could look at living things in far more detail. Scientists found ways to compare much smaller features of living things, including a tiny **molecule** called **DNA**, found inside almost every **cell** of every living thing. A creature's DNA acts as a set of "instructions" for growth and development. For example, a shark's DNA guides a shark's cells to grow into a shark, rather than a crocodile, a daffodil, or a human. A complete set of a creature's DNA instructions is known as a **genome**.

This is a short section of a very long DNA molecule

Today we can compare the DNA of any two living things and find out exactly how much of their genetic information they share. This is a much better way to find out how closely related two living things are. All this new information is helping scientists to draw more accurate trees of life, known as evolutionary trees or **phylogenetic** trees. By comparing the DNA and other molecules of any set of creatures, we can draw a phylogenetic tree to show how they are most likely related to one another.

SURPRISING SECRETS

Evolutionary trees have revealed that some creatures are not as closely related as we once thought. For example, crocodiles turned out to be more closely related to birds than they are to lizards or tortoises. The "reptiles" are not really a group of relatives on the family tree of life, unless we count birds as reptiles too. Find out more on page 176.

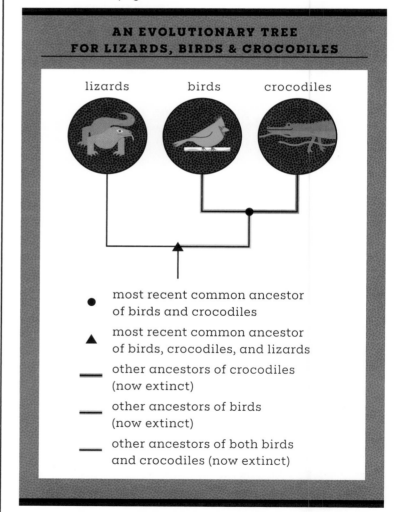

AN EVOLUTIONARY TREE FOR LIZARDS, BIRDS & CROCODILES

lizards　　birds　　crocodiles

● most recent common ancestor of birds and crocodiles

▲ most recent common ancestor of birds, crocodiles, and lizards

▬ other ancestors of crocodiles (now extinct)

▬ other ancestors of birds (now extinct)

▬ other ancestors of both birds and crocodiles (now extinct)

Other living things turned out to be more closely related than scientists once thought. For example, the DNA of fungi turned out to have more in common with animal DNA than plant DNA. This tells us that mushrooms are more closely related to humans than to plants! A tree of life can tell you how closely related you are to trees, toadstools, tiny amoebas, and every other living thing.

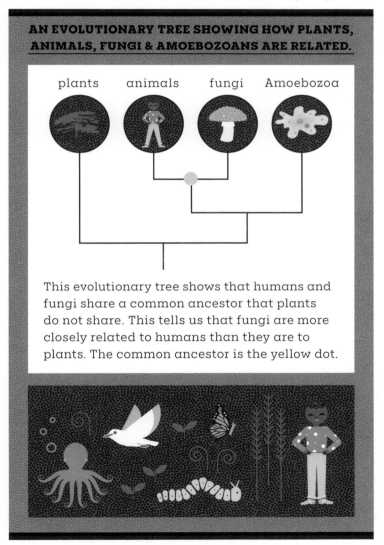

AN EVOLUTIONARY TREE SHOWING HOW PLANTS, ANIMALS, FUNGI & AMOEBOZOANS ARE RELATED.

plants   animals   fungi   Amoebozoa

This evolutionary tree shows that humans and fungi share a common ancestor that plants do not share. This tells us that fungi are more closely related to humans than they are to plants. The common ancestor is the yellow dot.

ORDER FROM CHAOS

Over the last 3.8 billion years, there have been millions of different species that have called this planet home. This dazzling diversity is a result of evolution, when living things adapt different ways of feeding, moving, hiding, and reproducing to better survive in different **habitats**.

This book uses a simple evolutionary tree as a starting point for exploring Earth's mind-boggling biodiversity. Although we only focus on living species that can be found on Earth today, it is still impossible to include every living species on a single tree of life, or in a single book—even a book as big as this one! More than 2 million living species have been named so far and there are no trees big enough to hold that many leaves. Even an enormous real-life oak tree only has around 100,000 leaves at its tips! Instead, this book begins with a simple tree of life that shows some of the main branches. We will zoom in and out of this tree of life, stopping to look more closely at some of the weirdest and most wonderful boughs, twigs, and leaves in more detail.

READING OUR TREE OF LIFE

Each of the branches on our tree of life represents a major group of living things. These branches have been color-coded to show which of the three main types—or "domains"—of living things they belong to: the true bacteria, archaea, or eukaryotes.

Members of the first two domains are all **microbes**—tiny creatures made up of just one cell. You can read more about cells, the building blocks of living things, on page 207. All other living things belong to the third domain, the eukaryotes. This domain includes plants, fungi, and animals—including humans. Most

eukaryotes are far larger than microbes, with bodies made up of billions or even trillions of cells.

As you explore the three main sections of this book, you'll discover examples of the huge variety of life in each domain. Most of the species scientists have named so far are eukaryotes, so section three is the longest section. It has been split into shorter chapters, each exploring one or more major branches of the eukaryote tree of life: plants and algae; animals, fungi, and relatives; and other eukaryotes, most of which are microscopic creatures known as protozoans.

DOMAINS OF LIFE

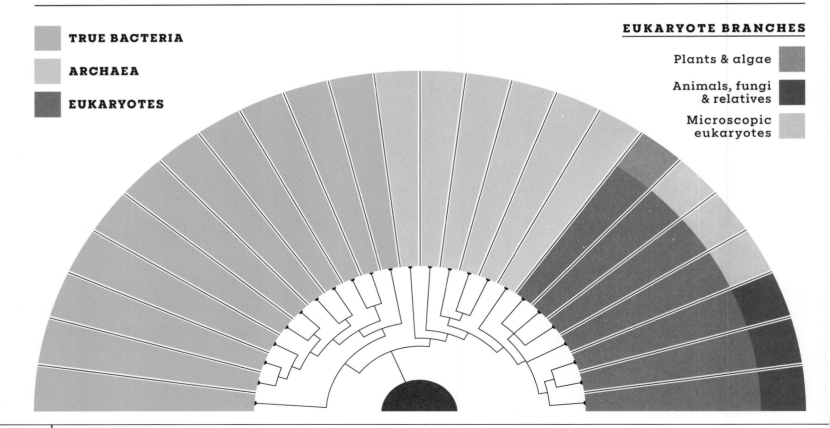

TRUE BACTERIA

ARCHAEA

EUKARYOTES

EUKARYOTE BRANCHES

Plants & algae

Animals, fungi & relatives

Microscopic eukaryotes

On a tree of life, a group of all the living things that share one single common ancestor is known as a **clade**. You can think of clades as boughs, branches, and twigs on the tree of life. All the leaves—or species—sprouting from that bough, branch, or twig are more closely related to each other than to leaves sprouting from other boughs, branches, or twigs. Smaller clades are nested inside larger clades, so a clade might contain hundreds of thousands of species, or only two. Smaller clades may be a part of many larger clades.

If our tree of life were a real tree, we could choose to focus on a large branch (or clade) with lots of stems and leaves attached, or a much smaller one. It's the same with the tree of life. In this book we will zoom in and out to focus on clades of different sizes. Every spread focuses on one clade. Some are large clades, with millions of related species. We will also zoom in on some of the smaller clades nested inside major branches of the tree of life and meet a few of the most fascinating species from each clade.

A CLADE IS A GROUP OF LIVING THINGS THAT ALL SHARE A COMMON ANCESTOR

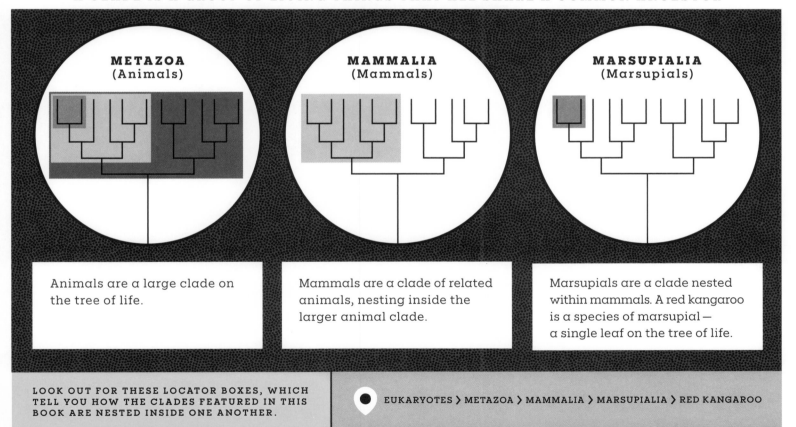

METAZOA (Animals)

MAMMALIA (Mammals)

MARSUPIALIA (Marsupials)

Animals are a large clade on the tree of life.

Mammals are a clade of related animals, nesting inside the larger animal clade.

Marsupials are a clade nested within mammals. A red kangaroo is a species of marsupial — a single leaf on the tree of life.

LOOK OUT FOR THESE LOCATOR BOXES, WHICH TELL YOU HOW THE CLADES FEATURED IN THIS BOOK ARE NESTED INSIDE ONE ANOTHER.

EUKARYOTES > METAZOA > MAMMALIA > MARSUPIALIA > RED KANGAROO

TREE OF LIFE

This tree of life shows how the large groups of living things explored in this book are likely to be related to one another, and to the last common ancestor of all living things (known as LUCA). You can find the sources used to construct this tree on page 2. To make Earth's mind-boggling biodiversity a little easier to explore, we have only included the clades featured in this book in the tree. You will find an entry for each main branch or segment. In section three, you will be able to clamber even further along three of the main branches of the eukaryote tree of life, exploring some of the smaller clades that sit within this huge group of living things.

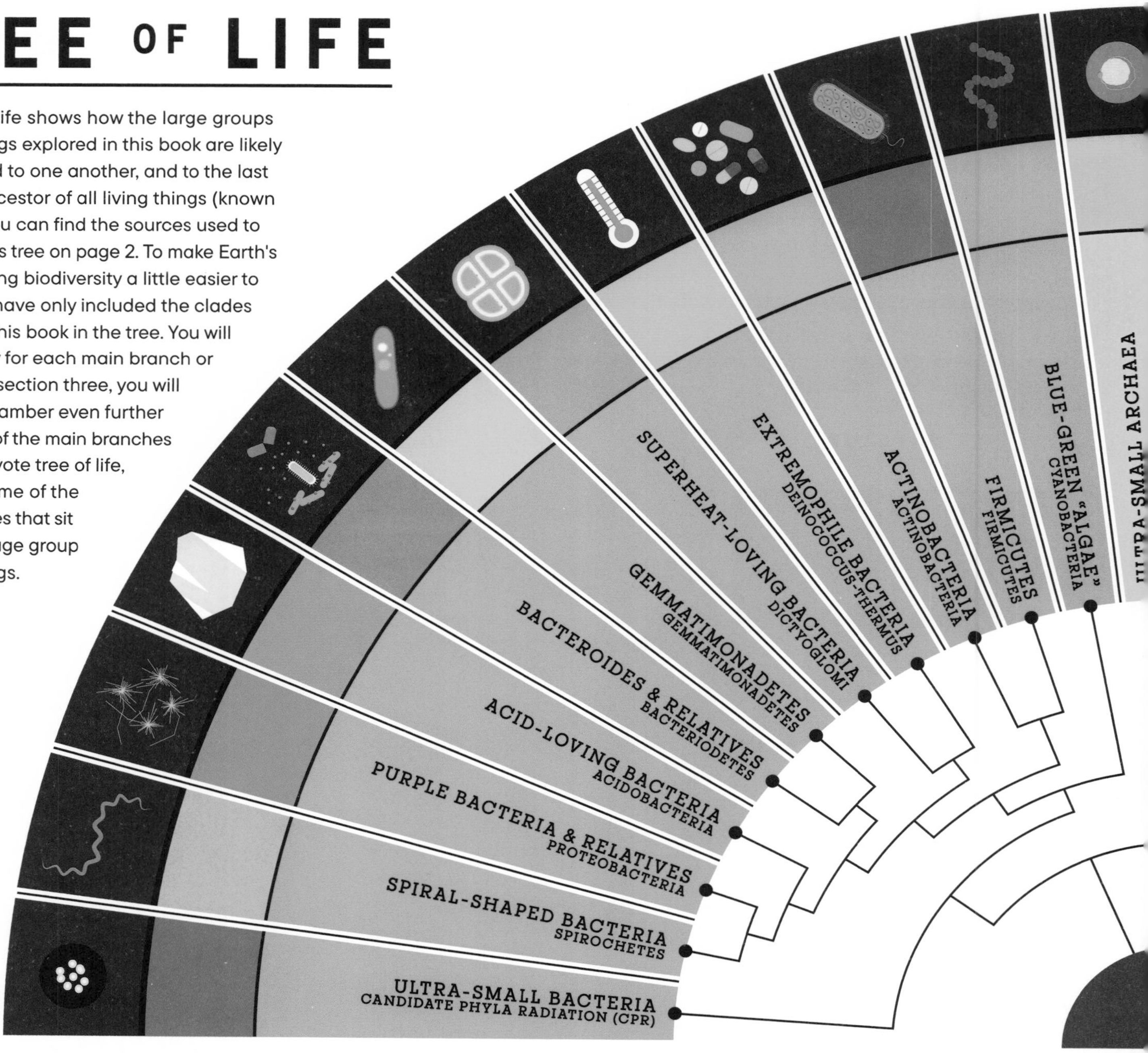

ULTRA-SMALL ARCHAEA

BLUE-GREEN "ALGAE"
CYANOBACTERIA

FIRMICUTES
FIRMICUTES

ACTINOBACTERIA
ACTINOBACTERIA

EXTREMOPHILE BACTERIA
DEINOCOCCUS-THERMUS

SUPERHEAT-LOVING BACTERIA
DICTYOGLOMI

GEMMATIMONADETES
GEMMATIMONADETES

BACTEROIDES & RELATIVES
BACTERIODETES

ACID-LOVING BACTERIA
ACIDOBACTERIA

PURPLE BACTERIA & RELATIVES
PROTEOBACTERIA

SPIRAL-SHAPED BACTERIA
SPIROCHETES

ULTRA-SMALL BACTERIA
CANDIDATE PHYLA RADIATION (CPR)

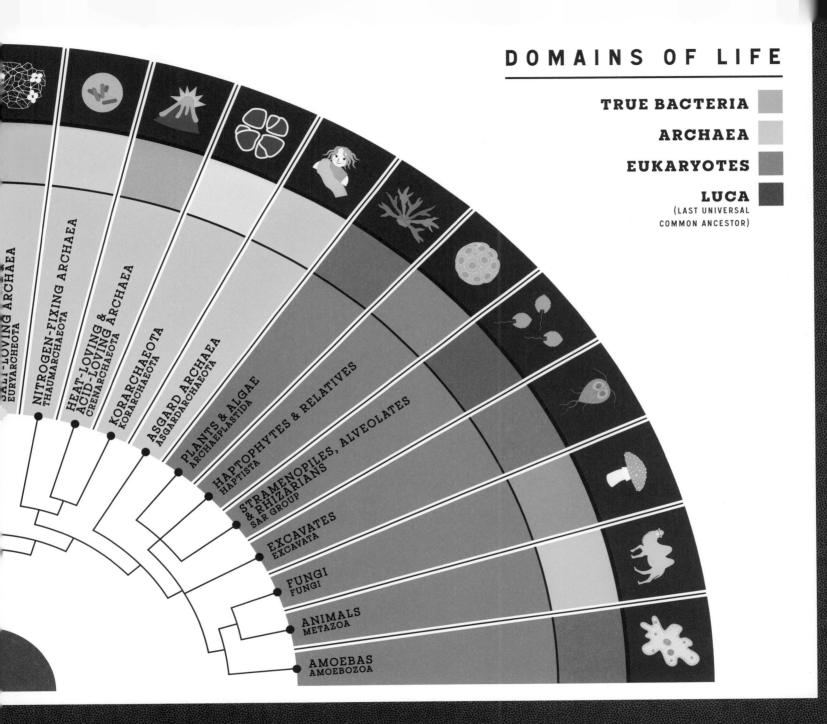

DOMAINS OF LIFE

TRUE BACTERIA

ARCHAEA

EUKARYOTES

LUCA
(LAST UNIVERSAL
COMMON ANCESTOR)

SALT-LOVING ARCHAEA
EURYARCHEOTA

NITROGEN-FIXING ARCHAEA
THAUMARCHAEOTA

HEAT-LOVING
ACID-LOVING ARCHAEA
CRENARCHAEOTA

KORARCHAEOTA
KORARCHAEOTA

ASGARD ARCHAEA
ASGARDARCHAEOTA

PLANTS & ALGAE
ARCHAEPLASTIDA

HAPTOPHYTES & RELATIVES
HAPTISTA

STRAMENOPILES, ALVEOLATES
& RHIZARIANS
SAR GROUP

EXCAVATES
EXCAVATA

FUNGI
FUNGI

ANIMALS
METAZOA

AMOEBAS
AMOEBOZOA

MARSUPIALS

MARSUPIALIA

YOU ARE HERE

EUKARYOTA

AMORPHEA

Baby marsupials are the only animals to be born twice! After leaving their mother's womb, they continue to develop inside a special pouch in her skin.

ALL ABOUT

A developing marsupial spends a short time in their mother's womb (from 12 to 42 days) then crawls to a special pouch where they finish growing while being fed with milk. After a few months, the baby marsupial, known as a joey, is "born" a second time—by simply emerging from the pouch!

Apart from this, marsupials mirror other mammals in most ways. They include marsupial versions of moles, flying squirrels, wolves, rodents, cats, and anteaters. In the past, there were even marsupial versions of a saber-toothed tiger!

Fossils of marsupials are found all around the world, but today marsupials are only found in Australasia and the Americas. In Australia, many marsupials are threatened by animals such as foxes, cats, and rats, which were all introduced from other parts of the world. Scientists are still figuring out about when exactly marsupials last shared a common ancestor with other mammals—and what happened to set them off and keep them on different evolutionary paths! Marsupials probably evolved in isolation in the Southern Hemisphere for millions of years, after becoming separated by great oceans or impassable land. Meanwhile, marsupials left in the Northern Hemisphere may have been outcompeted by other types of mammals.

KEY FACTS

- Around 335 species
- From tiny 10-cm (4-in) Ningbings to red kangaroos over 2 m (6.5 ft) tall
- Marsupial fossils are found all over the world, but living marsupials are only found in Australasia and the Americas

SPECIMEN

RED-NECKED WALLABY

SHARED FEATURES

- Thick fur
- Mammary glands and nipples are hidden in a fold of skin called a pouch
- Lower body temperature than other mammals
- Born early and continue to develop in a pouch while attached to the nipples

GOOD NEIGHBORS?

In Australasia, marsupials are found at almost every link in the food chain—just like eutherian mammals in other parts of the world. Recently, scientists discovered that humans and marsupials share a feature of their genomes that could be key to understanding and treating certain human diseases.

USING THIS BOOK

Each spread of this book focuses on one clade—a group of living things that share a common ancestor. In some cases, the following pages zoom in to that clade, looking in more detail at some of the smaller clades nested within.

You'll find out what members of each clade have in common and meet some of the weird and wonderful species within it—the "leaves" on that branch of the tree of life.

Some clades were chosen because they are very diverse (evolution has led to many different species). Some were chosen because they include creatures with particularly unusual and incredible features. And some clades are explored because they have become an important part of human lives.

The book finishes by looking at nonliving particles such as viruses. These are not made of cells, so they are not officially living things. But they have had (and still have) a huge impact on life on Earth, so we have included them in this book.

HOW TO READ EACH ENTRY

1 How this clade nests within other clades in this book
2 The clade or group's common name and scientific name
3 Its location on the tree of life
4 Which domain of life this group of creatures belong to
5 Which kingdom it was traditionally classified into
6 The size of the smallest and largest species, and typical habitats
7 A typical species within this clade
8 All about this group of living things
9 Key features shared by members of this clade
10 How creatures in this clade have become a part of human lives

Words highlighted in **bold** are described in the glossary at the back of the book (p216–219).

Each entry also includes a gallery of illustrations and captions, highlighting famous, weird, or wonderful members of that clade.

At school, we learn that living things belong to one of five "kingdoms" of life: plants, animals, fungi, monera, and protists. This traditional classification system groups creatures based on features of their bodies or cells. Today's biologists (and this book) use evolutionary trees to group living things, but five-kingdom classification is still a useful tool for helping us to describe biodiversity. Look out for these symbols, which link the creatures in each clade to one of the five kingdoms.

 Plants: The plant kingdom includes creatures that are green, made up of many cells, and don't move (much). They can make their own food.

 Animals: The animal kingdom includes creatures made up of more than one cell. Animals can move around and get **nutrients** by ingesting (eating) them.

 Fungi: The fungi kingdom includes both single-celled and multicellular creatures. They don't eat like animals or make their own food like plants. Instead, they soak up nutrients from their surroundings.

 Monera: The monera kingdom includes all the prokaryotes—single-celled creatures with much simpler cells than other living things.

 Protists: The protist kingdom was where biologists put microscopic single-celled creatures that didn't seem to fit anywhere else! Their cells have lots in common with the cells of plants, animals, and fungi. They tend to be bigger than the monera.

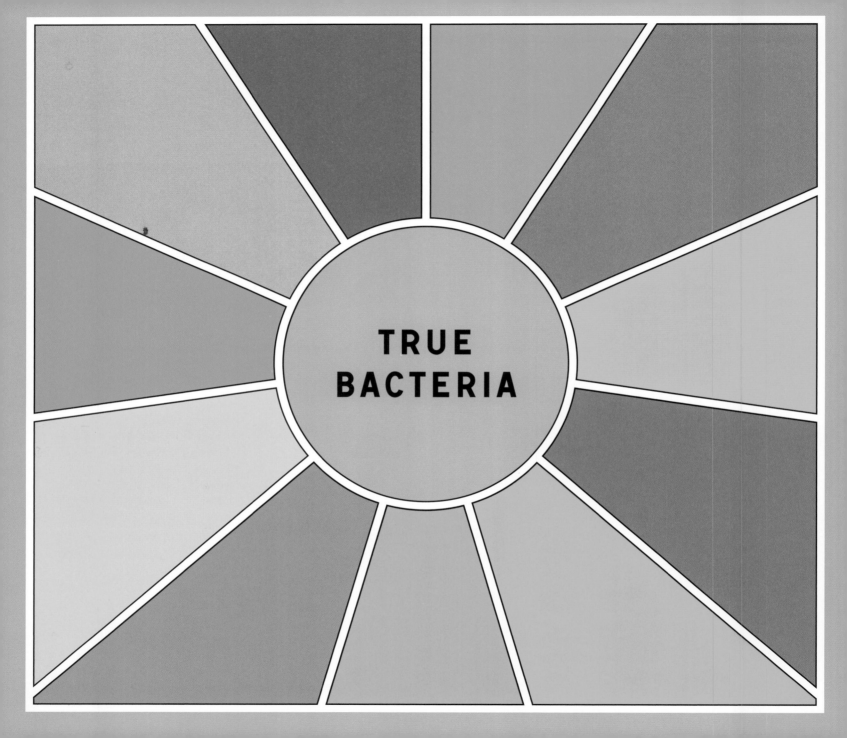

TRUE
BACTERIA

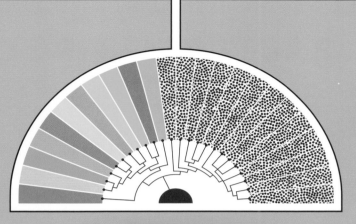

EUBACTERIA

BACTERIA ARE SOME OF THE TINIEST LIVING THINGS. EACH BACTERIUM IS MADE UP OF JUST A SINGLE, SIMPLE **CELL** AND MOST CAN ONLY BE SEEN WITH A MICROSCOPE. HOWEVER, WHAT BACTERIA LACK IN SIZE THEY MAKE UP FOR IN NUMBERS. BACTERIA ARE THE MOST ABUNDANT LIVING THINGS ON EARTH AND PLAY A STARRING ROLE IN EVERY **ECOSYSTEM.**

Scientists have recorded around 11,000 living **species** of bacteria but think there could be millions more. Although different species of bacteria don't look as different from one another as an oak tree and a rose, or a zebra and a starfish, their genes tell a different story. Bacteria were some of the very first living things on Earth and have spent the last 3.7 billion years adapting to life here.

Many have evolved unique ways to get ahold of energy and **nutrients.** Some can make their own food by capturing the energy in sunlight or from the chemicals spewed by superheated ocean vents. This allows bacteria to survive in almost every **habitat** you can imagine, from hot volcanoes and frozen Arctic snow to toxic mud or the air above our heads! There is even a species of bacteria that "breathes" arsenic, a substance that is toxic to most living things.

Most bacteria must find rather than make their food, so they like to live in habitats where there is plenty to feed on. This is one reason that colonies of billions of bacteria are found inside animal intestines. We know most about bacteria like these. This includes bacteria used to grow and prepare human foods, bacteria used to make medicines, and bacteria that cause diseases.

In their time on this planet, bacteria have reshaped Earth's soils, water, and air to create the conditions that allow millions of plants, animals, fungi, and protists to survive too. These other living things may be larger, louder, and faster, but they will never outnumber bacteria. The planet still belongs to bacteria and nothing could survive without them.

PURPLE BACTERIA & RELATIVES

PROTEOBACTERIA

YOU ARE HERE

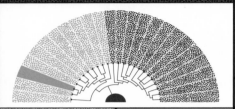

EUBACTERIA

This supergroup was named after Proteus, a shape-shifting character from Greek myths. It's a good way to describe creatures that live in a mind-boggling number of different ways!

KEY FACTS

- More than 1,600 species
- Includes many "typical" sized bacteria, such as *E. coli* at 1 to 2 μm (micrometers) long, but also "giant" species up to 0.75 mm (0.3 in) across
- Found everywhere from soils and sewage works to the roots, skin, and intestines of plants or animals

SPECIMEN

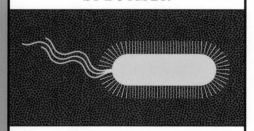

ESCHERICHIA COLI

ALL ABOUT

We know more about Proteobacteria than any other type of bacteria. They have shaped human lives since ancient times. The first species of Proteobacteria that humans noticed were the ones that cause disease in people, animals, and plants. They include *Yersinia pestis*, infamous for causing the bubonic plague—the Black Death. They also include *Escherichia coli*—*E. coli* for short—which can cause food poisoning. Infections such as food poisoning may be caused by bacteria finding themselves in the wrong habitat at the wrong time, for example when bacteria from our digestive system get into our blood. Some Proteobacteria are even adapted to live as **parasites**—creatures that spend their whole lives inside plants or animals, taking food and resources without giving anything back.

However, most Proteobacteria—including most strains of *E. coli*—are harmless to humans. Some even live happily inside people, plants, or animals, helping to support life in our bodies. This is known as a symbiotic relationship.

Most important of all are the **nitrifying** Proteobacteria bacteria found in soils. These can capture or "fix" **nitrogen** from the air. Nitrogen is one of the main building blocks of **proteins** and is needed by all living things. The bacteria turn the nitrogen into nutrients that plants can soak up through their roots. These nutrients are then passed on up the food chain. Almost all the nitrogen in your food was originally "fixed" from the air by bacteria.

SHARED FEATURES

- A huge range of shapes, from straight rods to rings, spirals, and spherical or egg-shaped **"cocci"**
- Some have "tails" called **flagella** used for moving around
- They are known as **Gram-negative** bacteria because they turn red or pink when stained using certain chemicals

GOOD NEIGHBORS?

Proteobacteria are notorious for causing nasty diseases in humans, including meningitis, whooping cough, typhoid fever, dysentery, and cholera. But this group also includes some of the "friendly" bacteria in our guts. Bacteria from this branch of the tree of life are also vital for food production and for breaking down sewage in water-treatment plants.

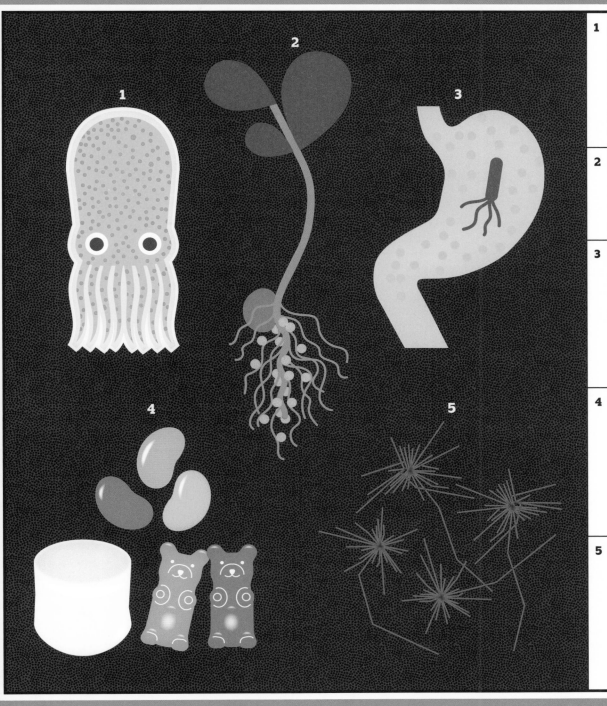

1. **GET YOUR GLOW ON**
Some Proteobacteria can make their own light. These **bioluminescent** bacteria sometimes live in the skin of sea animals, such as Hawaiian bobtail squid. The bacteria get food and protection, and the squid gets a glow-in-the-dark outfit to scare off predators!

2. **NOURISHING PLANTS**
Some plants have evolved to let nitrogen-fixing Proteobacteria live inside their roots. The bacteria get sugar and protection in return for some of the nitrogen they capture.

3. **STOMACH-CHURNING**
Your stomach is one of the most acidic environments on the planet! It protects us by killing most living things that we swallow. *Helicobacter pylori* not only survives but *lives* in this horrible habitat! In some people, it irritates the stomach lining, causing stomach ulcers and even cancer.

4. **CHEWY CANDY**
Some types of Proteobacteria are used to make food additives by adding the Proteobacteria to a sugar source and fermenting it. Gellan gum is used to make jelly candy, chewing gum, and to help thicken vegan foods. Xanthan gum is used to thicken ice cream, toothpaste, and ketchup.

5. **SULFUR, SO GOOD**
Sewage wastewater might be the last place you'd look for life, but it's bursting with bacteria! This purple sulfur bacteria is adapted to get energy and nutrients in a different way to most living things—chemical reactions involving stinky sulfur.

FIRMICUTES

FIRMICUTES

This group includes types of bacteria that are a huge part of our daily lives. Although you never see them, billions of Firmicutes call your skin and intestines their home!

YOU ARE HERE

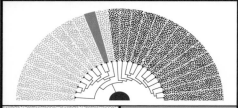

EUBACTERIA

KEY FACTS

- At least 2,475 species in our guts alone
- Includes some true "giants," up to 0.6 mm (0.02 in) long
- Found everywhere in nature—especially in soils, and on and inside animals and plants

SPECIMEN

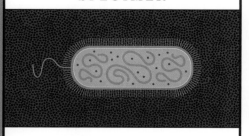

BACILLUS ANTHRACIS

ALL ABOUT

Firmicutes means "strong skin," and these bacteria have thick **cell** walls for protection. Many Firmicutes can also form **spores**—a sort of "survival" form that can stand up to tough conditions. In spore form, a bacterial cell is resting or dormant, helping it to survive high temperatures, dangerous radiation, toxic chemicals, or a total lack of water. When conditions improve, the spores quickly form normal cells that get on with the business of living—feeding, excreting waste substances, and reproducing.

Robert Koch discovered this strange life cycle while studying anthrax, which is a deadly disease. He proved that the disease was spread by spores of anthrax bacteria, which can lodge in the skin or lungs. Once people knew diseases were caused by **microbes**, they understood how simple hygiene measures such as washing our hands and food could prevent infections from spreading and save hundreds of thousands of lives.

Like all bacteria, Firmicutes produce **enzymes** and other substances as they go about their lives. These include **toxins**—chemicals that can harm or kill other living things and are made by the bacteria for self-defense. Because of their dramatic effects on our cells, these toxins can be useful for making medicines. Humans use substances produced by Firmicutes in hundreds of different ways.

SHARED FEATURES

- Most are known as **Gram-positive** bacteria because their thick cell walls turn blue under a microscope when stained using certain chemicals
- Some are spherical or rod-shaped, but others form long, branching filaments

GOOD NEIGHBORS?

Although Firmicutes cause disease, they are one of two main groups of friendly bacteria that make up our body **"microbiome."** The other group is the Bacteroidetes (see page 26). Plants have microbiomes too, and Firmicutes are a big part of these. This makes Firmicutes vital for farming and for food production.

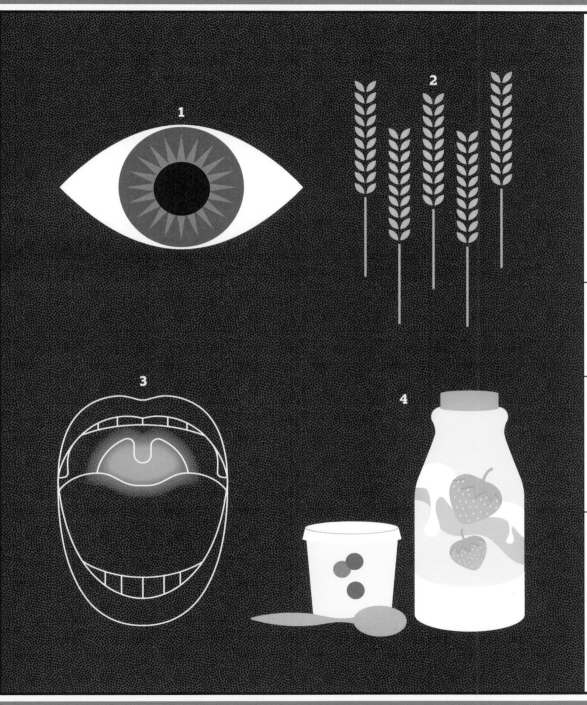

1 DEADLY TOXINS

Clostridium bacteria like to grow where there is no oxygen. Certain species cause infections in humans, including food poisoning, botulism, tetanus, and gangrene. Their spores can resist high temperatures, making them very difficult to destroy. The toxins made by *Clostridium botulinum* (Botox) are some of the deadliest natural poisons. Just 4.4 pounds of botulism toxin would be enough to kill everyone on Earth. But "Botox" can also be turned into medicines to treat eye problems such as migraines, squints, blurred vision, and dry eyes. Botox is even used to smooth out wrinkled skin.

2 HEALTHY PLANTS

Certain *Bacillus* species are even used as naturally occurring alternatives to chemical pesticides and fertilizers. This makes them very important for crop farming.

3 FRIEND AND FOE

Certain Firmicute bacteria live on our skin and in our mouths, throats, and intestines in huge numbers. They are usually a healthy part of our microbiome, but sometimes cause diseases, such as tooth **decay**, strep throat, blood infections, and wound infections.

4 DAIRY FOODS

The Firmicutes include bacteria that play an important role in making dairy products such as cheese, yogurt, kefir, and other fermented foods. These bacteria produce lactic acid as they feed on sugars. Lactic acid helps gives the foods their special tastes and stops some dangerous types of microbes from growing.

ACTINOBACTERIA

ACTINOBACTERIA

ACTINOBACTERIA

YOU ARE HERE

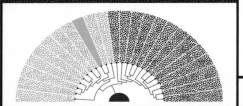

EUBACTERIA

KEY FACTS

- More than 1,100 species
- Includes ultramicrobacteria so small that 100 could fit inside a single *E. coli* cell
- Found in soils, fresh water, salt water, and even in the air

SPECIMEN

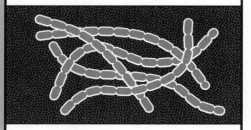

STREPTOMYCES GRISEUS

These super-soil dwellers are recyclers of carbon, the source of most antibiotics, and the secret behind the smell of rain!

ALL ABOUT

Most Actinobacteria are found in soil, up to 2 meters (6.5 feet) underground, where they live and feed on dead plant and animal matter. The bacteria break down certain substances in the dead matter so they can be absorbed as food. This is what brings about decay, unlocking nutrients such as carbon so that other living things can use them. It makes Actinobacteria a key part of ecosystems. The group also includes bacteria that live in **symbiosis** with living plants and animals, as well as a few **pathogens.** Together, the Actinobacteria make an incredible range of enzymes and other chemicals as they go about their daily lives. Humans have found many ways to harness the power of these substances.

A team of scientists led by Selman Waksman spent years hunting for other natural chemicals that could kill bacteria without harming humans. After four years, they discovered one! It is a substance made by the actinobacterium species *Streptomyces griseus*, used to defend itself from other microbes. They turned it into an antibiotic that can fight the bacteria that cause illnesses such as tuberculosis, typhoid, and cholera.

We have also harnessed the waste-pulverizing powers of Actinobacteria to clean up water and soil that have been polluted with toxic chemicals. Scientists are even exploring ways to use Actinobacteria to break down crops to make biofuels—an alternative to burning **fossil fuels**.

SHARED FEATURES

- Some grow branching filaments that form networks, linking different bacteria together so they can cooperate, like the cells of a large organism
- Some multiply by producing spores
- Their spores may have one or more tiny "tails" to help them move around

GOOD NEIGHBORS?

Some species of Actinobacteria can take advantage of a wound or a weakened **immune system** and cause diseases in people or animals. However, most of the time they live in soil without causing humans or other animals any harm. Actinobacteria are routinely used to produce substances important to farming, biotechnology, and medicine, including most antibiotics.

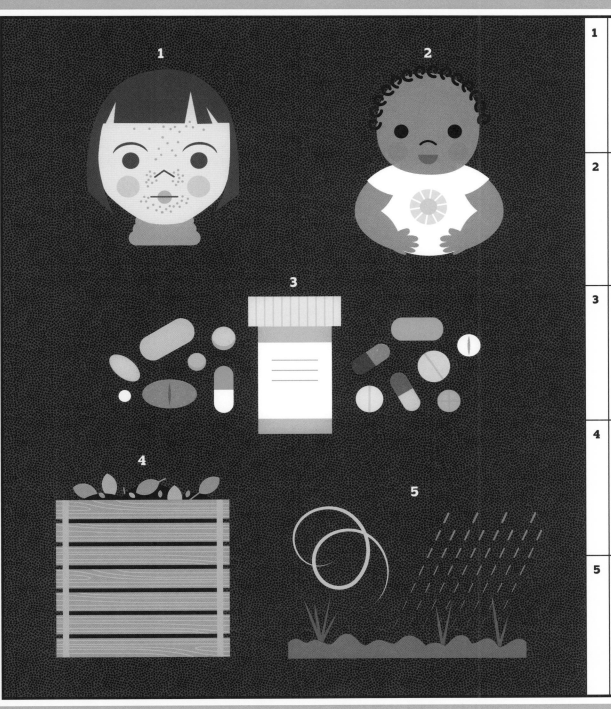

1	**ANGRY SKIN**
	One species of Actinobacteria is part of the microbe mix that lives on our skin and helps to keep it healthy. However, if the normal balance of this microbe is upset (for example by hormone changes, or stress) it can **colonize** skin follicles and cause acne.

2	**HUMAN HOSTS**
	Bifidobacterium bifidum are one of the first bacterial species to set up camp in human babies' intestines. These probiotics help to keep us healthy! They break down foods, make important nutrients such as folic acid, and help our immune system.

3	**AMAZING ANTIBIOTICS**
	Streptomyces bacteria and their relatives produce more than 10,000 different bacteria-fighting chemicals. They are the source of most of the world's antibiotics, as well as medicine to fight cancer and infections caused by parasites and fungi.

4	**COMPOSTING CHAMPIONS**
	Thermobifida bacteria grow best at warm temperatures, around 131°F. In compost heaps and manure piles, they are some of the main microbes that break down the tough cell walls of plants (page 48), releasing carbon and other nutrients that new life needs to grow.

5	**THE SMELL OF RAIN**
	Certain Actinobacteria produce chemicals called terpenoids, which have an earthy, musty smell. The best-known is geosmin, which our nose is very good at detecting. It's what you can smell in the air after rain disturbs the soil where the bacteria live!

BLUE-GREEN "ALGAE"

CYANOBACTERIA

These "living fossils" have called Earth home for more than 3.5 billion years. In that time, they have reshaped the planet, helping create the conditions that today's living things rely on.

YOU ARE HERE

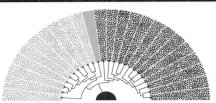

EUBACTERIA

KEY FACTS

- Around 2,700 species
- From tiny Picocyanobacteria just 0.5 μm wide, to "giants" 100 μm long
- Found in most inland waters, including hot springs and beneath icy lakes; all kinds of land habitats, including cracks in dry desert rocks, and inside other living things

SPECIMEN

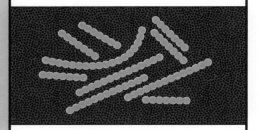

ANABAENA CIRCINALIS

ALL ABOUT

The bacteria in this group have a very special ability. Thanks to colorful **pigments** in their cells, they can capture the energy of sunlight and use it to assemble their own food from very simple building blocks. This is called **photosynthesis** and it's a superpower shared by plants. It's the reason that Cyanobacteria were classified as a type of algae by early **naturalists**. Their old name, "blue-green algae," is still used today.

As Cyanobacteria carry out photosynthesis, they take in **carbon dioxide** and release oxygen. Billions of years ago (long before plants evolved) this was the main source of oxygen in the Earth's atmosphere. It changed the chemistry of the air, causing the extinction of some early types of life but creating the conditions that today's living things rely on.

Today, Cyanobacteria are found in almost all watery habitats. Some species live alone, while others team up to form large colonies. They include the slimy **biofilms** that can be spotted growing around drains in dirty sinks!

Cyanobacteria are a huge part of healthy ecosystems, but if waste such as sewage or fertilizer gets into water, Cyanobacteria may begin to grow too quickly, in massive "blooms." This uses up oxygen needed by fish and other creatures. The bacteria can also release toxins that are poisonous to land animals that drink or swim in the water.

SHARED FEATURES

- A variety of shapes and sizes
- Contain colorful pigments, including green **chlorophyll**, which can harvest light energy for photosynthesis
- Some species have pink, brown, or red pigments too
- Often have a very thick cell wall
- Lack flagella (or "tails") but many can spread by producing tiny gliding filaments

GOOD NEIGHBORS?

Cyanobacteria play a huge role in the cycles of nutrients needed by all living things, such as oxygen, carbon, and nitrogen. Many have the ability to "fix" these elements, by converting them into substances that other living things can then use. Blue-green algal blooms can be toxic for human swimmers. Cyanobacteria can also cause itchy skin after swimming in the wild.

1 LIVING IN LICHENS

Some lichens that grow on tree trunks, rocks, and other surfaces are complicated creatures, made up of a fungus and Cyanobacteria or algae, living in symbiosis. Each helps the other to survive.

2 FLAMINGO FEATHERS

The bright pigments in Cyanobacteria are often easy to see in the water—or creatures—they live in. The Red Sea is named after occasional blooms of red-colored Cyanobacteria. Brine shrimp and flamingos become pink thanks to pigments from Cyanobacteria they eat in the salty lakes where they live.

3 FEEDING THE OCEANS

Cyanobacteria are hugely important to the ocean's ecosystems. They capture sunlight energy to make their own food, which is then passed on up ocean food chains. Cyanobacteria also lie at the bottom of food chains in many extreme land habitats where plants can't survive, from deserts to hot springs and salty marshes.

4 PLANTS

Some plants, such as floating ferns, host Cyanobacteria that can capture nitrogen from the air. They act as natural fertilizers that help plants survive in poor soils.

5 SPIRULINA SNACKS

Spirulina is a food made from Cyanobacteria. It has as much protein as eggs and is packed with other nutrients. It can be easily grown in ponds and has been eaten for centuries in Africa, Mexico, and Central America.

BACTEROIDES & RELATIVES

BACTEROIDETES

YOU ARE HERE

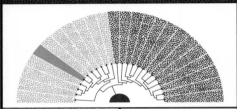

EUBACTERIA

KEY FACTS

- Around 7,000 species
- 0.5–1.5 µm long
- Found in animal intestines (especially mammals) as well as all kinds of other habitats around the world, from soil and ocean silt to fresh water and seawater

SPECIMEN

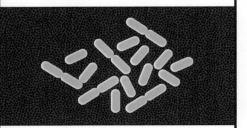

BACTEROIDES FRAGILIS

Friend or foe? This group includes some of the main bacteria living in animals' digestive tracts, including ours. But they also include some of the world's nastiest germs.

ALL ABOUT

This large group of bacteria includes species that love to live in habitats without oxygen—especially the warm, moist digestive tracts of mammals, where their next meal is never far away. Billions are happily at home in your mouth and intestines right now. They feed by breaking down different kinds of foods, including fiber and starch.

Doctors and scientists are learning that the gut microbiome is essential to keeping us healthy. But they still aren't sure which species of Bacteroidetes are friends or "frenemies." Some may be both, depending on the environment inside our bodies. One problem is that some of these bacteria break down proteins in our diet, releasing toxic chemicals. This triggers our immune system to leap into action, causing painful inflammation.

Scientists have noticed that as people get older, the number of *Bacteroides* species in their gut increases compared to Firmicutes (see page 20). *Bacteroides* have also been linked with obesity, which is a condition where a person's body is storing too much fat, affecting their health in different ways. Figuring out exactly what impact they have may help us to invent new ways to improve human health.

Elsewhere in nature, there is no doubt that Bacteroidetes are friends. Their ability to break down tough plant materials such as **cellulose** is vital for ecosystems, as it releases the nutrients needed by new living things.

SHARED FEATURES

- Bacteroidetes have an unusual way of moving, which makes them appear to glide along
- Some need oxygen to live, while others are only found in habitats where there is no oxygen at all
- Gram-negative

GOOD NEIGHBORS?

These bacteria live in the bodies of many of the grass-eating animals we farm. Without them, these animals would not be able to unlock the energy and nutrients in plants. However, some species are known to cause nasty infections if they get in the wrong part of the body, or if the environment in our guts is thrown out of balance.

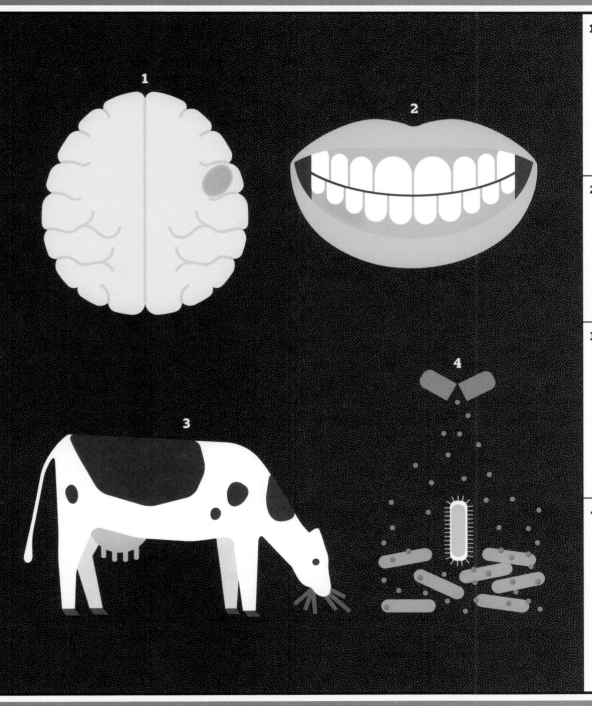

1 **LOCATION, LOCATION**
If it finds itself in the wrong place, *Bacteroides fragilis* is one of the most harmful species of bacteria. For example, if it escapes the gut during surgery, it might travel around a patient's bloodstream. It will set up camp in other parts of the body, such as the brain, causing dangerous swellings called abscesses.

2 **GUM DISEASE**
Sore, red, or bleeding gums can be a sign of gum disease caused by bacteria. Lots of Bacteroidetes species normally live in our mouths and on the surface of our teeth, and we control them by brushing twice a day. But if they get below the gum line, they can do lots of damage.

3 **STOMACH SUPERHEROES**
Bacteroides ruminicola lives in the rumen or "foregut" of animals that regurgitate their food to chew it a second time, including the cattle we rely on for meat and milk. The bacteria produce enzymes that can break down the toughest building blocks of plants. Without the bacteria, these animals would not be able to unlock the energy and nutrients in plants.

4 **ANTIBIOTIC RESISTANCE**
Around 100 years ago, scientists began using antibiotics to fight infections caused by bacteria. But bacteria are fighting back by developing resistance to these medicines. Certain species of *Bacteroides* have very high resistance rates, making them dangerous pathogens.

SPIRAL-SHAPED BACTERIA

SPIROCHETES

These tiny living squiggles are found in a range of places, from red coral reefs to insect intestines. We still have a lot to learn about their strange lives.

YOU ARE HERE

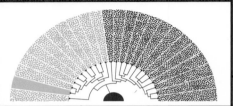

EUBACTERIA

KEY FACTS

- More than 90 species
- Long and thin; the biggest Spirochetes are up to half a millimeter (0.2 in) long!
- Found in many different liquids, from the mud that collects at the bottom of lakes and oceans, to the digestive tract of insects, mollusks, and mammals

SPECIMEN

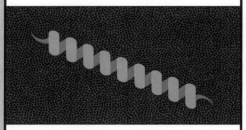

TREPONEMA PALLIDUM

ALL ABOUT

Spirochetes look and move very differently from other bacteria. Their long, thin cells spiral through liquids like a corkscrew. They can even spiral through very thick and gooey liquids such as mud. As they travel, Spirochetes feed on organic **molecules,** such as sugars and amino acids (the building blocks of proteins). The best place to find these foods is inside other living things, so some Spirochetes like to live in blood and other body fluids.

Sometimes Spirochetes live in harmony with insect hosts. Termites, for example, need the Spirochetes inside them to survive, but scientists still haven't figured out why. One clue lies in where the Spirochetes are found… attached to the surface of larger microbes that live in the termites' guts. By working like tiny outboard motors, they may help the larger microbes to move about inside the termites, helping with digestion.

Not all of today's Spirochetes are helpful. Certain species are adapted to live as parasites, taking from their host but not giving anything back. They cause disease in animals, including humans, and the "sock" that covers each bacterium acts as a disguise that makes it hard for our immune systems to track them down and fight back.

SHARED FEATURES

- Around a hundred tails, called flagella, fold back inside the cell and join themselves to the other end
- The whole cell is covered by a flexible "sock"
- As the flagella move, the cell spirals around, helping it move
- Spiral-shaped
- Gram-negative

GOOD NEIGHBORS?

Some Spirochetes species cause nasty diseases such as syphilis, Lyme disease, and yaws in humans, as well as disease in pets, farm animals, and wild mammals. These diseases affect millions of people and animals every year.

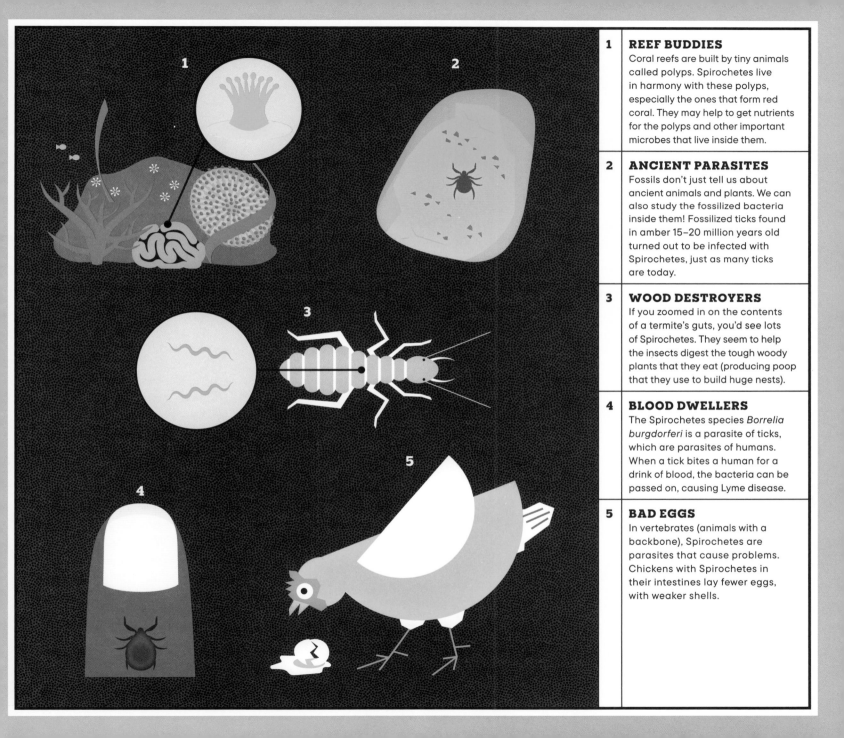

1 REEF BUDDIES
Coral reefs are built by tiny animals called polyps. Spirochetes live in harmony with these polyps, especially the ones that form red coral. They may help to get nutrients for the polyps and other important microbes that live inside them.

2 ANCIENT PARASITES
Fossils don't just tell us about ancient animals and plants. We can also study the fossilized bacteria inside them! Fossilized ticks found in amber 15–20 million years old turned out to be infected with Spirochetes, just as many ticks are today.

3 WOOD DESTROYERS
If you zoomed in on the contents of a termite's guts, you'd see lots of Spirochetes. They seem to help the insects digest the tough woody plants that they eat (producing poop that they use to build huge nests).

4 BLOOD DWELLERS
The Spirochetes species *Borrelia burgdorferi* is a parasite of ticks, which are parasites of humans. When a tick bites a human for a drink of blood, the bacteria can be passed on, causing Lyme disease.

5 BAD EGGS
In vertebrates (animals with a backbone), Spirochetes are parasites that cause problems. Chickens with Spirochetes in their intestines lay fewer eggs, with weaker shells.

EXTREMOPHILE BACTERIA

DEINOCOCCUS-THERMUS

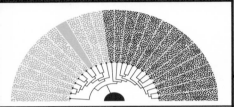

EUBACTERIA

KEY FACTS

· Around 50 species
· 0.5 to 10 μm long/wide
· Found everywhere, including the
  most extreme places on the planet

SPECIMEN

DEINOCOCCUS

If an asteroid or natural disaster struck planet Earth, the bacteria in this group might be the creatures most likely to survive!

ALL ABOUT

Bacteria in this group are found everywhere from air and fresh water to animal poop. They have been found in the hot, dry Saharan desert, in toxic geothermal springs, in the human gut, in radioactive waste, and in many other places, too.

These "extremophile" bacteria can survive such extreme habitats because they are incredibly tough. Toughest of all is *Deinococcus radiodurans*, which survives almost anything scientists throw at it: a total lack of air in space, six years without water, extreme hot and cold, strong UV light, and nuclear radiation that kills almost every other living thing.

Its secret to survival is its ability to repair any of its genes that get damaged. *Deinococcus* bacteria store up to ten copies of their **genome**, which act as backups. If a gene gets damaged (for example, by radiation), the cell has a way to repair it—or at least eject it—so it doesn't give the cell faulty instructions to follow!

Lots of researchers are studying these bacteria, figuring out ways to harness their incredible powers. For example, they may one day help us find a way to break down the dangerous radioactive waste from nuclear power stations more quickly. At the moment, this takes hundreds or even thousands of years.

SHARED FEATURES

· Shaped like rods or spheres
· Often hang out in pairs, or
  groups of four called tetrads
· The pink pigment of Deinococcales
  acts as a shield against dangerous
  nuclear and UV radiation
· Thick cell walls stain Gram-
  positive, but cells also share
  features of Gram-negative bacteria
· Do not have a way to move
  themselves about

GOOD NEIGHBORS?

Scientists are very interested in extremophile bacteria and their adaptations. They are even helping us to figure out how life on the planet may have begun. Billions of years ago, conditions on Earth's surface may have been like conditions in today's geothermal springs.

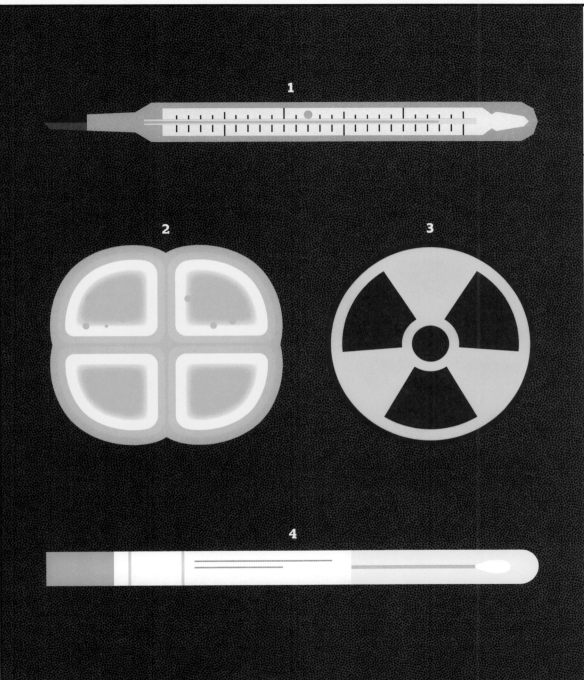

1	**IN HOT WATER** Unlike most living things, *Thermus* bacteria are at their happiest in hot water, between 122°F and 176°F. They are found in hot springs around the world. Most proteins get scrambled if they are heated much above 98.6°F, but *Thermus* bacteria produce special proteins that can cope with the heat.
2	**RADIATION RESISTANT** *Deinococcus radiodurans* was discovered in 1956 in meat that had been exposed to lethal gamma radiation. Nuclear radiation harms living things by breaking apart their genes. But these bacteria were still alive and well!
3	**RECORD BREAKERS** The size of a dose of radiation is measured in "grays" (Gy). Five Gy would kill a human, and about 800 Gy kills *Escherichia coli* bacteria. *Deinococcus radiodurans* have amazed scientists by living through doses of 5,000 to 15,000 Gy! No wonder they're listed as the world's toughest bacteria in *The Guinness Book of World Records*.
4	**PCR SUPERSTAR** The species *Thermus aquaticus* produces a particularly robust and speedy enzyme called **DNA** polymerase, which has become world famous. It can be used in labs to make millions of copies of any strand of DNA. This method is known as polymerase chain reaction (PCR) and is used for all kinds of different things—including the PCR tests that detect DNA belonging to the coronavirus that causes COVID-19.

ACID-LOVING BACTERIA

ACIDOBACTERIA

YOU ARE HERE

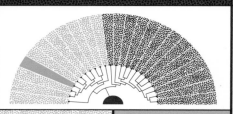

EUBACTERIA

ALL ABOUT

This group of bacteria were only discovered in 1991, but are turning up everywhere. In certain soils, more than half of the bacteria belong to this group! We are only just starting to learn about their role in ecosystems. Unfortunately, Acidobacteria are very hard to grow in a lab, which makes this difficult.

Scientists have been able to collect genetic information from the Acidobacteria that live in soils in order to "read" their genes. They tell us that this group is very diverse and may help soil clump together and trap water and nutrients. Acidobacteria also seem to have lots of features that help them compete with and even control other bacteria, helping them to survive in harsh conditions.

1 FROZEN SURVIVORS
The McMurdo Dry Valleys in Antarctica have some of the harshest conditions on the planet. Yet Acidobacteria seem to thrive there! There are no plants or animals in these valleys, but the soils contain so many bacteria, scientists are eager to learn more about the adaptations that help them cope with life in a natural freezer.

SUPERHEAT-LOVING BACTERIA

DICTYOGLOMI

ALL ABOUT

Just two species of Dictyoglomi have been named so far, and they are so different from other bacteria it's a bit like looking at alien life-forms. These bacteria are survivors that thrive in superheated, oxygen-free habitats such as hot springs. As well as standing up to heat, they make enzymes that seem able to break down a whole host of carbohydrates for food. These enzymes are being used in papermaking, to break down colored chemicals in wood pulp and bleach the paper white.

YOU ARE HERE

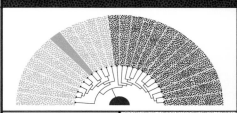

EUBACTERIA

GEMMATIMONADETES

GEMMATIMONADETES

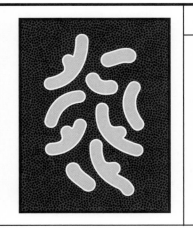

ALL ABOUT

This group of bacteria are most mysterious of all. Scientists have barely found any living examples, but their DNA seems to be everywhere, from soils and seas to mountain streams and sewage works. They must be important, but we don't yet know why. The first example was found feeding on chemicals in the stinky sludge of a wastewater-treatment plant. Others can use light energy to assemble their own food, and one species can even break down damaging greenhouse gases. Perhaps one day they will help us find new ways to tackle the climate emergency.

YOU ARE HERE

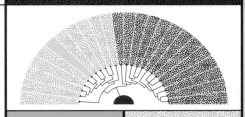

EUBACTERIA

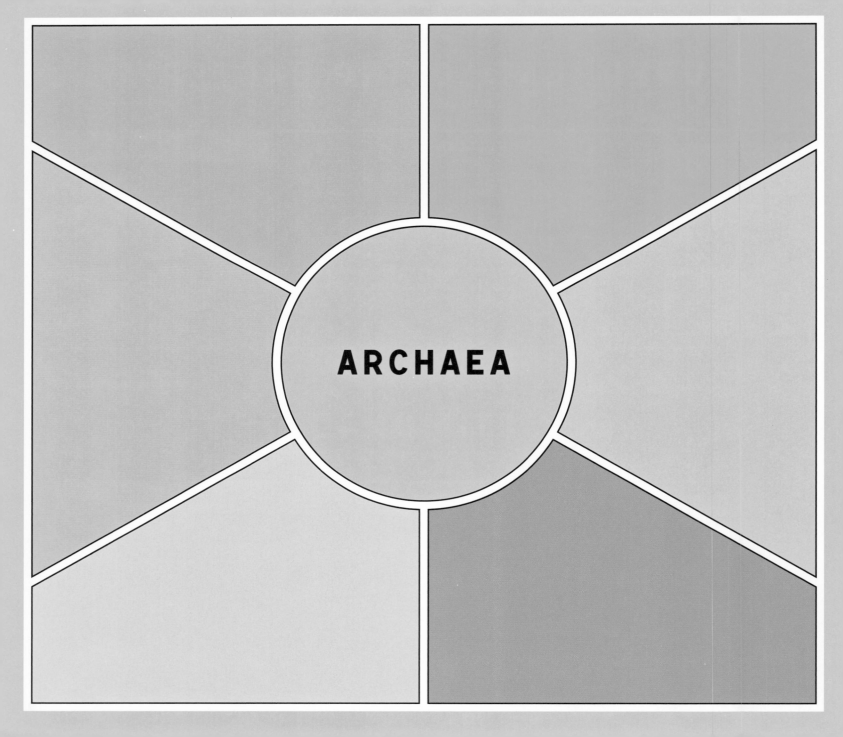

ARCHAEA

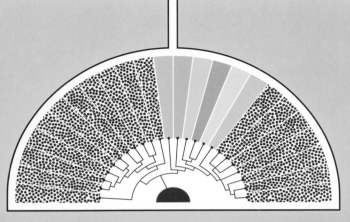

ARCHAEA

FOR A LONG TIME, SCIENTISTS OVERLOOKED ARCHAEA, THINKING OF THEM AS JUST ANOTHER TYPE OF BACTERIA WITH THE SAME SIMPLE CELLS. BUT EVERYTHING CHANGED WHEN THE TOOLS TO READ GENES WERE INVENTED. ARCHAEA TURNED OUT BE MUCH MORE LIKE THE CELLS OF ANIMALS AND PLANTS. ANCIENT ARCHAEA MAY EVEN BE OUR ANCESTORS.

If every living thing on Earth were weighed, archaea would make up a fifth of the total. Archaea are tiny **microbes** yet they outnumber most other creatures on Earth! This makes them a key part of most **ecosystems**.

Now that we know that archaea have a key position in the tree of life, scientists are rushing to find out more about them. Only around 500 **species** of archaea have been named so far. They have been discovered in a wider range of habitats than any other living thing. Some species thrive in places with mild conditions, such as soils, oceans, and animal intestines. But many archaea are extremophiles. They prefer harsh **habitats** that would kill most other living things—extremely hot geysers, freezing Antarctic waters, corrosive or salty lakes, toxic mines, and deep underneath oceans in crushing pressure and total darkness. The more we explore these unfriendly places, the more types of archaea we find.

To survive in such places, archaea have evolved a mind-boggling range of ways to capture and use energy. Some release energy locked inside toxic **minerals**, such as stinky hydrogen sulfide or ammonia. Some capture carbon from the air itself. Others use sunlight as a source of energy. Archaea waste products are unique too. The methane gas that escapes from the intestines of farm animals (and humans) is formed by archaea living inside them! Archaea are a part of many animal **microbiomes**, but unlike other microbes, they rarely cause disease. This is one reason that it took us so long to discover them. Another is that the archaea's love of extreme conditions makes it very hard to grow and study most species in a lab.

We still have lots to learn about how different types of archaea are related to each other and to other living things. This chapter explores some of the largest and most important groups of archaea identified so far, but their exact grouping on the tree of life is far from certain.

METHANE-MAKING & SALT-LOVING ARCHAEA

EURYARCHAEOTA

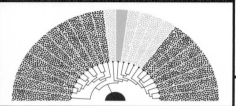

ARCHAEA

KEY FACTS

- Several hundred species
- Most are unimaginably tiny, at less than 1 μm long
- Everywhere from deep-sea vents to animal intestines, landfills, dry deserts, salt lakes, oil wells, and mines deep below Earth's surface

SPECIMEN

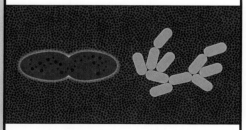

HALOBACTERIUM SALINARUM

This group of microbes are the creatures behind several strange phenomena, from spooky lights and purple lakes to belching cows!

ALL ABOUT

Named after a Greek word for "large," this branch of the tree of life includes a huge range of different microbes. They can be sorted into three smaller groups—archaea that love high temperatures, archaea that grow best in very salty environments, and archaea that make methane. Some species have more than one of these abilities.

Euryarchaeota are found in some of the most extreme (and smelliest) environments on Earth—from **sulfur**-rich hot springs to deep under Greenland's subzero ice. Some scientists wonder if methane-making archaea may be found on Mars too one day: not only because they can survive tough conditions but because the mixture of gases they release is strangely similar to Martian air!

Another large group of Euryarchaeota, known as Halobacteria, are named after their love of salt. They grow best in places that are at least three times saltier than seawater, such as the Dead Sea, salty Antarctic lakes, and even inside salted fish. This is remarkable because most living things are harmed or killed by very salty environments (it's the reason that salt is used to preserve food in the first place). The adaptations that protect salt-loving **cells** from damage are very effective. The oldest **DNA** ever found belongs to an ancient species of *Halobacterium*. It was found inside salt crystals that are 419 million years old.

SHARED FEATURES

- A wide range of shapes and sizes, from ball-shaped **cocci** to rods and filaments and even triangle-shaped cells
- Unusually for archaea, some methane-making Euryarchaeota have a cell wall like those belonging to bacteria

GOOD NEIGHBORS?

The methane produced by some archaea is a greenhouse gas, known to cause global warming and climate change. However, other Euryarchaeota are busy removing methane, breaking it down as their source of carbon. Overall, these different species are an important part of the **carbon cycle** on Earth.

1 GHOST LIGHTS
Strange "ghost lights" seen hovering over bogs and swamps at night have inspired folk stories of ghostly creatures such as will-o'-the-wisp. Today, scientists explain these spooky lights as a glowing mixture of "marsh gas" produced by methane-making archaea that live in the mud.

2 GREENHOUSE GAS
Methane is a potent greenhouse gas. It's thought that almost a quarter of the methane produced around the world each year comes from Euryarchaeota growing in rice fields and other land habitats.

3 SALT LOVERS
The **cell** membranes of salt-loving Euryarchaeota contain the same pink and red pigments found in carrots and tomatoes! Salty lakes that are home to large groups of these archaea often look pink or purple.

4 METHANE MAKERS
Methane-making Euryarchaeota are often found in habitats where there is no oxygen but a buildup of hydrogen gas, such as piles of manure. The archaea use the hydrogen to produce methane gas. This chemical reaction releases energy, which the archaea use to live, grow, and reproduce.

5 EXCUSE ME!
Similar conditions are found inside the intestines of grass-eating farm animals and humans, so methane-making archaea thrive here too. The methane gas they produce is released when we pass gas (although most of the gas is just normal air that we swallow as we eat and drink).

HEAT-LOVING & ACID-LOVING ARCHAEA

CRENARCHAEOTA

YOU ARE HERE

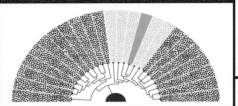

ARCHAEA

KEY FACTS

- Almost 50 species named so far
- Individual cells are less than 1 μm long, but they can link together to form filaments more than 100 μm long
- Found in hot water environments, from deep-sea **hydrothermal** vents to hot springs

SPECIMEN

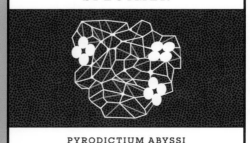

PYRODICTIUM ABYSSI

Tiny but mighty, the most extreme heat-loving microbes belong to this major group of archaea. They grow best in hot water up to 212°F—the same temperature as a boiling kettle.

ALL ABOUT

All Crenarchaeota live in water, but not just any old water. They like their habitats to be hot, hot, hot! Some types can grow at temperatures up to 235°F. They are found in water heated deep underground, near volcanoes or in hot springs. They are also found in the deep oceans, where superheated water floods out of **hydrothermal** vents.

Around volcanoes and hot springs, the mud and soil are often rich in sulfur, and many of these microbes depend on sulfur as a source of food and energy. Some use sulfur like we use oxygen, as part of the chemical reactions that help them unlock energy in food.

To help them survive in these hostile environments, many Crenarchaeota have adaptations that help them stand up to radiation or acid. Some species even prefer to live in solutions of hot, dilute sulfuric acid—a substance so corrosive that humans use it as a drain cleaner. Sulfuric acid can burn skin and dissolve metal, but for these archaea it's home sweet home.

The extremophile Crenarchaeota were the first of this group to be discovered and are so fascinating that scientists are learning lots about them. More recently we have learned that they have close relatives that enjoy lower temperatures in soil and oceans (see page 40).

SHARED FEATURES

- Many have unusually shaped cells, including lopsided discs, rectangular rods, and wonky spheres
- Some form large groups that cling together like a bunch of grapes or use wispy fibers to form a lattice of cells

GOOD NEIGHBORS?

The extreme habitats loved by these microbes may be similar to conditions on Earth when life began. Looking at Crenarchaeota may help us figure out how the earliest life-forms survived. The biotech industry is also interested in Crenarchaeota because the enzymes they produce could do useful jobs in extreme conditions.

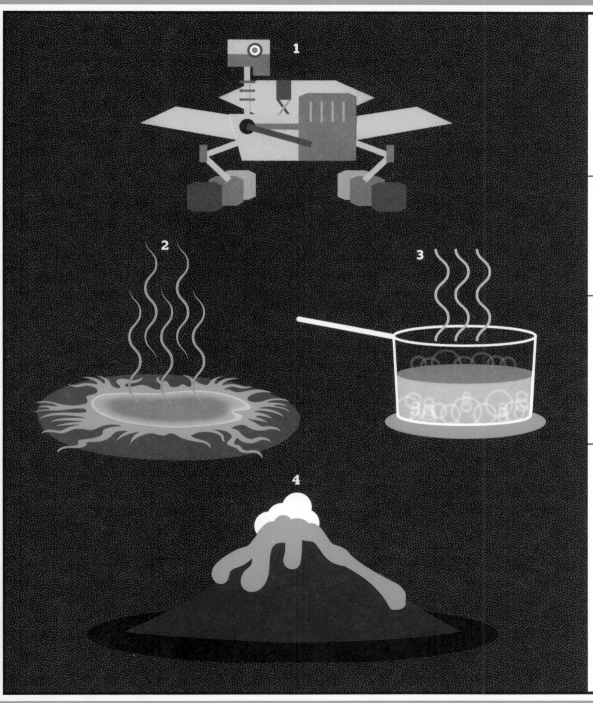

1 LIFE ON MARS?

Photographs of Mars taken from space show that the surface may once have been covered in hot springs. Robot rovers sent to Mars have been searching for traces of ancient Martian microbes. If they are found one day, they may have similar features to the Crenarchaeota that can live in the hot springs.

2 SULFUR-LOVING

Thermoproteales are found in sulfur-rich hot springs, bathed in acid at up to 207°F. Some depend on sulfur as a source of food and energy. They produce stinky hydrogen sulfide, which smells like rotten eggs.

3 IN HOT WATER

Desulfurococcales hold the world record for heat resistance! They grow around deep-sea hydrothermal vents at temperatures up to 235°F. They are happiest at 221°F, which is hotter than boiling water (although the crushing pressure of the deep ocean stops the superheated water from turning into gas).

4 VOLCANO DWELLERS

An active volcano might not be the first place you look for life, but biologists have been amazed to find the archaeon *Sulfolobus* living in the gloopy mud around Mount Vesuvius in Italy. It thrives where the **pH** is 2, as acidic as lemon juice, thanks to sulfuric acid made by the archaea themselves. An amazing range of viruses are also found inside *Sulfolobus*!

NITROGEN-FIXING ARCHAEA

THAUMARCHAEOTA

At least a fifth of all microbes in the ocean belong to this group. As they go about their lives, they play a huge role in Earth's nitrogen and carbon cycles.

YOU ARE HERE

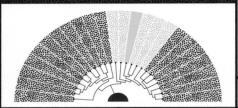

ARCHAEA

KEY FACTS

- Scientists have found evidence of at least 80 species, but very few have been named or studied
- Includes some giant species for archaea, up to 10 μm wide and 24 μm long
- Deep oceans, the muddy Amazon river, soils (especially deep soils and peats), and mangrove swamps

SPECIMEN

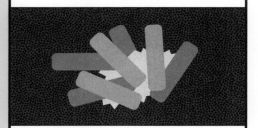

NITROSOPUMILUS MARITIMUS

ALL ABOUT

Seas and oceans are Earth's largest habitats for living things. Near the ocean surface, plants (page 46) and Cyanobacteria (page 24) lie at the bottom of most food chains. Here they can capture sunlight energy and convert it to chemical energy in food. However, the average depth of the world's oceans is 3.7 kilometers (2.3 miles), far beyond the reach of the sun's rays, meaning that 95% of this vast habitat is completely dark.

For a long time, scientists were puzzled about where deep-sea creatures got their food. Could they really survive on scraps drifting down from above? Or nibble the food made by microbes living around hot water vents? The discovery of huge numbers of Thaumarchaeota in deep oceans solved the mystery.

Thaumarchaeota thrive in the very deepest oceans, including the hadal zone between 6 and 11 kilometers (3.7 and 6.8 miles) under the surface—one of the most hostile habitats on the planet. The Thaumarchaeota are some of the only plankton in this zone and are gobbled up in vast numbers by strange deep-sea creatures who have very little else to eat.

When Thaumarchaeota were first discovered, biologists assumed they were part of the Crenarchaeota branch of the tree of life. As we found out more about their genes, we realized they make up a branch of their own—one of the most important on Earth.

SHARED FEATURES

- Many have archaella, skinny whip-like hairs or "tails" sticking out from their cell surface
- The archaella are used to help the cell move around and interact with other cells
- The cells of some species link together to form filaments up to 30 mm (1.18 in) long

GOOD NEIGHBORS?

These microbes help to drive the cycles of carbon and **nitrogen** on Earth that all life relies on. Humans are learning how to use their extraordinary abilities in different ways. For example, some Thaumarchaeota get ahold of nitrogen and energy by breaking apart ammonia, which is toxic to fish. They play an important role in keeping fish tanks and aquariums healthy.

1 MARIANA TRENCH
In the deepest oceans, Thaumarchaeota can turn chemicals found in decaying organic matter into nutrients needed by new ocean life, and they don't need light to do it. This makes them a huge part of ocean ecosystems.

2 SPONGE BUDDIES
Some Thaumarchaeota live in symbiosis with ocean animals called sponges (page 104). They have adaptations that allow them to live inside the sponges without getting digested. In fact, more than a third of each sponge can be microbes! Thaumarchaeota carry out chemical reactions that help the sponges. These include defending them against predators, making nutrients the sponge needs, and getting rid of toxic waste products. It helps explain why sponges are such successful ocean animals.

3 HARD TO STUDY
It's difficult to extract Thaumarchaeota from oceans and then grow them in a lab, so only a few species have been studied closely. The first to be successfully grown was in a tropical aquarium in Seattle, Washington.

4 SOIL SUPERHEROES
The group also includes land-based species, which break down dead plants in forest soils.

5 MANGROVE MICROBES
Giant Thaumarchaeota have been found living on the sunken roots of mangrove swamps, and may play a vital role in recycling the building blocks of life in these important ecosystems.

KORARCHAEOTA

KORARCHAEOTA

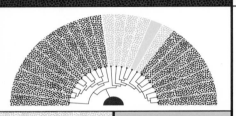

ARCHAEA

ALL ABOUT

The harder we hunt for archaea, the more we are realizing just how many different groups are out there. Korarchaeota were the third main group to be identified and their genes have revealed some surprises. Most living things have just one way to get food or energy. Some Korarchaeota species have genes that code for two ways of getting food and energy. This means they may be able to switch their source of food and energy depending on the conditions they find themselves in. So far Korarchaeota have been found in very hot habitats near **hydrothermal vents** in the deep ocean, and hot springs on land.

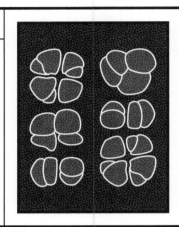

ULTRA-SMALL ARCHAEA

NANOARCHAEOTA

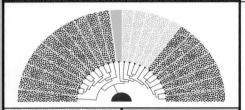

ARCHAEA

ALL ABOUT

Nanoarchaeota belong to a larger group of very small archaea known by the acronym DPANN. This branch of the tree of life includes the smallest living creatures ever discovered. Each *Nanoarchaeum equitans* cell is just a hundredth of the size of an *Escherichia coli* bacterium. They live as parasites on the surface of larger, heat-loving archaea! Without their hosts, these tiny microbes could not survive. They have the smallest **genome** or "instruction book" that scientists have ever found in a living thing. They rely on their hosts to make many of the substances they need to live and make copies of themselves.

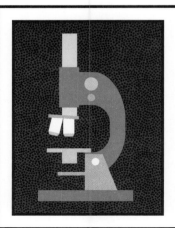

ASGARD ARCHAEA

ASGARDARCHAEOTA

ALL ABOUT

1 THOR

Asgard archaea are hard to find in nature and even harder to cultivate and study in a lab. Growing Asgard archaea in a lab for the first time took 12 years! First, scientists dug samples out of mud beneath the Pacific Ocean. Next, they spent five years re-creating this methane-rich habitat in the lab. Even then, the microbes took up to 25 days to double in number (most bacteria double every hour or less). It was worth the wait. Under the microscope, they saw bizarre cells with tentacles that the archaea may use to hug other microbes, so that they can work together to survive!

The first of these strange archaea were discovered in 2015, 3.3 kilometers (2 miles) below the Atlantic Ocean. They were found near a group of hydrothermal vents called Loki's Castle. Since then, the Lokiarchaeota—and their close relatives, the Thor-, Odin- and Heimdallarchaeota—have all been named after gods and places from Norse mythology.

Amazingly, these "Asgard archaea" turned out to have the instructions for making proteins once thought to only be found in plants, animals, fungi, and protists. This suggests that the **common ancestor** of all eukaryotes is an archaeon, changing the way biologists think about life on Earth.

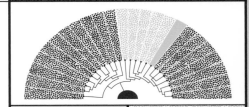

ARCHAEA

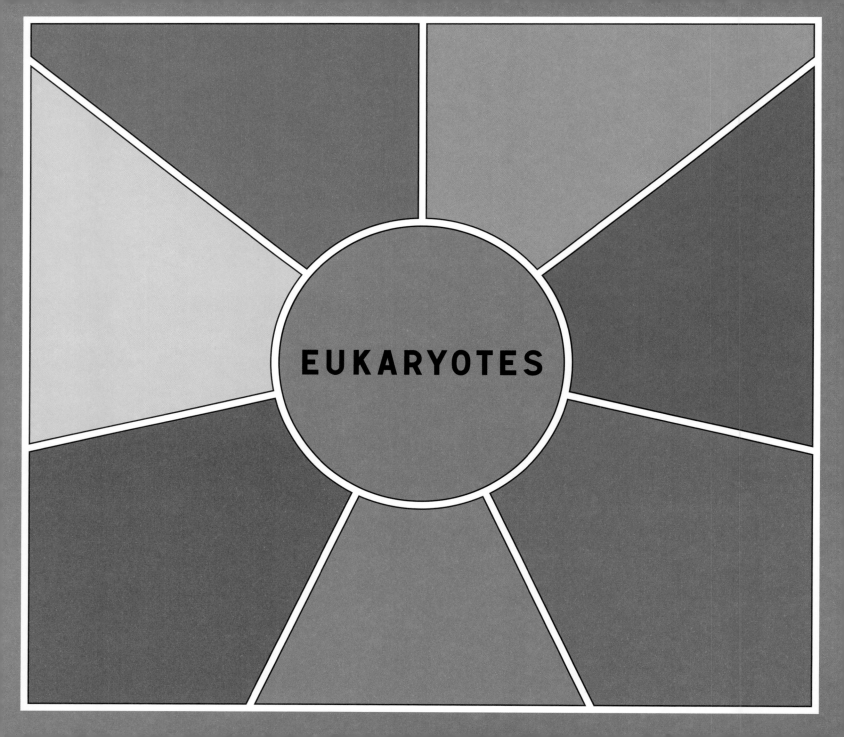

EUKARYOTES

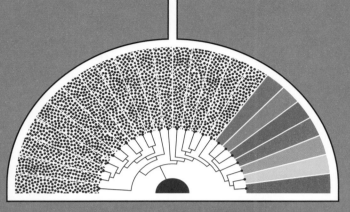

EUKARYOTA

WELCOME TO THE LARGEST DOMAIN OF LIFE. ALMOST 2 MILLION DIFFERENT EUKARYOTES HAVE BEEN NAMED SO FAR AND THEY INCLUDE ALMOST ALL THE CREATURES YOU SEE AROUND YOU—PLANTS, ALGAE, FUNGI, AND ANIMALS.

This domain includes the largest living things, such as blue whales and towering trees. It also includes microscopic single-celled creatures, such as yeasts and amoebas.

Eukaryotes may look and behave very differently from one another on the surface, but they are united by their similar **cells**. Eukaryote cells are more complex and organized than the "prokaryote" cells of the bacteria and archaea we met in the first two sections of this book. Eukaryote cells are packed with different compartments and with tiny structures called organelles, which carry out a host of different jobs.

The eukaryote domain of life is so large that this section has been split into three chapters. The first explores the clade of creatures known as plants and algae. Their cells have the amazing ability to capture sunlight energy and make their own food. By doing so, they support most other life-forms on Earth.

The second explores the biggest branch on the tree of life as we know it—the clade of animals and fungi. Like plants, most fungi and all animals are multicellular creatures, made up of billions or trillions of cells. They have evolved a dazzling diversity of forms and lifestyles.

The eukaryote domain of life also includes a host of microscopic single-celled creatures known as protozoans. Some are so bizarre that for a long time they baffled scientists and were lumped together in the "kingdom" known as protists. The third chapter explores some of the key clades of protozoans on the eukaryote branches of the tree of life. Although they are gathered together in this book, peering at their **DNA** has revealed that two protozoans from different clades are just as diverse as plants and animals.

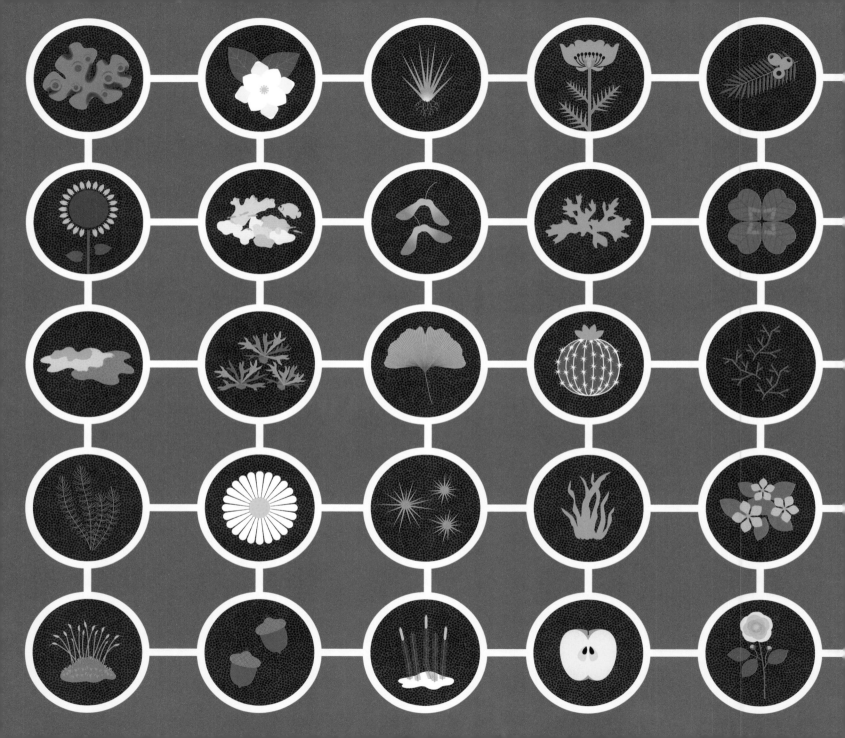

PLANTS & ALGAE
ARCHAEPLASTIDA

DON'T LOOK NOW, BUT YOU'RE SURROUNDED! PLANTS AND ALGAE HAVE COLONIZED EVERY PART OF EARTH'S SURFACE. YOU CAN SPOT THEM ON SEASHORES AND MOUNTAIN SUMMITS, CROWDED TOGETHER IN RAIN FORESTS, AND DEFENDING THEMSELVES IN DESERTS.

You may be pretty good at spotting plants, but could you tell an algae apart from an amoebozoan? Why are trees in this group and not toadstools? The secret is deep inside plant and algae cells.

These cells all contain tiny structures called plastids, which use sunlight energy to make food for the plant. This superpower, known as **photosynthesis**, is ancient and very useful. Plants and algae have been living on planet Earth for more than a billion years, and most still rely on photosynthesis as their only source of food. The group Archaeplastida is even named after their plastids.

This massive group of eukaryotes has helped to shape life on Earth. When the ancestors of today's green algae and plants first began living on land, they reshaped the air and climate and formed brand-new **habitats**. This made it possible for animals to move from oceans to land too. Today animals depend on plants and algae for just about everything, including food. Life as we know it would be impossible without them.

Get ready to explore the greenest branch of the tree of life and learn how plants and algae shape our world.

RED ALGAE
RHODOPHYTES

Red algae turn up in all kinds of surprising places, from science labs to ice cream parlors and sushi restaurants!

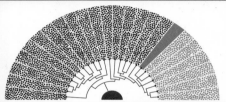

EUKARYOTA

ARCHAEPLASTIDA

KEY FACTS

- More than 5,000 species
- From long seaweeds to microscopic single-celled algae
- Most live in salt water, near coasts, but a few species are found in fresh water habitats

SPECIMEN

PYROPIA

ALL ABOUT

If you've ever spotted red seaweed in a rock pool or washed up on a beach, you've met a member of this ancient group of algae—simple plant-like organisms that don't have the roots, stems, or leaves of true plants. The oldest red algae fossils are thought be more than a billion years old!

Most red seaweeds are—unsurprisingly—found in saltwater habitats. Like plants on land, they rely on sunlight to make their own food, so they grow around coasts, where the water is shallow enough for some sunlight to reach them.

To carry out photosynthesis, red algae depend on colorful chemicals called pigments to soak up the sunlight energy. The main pigment found in plants and algae is green **chlorophyll**. As well as chlorophyll, red algae contain red and brown **pigments** that capture a wider range of the energy in sunlight. In particular they can soak up blue light—the color that can travel farthest through water. This allows red algae to live in deeper water than green plants and algae. In fact, some red algae live deeper than any other photosynthetic creatures—up to 270 meters (885 feet) underwater, which is almost the height of the Eiffel Tower.

Their ability to capture so much energy from sunlight means that red algae play a huge part in watery food chains, providing food for fish, worms, and many other creatures. They are an important source of oxygen in seawater too.

SHARED FEATURES

- Complex life cycles with three stages
- Super-tough cell walls protect them from germs, churning waves, sunshine, and other things
- Contains green, red, and brown pigments

GOOD NEIGHBORS?

Red algae are an important food in some parts of the world. They are also the source of substances that are used in medicine or added to foods and cosmetics to change their color or texture. Red seaweeds are also the source of an important gel called agar.

1	**AGAR** Red algae are also used to make agar. This jelly-like substance is used by biologists for growing **microbes,** so they can be studied more closely.
2	**REEF BUILDERS** Some red algae have helped corals to build tropical reefs over millions of years. Single-celled algae, like these coralline algae, make themselves a hard shell, which stays in place long after they have died. They are so good at doing this, they have even been used to grow replacement bones for humans!
3	**SUPER SOAKERS** Seaweeds are algae that live in salt water and are big enough to see without a microscope. Red seaweeds anchor themselves on rocks, on the shells of clams or sea snails, and even other seaweeds where they soak up the sunlight that makes it through the water. Red seaweeds can soak up most colors in sunlight except red light, which is why they look red to our eyes.
4	**FOOD ADDITIVES** Certain substances in the tough cell walls of red algae form gels when they are mixed with water. We use them to make foods thick and gloopy—including yogurt, ice cream, bubble tea, and jams!
5	**SUSHI WRAPPERS** Edible red seaweeds are packed with vitamins and proteins. Nori, a red seaweed that turns green and crispy when dried and toasted, is the most famous. It is used as an edible wrapper for sushi.

GREEN ALGAE & LAND PLANTS

CHLOROPLASTIDA

YOU ARE HERE

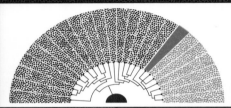

	EUKARYOTA
	ARCHAEPLASTIDA

KEY FACTS

- Up to 12,000 species of green algae and more than 435,000 species of land plants
- Green algae range from tiny plankton just 0.2 μm across to giant seaweeds with 60-m (196-ft) fronds. Some land plants grow even bigger than this
- Found everywhere on land and in water

SPECIMEN

COMMON LIVERWORT

It's good to be green! This is one of the largest and most important groups of living things in the world, and its members are found everywhere.

ALL ABOUT

Members of this **clade** are easy to spot because they are usually green! The color comes from a pigment called chlorophyll, found inside the cells of every species—from tiny, single-celled algae to towering trees. Green algae and plants use chlorophyll to soak up sunlight energy and make their own food, which they can store for later.

Green algae likely evolved first in the oceans and most green algae still live in water. Some anchor themselves on stones or other objects underwater. Others float freely, sometimes turning the surface of stagnant water green as part of pond "scum." They are an important source of food and oxygen for creatures that live in water.

Around 470 million years ago, some green algae made the move from water to land. What happened next transformed the planet. Those ancient algae are the ancestors of all the land plants we see today. Over millions of years, plants have reshaped Earth's atmosphere and land, creating landscapes where all kinds of other land creatures could evolve.

Some green algae species still grow above water—on tree trunks, in soil, and on rocks surrounded by air. But today, land plants outnumber their algae ancestors. They are the main type of living things found in most land habitats. The rest of this chapter is devoted to exploring their diversity in depth.

SHARED FEATURES

- The cells contain two types of the green pigment chlorophyll, plus yellow and brown pigments
- The starchy food they make is stored and converted to sugar when needed
- Their cell walls are strengthened by **cellulose**, which helps plants and algae to keep their shape and stay stiff and upright

GOOD NEIGHBORS?

Almost every food chain in the world begins with members of this group. We also use green algae and land plants to make clothes, buildings, medicines, fuels, and just about everything else you can think of! Pigments from green algae are even being used to help prevent cancer in humans.

| 1 | **GREEN SEAWEEDS** |
| | The easiest green algae to spot are seaweeds, such as sea lettuce grazed on by giant dugong. Although they look leafy, these large green algae are simpler than most land plants, without real roots, stems, or leaves. |

| 2 | **PHYTOPLANKTON** |
| | Algae capture **carbon dioxide** from the air just like land plants, but algae grow much faster. A single cubic meter (35 cubic feet) of algae can capture as much carbon as 100 square meters (more than 1,000 square feet) of forest. The smallest green algae are important phytoplankton. The energy and **nutrients** they capture are passed on up ocean food chains. |

| 3 | **LAND PLANTS** |
| | Land plants have been so successful at finding ways to survive on land, there are now hundreds of thousands of species. The rest of this chapter explores some of the main groups. |

| 4 | **LICHENS** |
| | Have you ever spotted curly, crispy, or stringy lichen growing on trees or stones? It's a hybrid of two different living things—green algae living in partnership with fungi! Look closely and you might also spot a peppered moth camouflaged against the lichen! |

| 5 | **STRANGE HABITATS** |
| | Some green algae live on or inside other creatures—including on the fur of sloths! The algae get shelter and water from the sponge-like fur. In return, they may provide the sloth with nutrients or help to camouflage the slow-moving sloths. |

LAND PLANTS

EMBRYOPHYTES

YOU ARE HERE

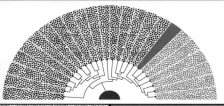

| EUKARYOTA |
| ARCHAEPLASTIDA |

KEY FACTS

- 435,000 species
- From tiny watermeal plants less than 1 mm (0.04 in) wide to towering trees more than 100 m (328 ft) tall
- Found on every landmass, including the coasts of Antarctica

SPECIMEN

CROCUS

Plants began living on land about 3 billion years after life began in the oceans, but they quickly made the planet their own.

ALL ABOUT

The land plants are such a big and important group of living things, that it's fascinating to gaze back in time and find out how they conquered planet Earth. Fossils show us that green plants began living on land around 470 million years ago, during a period known as the Ordovician. Earth's shallow seas were already getting crowded with life, all competing for the same energy, space, and nutrients. Certain green algae found success spending more time out of the water—clinging to the rocky coastline—where they were bathed in the sunlight needed to make their own food.

When these algae died, they formed **sediments** that washed up and collected in sheltered places—such as the estuaries where rivers meet seas. These decaying algae formed the first soils, creating habitats where new types of land plants could get started. Since then, thousands of different land plants have evolved, turning the planet's landmasses green.

The first land plants had to adapt to being surrounded by air instead of water. The challenge was keeping ahold of the water inside their cells, which evaporates quickly in the sun and wind. Plants evolved a protective layer called a **cuticle**, to keep water locked inside. This is the waxy, shiny layer you can spot on many leaves. The drier the environment, the thicker a plant's cuticle tends to be!

SHARED FEATURES

- Green pigments often give them a bright green color
- Cells contain other pigments too
- Food is stored as starch
- Cell walls contain cellulose
- Land plants have a stage of their life cycle known as the **embryo**, which algae don't have. This gives them their scientific name, Embryophytes

GOOD NEIGHBORS?

It's impossible to imagine life without land plants. We rely on members of this group for most of our food and much of the oxygen that we breathe. We also use plants to make clothes, buildings, medicines, fuels, and just about anything else you can think of. Even the text you are reading right now is printed on paper made from plants!

1 EXTREME SURVIVORS
Plants are found almost everywhere on land, except places permanently covered in ice and snow. Antarctica is the only continent without trees or shrubs, but even there you'll find mosses (see page 56), liverworts (see page 54), and grasses (see page 76).

2 SIMPLE PLANTS
Liverworts, mosses, and hornworts look small and simple compared to most land plants, but under a microscope they are amazingly complex and beautiful.

3 SEED PLANTS
Seed plants produce seeds. A seed is a special type of embryo that rests until it finds itself in the right conditions to grow. Many plants that make seeds can also make a super-tough tissue called wood, which lets them grow taller than other types of plants—all the better for capturing sunlight!

4 VASCULAR PLANTS
Most land plants have special **tissues** (called xylem and phloem) for transporting water and food all around the plant. You can see this in action by placing a celery stalk in a cup of diluted ink or food coloring. Don't eat the celery afterward!

5 ALWAYS GROWING
Unlike most living things, land plants have special cells that keep on dividing for as long as the plant is alive—meaning that a plant never stops growing until it dies. Just as well when you're being nibbled by hungry herbivores.

LIVERWORTS

MARCHANTIOPHYTES

Small but mighty, these dinosaurs of the plant world are helping us to explain how plants first conquered the land.

YOU ARE HERE

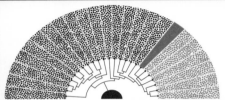

EUKARYOTA

ARCHAEPLASTIDA

KEY FACTS

- More than 9,000 species
- From less than 1 mm (0.04 in) to more than 5 cm (about 2 in) across
- Found around the world, especially in humid habitats such as tropical forests, swamps and bogs, rotting logs, and soggy soils

SPECIMEN

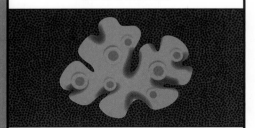

THALLOSE LIVERWORT

ALL ABOUT

Ancient liverwort fossils are the earliest evidence of land plants found so far. These micro-plants evolved long before the first dinosaurs appeared and are still going strong everywhere from deserts to the Arctic. For more than 200 years, biologists have used liverworts to help them unlock the secrets of plants—from understanding how their cells work to how plants know which way to grow.

Little liverworts tend to grow on the surface of damp things, such as rocks, trees, and the banks of streams. They are the tiny "weeds" that spring up as if by magic in the damp soil of house plants. Look closely and you'll see liverworts have no roots, seeds, flowers, or fruit—just rounded leaves, which may be as small as eyelashes. But liverworts are not as "weedy" as they seem. Liverworts gradually break down the rocks they grow on, helping to create soils. Liverworts also live closely alongside bacteria and fungi, relying on these microbes for all kinds of jobs, including anchoring the rootless plants in place.

Because they have such a long history, liverworts are interesting to scientists who are trying to figure out how plants began to grow on land. It's thought that today's liverworts look and behave more like the earliest land plants than any other group. Of course, liverworts have been evolving for just as long as any other plant—it's just that early on they found a formula that works well.

SHARED FEATURES

- No roots or veins to transport water through the plant
- Small size so they can soak up water from the surface they are sitting on (or even from the air)
- Reproduce by making **spores**, not seeds

GOOD NEIGHBORS?

Some gardeners see liverworts as weeds because they quickly steal air and light from growing seedlings. But liverworts are an important food for animals and also help dead logs to **decay**. The chemicals made inside their leaves are being investigated, with the hope that we can harness the liverworts' survival skills to help humans.

1	**TERRARIUM TROUBLE** Liverworts often take pride of place in terrariums, where they grow well in the damp conditions. But building too many terrariums is causing problems because people take plants from the wild.
2	**LIVER PLANTS** Some liverworts have branching lobes shaped a bit like livers, which is how this group got its name.
3	**SCIENCE STARS** When scientists are figuring out where a species belongs in the plant family tree, they often compare its genetic information to the **genome** of this common liverwort, *Marchantia polymorpha*. For more than 200 years, biologists have used a little liverwort species to help understand the inner workings of plants—from understanding how cells and chromosomes work to how plants know which way to grow.
4	**MURDER MYSTERY** Ötzi the Iceman is the famous frozen mummy of a prehistoric human murdered 5,300 years ago. By looking carefully at liverworts trapped in the ice alongside Ötzi, scientists were able to figure out where he had been walking before he died!
5	**LEAFY LIVERWORTS** Leafy liverworts are also known as "scale moss." They can be spotted growing on tree trunks or even leaves in humid tropical forests. Plants that grow on other plants are known as epiphytes.

MOSSES

BRYOPHYTES

Small and springy, mosses were some of the first plants to live on dry land!

YOU ARE HERE

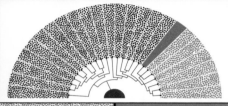

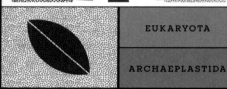

	EUKARYOTA
	ARCHAEPLASTIDA

KEY FACTS

- Around 12,000 species
- From 1 to 2 mm (0.04 to 0.08 in) to mounds more than 60 cm (about 2ft) tall
- Found everywhere except salt water, and especially in moist places because they have to be damp to reproduce

SPECIMEN

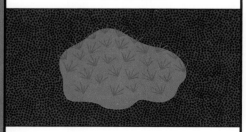

SPHAGNUM

ALL ABOUT

Mosses are small and simple plants without real roots, and without stems, flowers, or seeds. However, by growing closely together they can carpet huge areas of a forest floor and even form springy **"hummocks"** up to a meter (over 3 feet) high! Like liverworts, their small size is no barrier to success. Mosses may look simple, but scientists recently discovered that one moss species has about 10,000 more genes than a human does.

When a habitat is destroyed, mosses are some of the very first living things to reappear. Mosses aren't daunted by completely bare ground—even a rocky wall, rooftop, or pavement can become a home. This is because they don't rely on roots to soak up water. Instead, the entire moss acts like a giant sponge, soaking up and holding on to a huge volume of water when it rains. This can then be used by the moss when the weather is dry. Other creatures rely on this water too—especially small animals such as woodlice. Some birds love to tear moss up to get to the critters beneath.

By trapping water at the surface of the ground, mosses play a hugely important role in preventing soil erosion and maintaining the balance of water in a habitat, which helps other plants to grow. Mosses are the humble heroes that the world depends on. Because mosses are small, changes in acidity, temperature, and humidity affect them very quickly. They are becoming important for monitoring signs of air pollution, water pollution, and climate change.

SHARED FEATURES

- No roots
- Very small, thin leaves
- Anchor themselves to surfaces using thin brown **rhizoids**
- Reproduce by making spores, not seeds

GOOD NEIGHBORS?

In some parts of the world, peat—a thick layer of dead and slowly decaying moss— is dug up, dried, and burned as a fuel. Although it forms more quickly than coal, oil, and natural gas, peat still takes thousands of years to build up, so can be thought of as a fossil fuel. Living peat is often used for growing other plants, such as trees.

1 **PEATLANDS**

Peatlands are formed when *Sphagnum* moss dies in waterlogged bogs and slowly decays. They cover about 3% of Earth's land and provide an important habitat for thousands of creatures, including Bornean orangutans.

2 **GLOBAL TRAVELERS**

How do mosses get to mountainsides and rooftops in the first place? Scientists have discovered that they are carried long distances on the wind. The purple horn-toothed mosses are the most widespread, springing up everywhere from concrete buildings to glaciers.

3 **BOG MOSSES**

Sphagnum is the main kind of moss found in boglands, swamps, marshlands, and moorlands. These special habitats are like huge sponges that help to slow the flow of water across the land and prevent flooding in other areas.

4 **TINY WORLDS**

Mosses are home to a host of microscopic animals, such as tardigrades or "water bears" (see page 109). Like water bears, moss can often survive for many years without water, then spring back to life when wet again. Scientists recently revived moss that had been frozen in Antarctic ice for 1,500 years!

5 **CLIMATE CHANGE**

More carbon is locked away in peat than any other vegetation type, including all the world's forests. When peat is burned, this carbon forms carbon dioxide, one of the greenhouse gases that is causing global warming and climate change.

FERN ALLIES

LYCOPHYTES

YOU ARE HERE

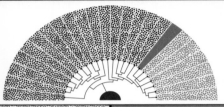

	EUKARYOTA
	ARCHAEPLASTIDA

KEY FACTS

- More than 1,200 species
- Today's species range from 1 cm (0.39 in) to several centimeters (several inches)
- Found everywhere except Antarctica, in all kinds of ecosystems

SPECIMEN

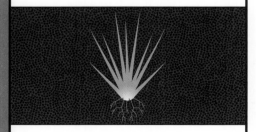

QUILLWORT

If you're looking for plants that can stick their tongue out at you or explode like fireworks, you've come to the right page!

ALL ABOUT

At first, many plants in this group were thought to be types of mosses or ferns. After all, they were small and seedless. They grow a bit like mosses and look a bit like ferns. But when scientists found fossils of ancient tree-sized lycophytes, they began to realize they'd gotten these plants completely wrong!

Lycophytes have an important feature that mosses (and liverworts) don't share—special tissues for transporting water and food all around the plant. These tissues (called xylem and phloem) are found in all "vascular plants" and allow them to grow MUCH bigger than liverworts and mosses, which have to painstakingly pass water on from cell to cell.

Plants use xylem tissue to transport water from the place it is soaked up to a place that needs it. They use phloem tissue to transport food far from the leaves where it is made. This means vascular plants can get as big as buildings and still get food and water to every cell.

Today's lycophytes are not nearly as big but they are the oldest group of vascular plants (around 400 million years old), which makes them very interesting to study. They do things a bit differently from other types of plants, and because of this, genetic engineers are looking at how to transfer genes from the lycophytes species to other crops to create better renewable fuels.

SHARED FEATURES

- Reproduce by making microscopic spores, not seeds
- Their spores are spread by the wind
- Their leaves have just one vein, which runs down the whole leaf

GOOD NEIGHBORS?

The remains of ancient lycophytes formed most of the world's coal—a fossil fuel that many countries still rely on for energy today. Burning coal is one cause of global warming and climate change, but *today's* lycophytes are helping scientists to bioengineer greener fuels for the future.

1	**SPIKEMOSSES** *Selaginella* or "spikemoss" forms green carpets in tropical forests. It's named after the spiky "tongue" that grows out from its leaves. This tongue may make a type of slime to keep young leaves damp!
2	**STRANGE SOCIAL LIVES** Scientists recently realized that huge colonies of staghorn ferns in Australia live a bit like ants or bees (see page 136). They divide up jobs such as collecting water, working for the good of the colony instead of themselves.
3	**QUILLWORTS** Quillworts grow in or near water, such as lakes and sleepy rivers. Their stems are totally underground—the only part we see is the leaves growing out of the top.
4	**CLUBMOSSES** Clubmosses were once popular winter decorations, perhaps because they look like tiny fir trees. But this proved dangerous, because their spores burn so quickly they explode! Lycopodium powder was once used to make bright camera flashes and fireworks.
5	**CLINGING ON** Many lycophytes live their lives attached to rain forest trees. The tree does the hard work of holding the lycophytes in a place where they can soak up sunlight.
6	**COAL CREATORS** Long before dinosaurs roamed Earth, lycophytes were the most successful plants on the planet. Some grew to more than 30 meters (98 feet) tall and today we still burn their ancient remains in the form of coal.

FERNS & HORSETAILS

MONILOPHYTES

YOU ARE HERE

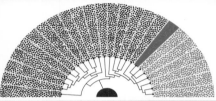

| EUKARYOTA |
| ARCHAEPLASTIDA |

KEY FACTS

- More than 11,500 species
- From aquatic ferns just 5 mm (0.2 in) tall to the Mexican giant horsetail, which can reach more than 7 m (23 ft)
- Found in all humid environments; ferns seem particularly fond of tropical and subtropical mountains. Many grow as epiphytes, on trees

SPECIMEN

OSTRICH FERN

This group of plants once dominated Earth. Their ancestors include giant trees as well as plants that wore down the teeth of the dinosaurs.

ALL ABOUT

The ancestors of today's ferns and horsetails lived on Earth at a time when all the world's continents were joined together as one supercontinent called Pangaea. This explains why they are found on every continent today, despite enormous oceans opening up in the meantime.

Ferns have large leaves called fronds, which begin as tightly coiled spirals. These "fiddleheads" unfurl to grow in a way that seems magical. Once they have unfurled, you can see that the fronds are made up of many smaller sections, arranged in a repeating pattern.

Like their ancient cousins the bryophytes and lycophytes, the ferns and horsetails produce spores and not seeds. Look underneath fern fronds and you might spot the spores developing on the surface of the leaf.

Ferns and horsetails are hardy plants. They can survive in spots where other plants would die, such as shady forest floors. Ferns and horsetails are also some of the first plants to spring back to life after forest fires or droughts. They can cope with substances in the soil that would poison other plants. The Chinese brake fern can soak up and store huge amounts of arsenic and lead from soil without being harmed. It's being used to help clean up contaminated soil, so the soil can be used safely in the future.

SHARED FEATURES

- Ferns have large leaves called fronds
- Fronds are made up of many smaller sections, arranged in a repeating pattern
- Reproduce by making spores, not seeds

GOOD NEIGHBORS?

Old books show that ferns were once used to try to treat dandruff and common colds! Today they are popular as garden and houseplants and millions of these are sold every year. But some ferns and horsetails are considered weeds because they outgrow other plants or are toxic to animals.

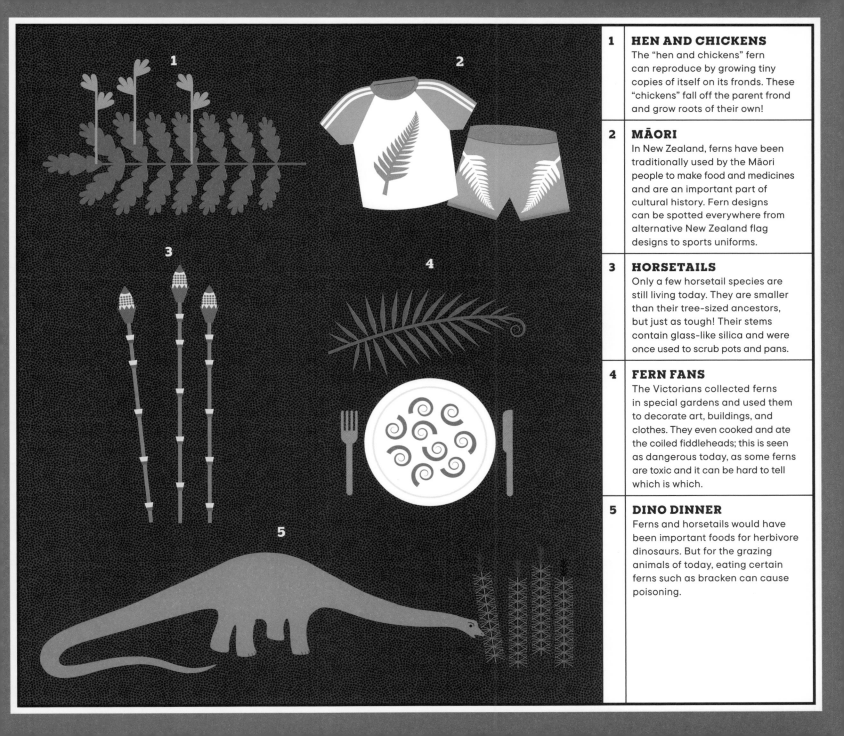

1 HEN AND CHICKENS
The "hen and chickens" fern can reproduce by growing tiny copies of itself on its fronds. These "chickens" fall off the parent frond and grow roots of their own!

2 MĀORI
In New Zealand, ferns have been traditionally used by the Māori people to make food and medicines and are an important part of cultural history. Fern designs can be spotted everywhere from alternative New Zealand flag designs to sports uniforms.

3 HORSETAILS
Only a few horsetail species are still living today. They are smaller than their tree-sized ancestors, but just as tough! Their stems contain glass-like silica and were once used to scrub pots and pans.

4 FERN FANS
The Victorians collected ferns in special gardens and used them to decorate art, buildings, and clothes. They even cooked and ate the coiled fiddleheads; this is seen as dangerous today, as some ferns are toxic and it can be hard to tell which is which.

5 DINO DINNER
Ferns and horsetails would have been important foods for herbivore dinosaurs. But for the grazing animals of today, eating certain ferns such as bracken can cause poisoning.

SEED PLANTS

SPERMATOPHYTES

The ability to produce seeds was a game-changer for plants. Today land is dominated by seed plants, and they are even found in parts of the ocean!

YOU ARE HERE

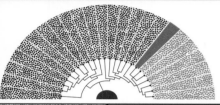

EUKARYOTA

ARCHAEPLASTIDA

KEY FACTS

- More than 300,000 species
- The largest seed plants are trees more than 90 m (295 ft) tall
- Found everywhere on land and even include ocean plants, such as seagrasses

SPECIMEN

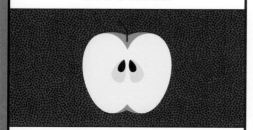

APPLE SEEDS

ALL ABOUT

Welcome to the largest clade of land plants. The spermatophytes are named after their ability to produce seeds, but that's not the only thing that sets them apart. Seed plants are said to be more "organized" than other types of plants in every way. While every part of a moss helps to soak up water, and every part of a fern carries out photosynthesis, a seed plant is divided up into lots of different parts, each with a different job to do.

This is one reason for their success. The other is the seeds themselves. Instead of sending thousands of microscopic spores off into the environment—in the hope that a few may land in the right place to grow—seed plants give their embryos a head start by packaging them up inside a seed.

Each seed includes nutrients and a protective coat. This helps the embryo travel farther from the parent plant. Some seeds travel for years before they begin to grow and may even cross oceans. This gives them a better chance of finding good conditions for growing, in a place where they won't compete with their parents and siblings for nutrients, light, and water.

Seed plants can be sorted into two subgroups. Gymnosperms include conifers, cycads, ginkgoes, and gnetophytes. These "naked seed" plants produce their seeds out in the open. The other, much larger group, are the angiosperms. These are plants that produce flowers and seeds that develop inside fruit, such as apples.

SHARED FEATURES

- Reproduce by making seeds
- Some produce wood to strengthen their stems
- Roots are good at sensing gravity and growing downward

GOOD NEIGHBORS?

Seed plants have shaped human history in all kinds of ways—from the everyday (a source of food, wood, and fibers to make clothes) to the unusual (the Ancient Egyptians used oil from cedar trees to mummify their dead). They are also grown and celebrated simply because they are beautiful.

1 GINKGOES

Ginkgoes were very common plants in the Jurassic, but just one species remains today. This "living fossil" almost became **extinct** too but was kept alive in the gardens of Chinese Buddhist monasteries. Today it is grown around the world and loved for its beautiful fan-shaped leaves.

2 GNETOPHYTES

This small but varied group of plants are known for surviving in strange places. Weirdest of all is the *Welwitschia*. This desert plant has two leaves that never stop growing, just like your fingernails!

3 FLOWERING PLANTS

Angiosperms are plants that produce flowers, and fruit with seeds inside. The first flowering plants only appeared about 130 million years ago, but since then they have successfully **colonized** just about every habitat in the world. Most plant species alive today are members of this group. Meet some of them on pages 68 to 87.

4 SEEDS OF ALL SIZES

Coconuts are some of the biggest seeds on the planet. The vanilla orchid (see page 74) produces the world's smallest seeds! They are the tiny black specks you might see in vanilla ice cream or custard.

5 CONIFERS

Conifers are a group of trees and shrubs that produce their seeds inside cones. They have leaves shaped like needles and can grow very tall. In colder forests, they are the main trees. Find out more on page 64.

CONIFERS

PINOPHYTES

The world's tallest, largest, and oldest living plants are all conifers. What's the secret to their success?

YOU ARE HERE

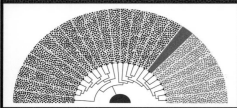

	EUKARYOTA
	ARCHAEPLASTIDA

KEY FACTS

- Around 630 species
- Fully grown conifers range from 30 cm (about 1 ft) to more than 100 m (328 ft) tall
- Found worldwide, in both **temperate** and humid climates; the main trees are found in cold climates

SPECIMEN

MARITIME PINE

ALL ABOUT

The pinophytes are a small group of seed plants with a BIG reach. Most are trees, including pine trees, fir trees, and many others. In the **Northern Hemisphere**, conifers are usually tall, with leaves shaped like needles. The needles are arranged in spirals around their branches and twigs, to capture as much light as possible all year-round. In the **Southern Hemisphere**, conifers are shorter and shaped more like bushes, with bigger, broader leaves.

Although there are just a few hundred species of conifers, they are like the world's lungs, taking in carbon dioxide and releasing huge volumes of oxygen during photosynthesis. In cooler areas, conifers are often the main plants—especially in the taiga, the vast northern forests that cover an amazing 17% of Earth's land. Together, these huge forests are the largest store of trapped carbon on land—beating even the rain forests. To cope with the cold winters, these evergreen trees grow in a cone shape with narrow tops and drooping branches, which helps snow slide off. They also make special chemicals that stop their needles from freezing!

If you've ever scratched the bark of a conifer, you may have noticed thick, sticky resin leaking out. Conifers produce resin to protect themselves from infections and insect attacks. The resin flows out and then sets hard to seal the wound. Resin often smells nice and can be used to make scented products as well as medicines, varnishes, and glues.

SHARED FEATURES

- Seeds form on the woody scales of a pine cone
- The pine cone protects the seeds
- When the seeds are ready, and the conditions are right, the scales open and the seeds fall out

GOOD NEIGHBORS?

Conifers are a hugely important source of wood for building. This "softwood" is also used for making paper and cardboard, paints and varnishes as well as food. People even make jewelry from the fossilized resin of conifers, known as amber. In some parts of the world, people use conifers and cones to decorate their homes in December.

1 GENTLE GIANTS
Sequoia trees (also known as redwoods) are the tallest living things in the world. Some grow to more than 100 meters (328 feet) tall and can measure more than 30 meters (98 feet) around the trunk.

2 DINOSAUR TREE
Wollemi pines, which date back to the time of the dinosaurs, are thought of as a "living fossils." These trees were thought to have gone extinct, until someone stumbled across one in an Australian canyon! Since then, their seeds have been planted around the world.

3 TOXIC TREES
The yew tree is toxic for humans. Eating just a few leaves or berries can be fatal. But these same toxic chemicals have been turned into powerful medicines, used to kill cancer cells.

4 RAW MATERIALS
Most wood, paper, and cardboard used in the northern hemisphere comes from the trunks of conifers.

5 ANCIENT AMBER
When fossilized pine resin is polished, it seems to glow orange-yellow. Sometimes the insects that attacked the tree and caused the resin to flow are found fossilized inside it!

6 LONG-LIVED
The oldest-known living thing on the planet is a 5,000-year-old bristlecone pine in California. It was a seedling at the very end of the Stone Age, when the great civilization of Ancient Egypt was just getting started.

CYCADS

CYCADOPHYTES

YOU ARE HERE

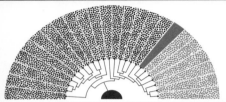

EUKARYOTA

ARCHAEPLASTIDA

KEY FACTS

- Around 300 species
- Most are shrub-sized, but some can reach 18 m (almost 60 ft) in height
- Found in tropical and subtropical areas of the Americas, Asia, and Australia

SPECIMEN

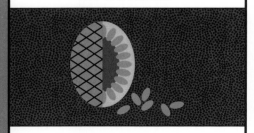

BURRAWANG SEEDS

Large, tough, and dangerous—cycads are the crocodiles of the plant world.

ALL ABOUT

Cycads look like palm trees crossed with ferns. The first cycads evolved just before the first dinosaurs, at least 280 million years ago. Perhaps that's why they adapted to become incredibly poisonous, to avoid being chomped by supersized herbivores! Many of today's cycads look very similar to their ancient ancestors and are very poisonous to mammals.

The main toxin found in a cycad's seeds, roots, and tough, leathery leaves is called cycasin. It's part of the plants' **immune system**, helping to protect them from infection by microbes. When cycasin is broken down in a mammal's body, poisons such as hydrogen cyanide, **nitrogen** gas, and formaldehyde are formed. Eating just one or two seeds can be fatal for a cat or dog. Despite this danger, cycad plants have been used as food and in traditional medicines in different parts of the world.

Most wild cycads are found in tropical and subtropical habitats, such as rain forests and grasslands. They can also live in extreme habitats where other plants struggle to survive, such as sand dunes and steep cliffs. Cycads are large plants and they live a long time—up to 1,000 years old! But many species are rare and becoming rarer. Cycads are popular garden plants because they are so beautiful, but this has led to illegal poaching of wild cycads. Some are facing extinction in the wild. International laws now ban the trade of certain wild cycad seeds. Protecting cycads will help to protect entire ecosystems.

SHARED FEATURES

- Unique "coralloid" roots, which branch like corals
- Crown of large leaves, each made up of many smaller leaves
- Seeds are produced inside cones
- Woody stems or trunks, without branches
- Has either male or female parts, rather than both

GOOD NEIGHBORS?

Cycads are wonderful neighbors for other plants, sharing nutrients such as nitrogen and carbon through the soil. As well as being an important source of flour in some parts of the world, cycads produce powerful toxins that can be turned into medicines to treat some diseases.

1	**BREAD TREES** Bread trees are cycads that only grow in the wild in Africa. They can cope with almost any weather, from high altitude, dry soil, and strong winds to freezing snow and ice. These beautiful cycads are critically endangered due to poaching of wild cycads and insect infestations.
2	**ROVING ROOTS** Cycads' amazing coralloid roots (shown here in yellow) grow up out of the soil, instead of down! This means the friendly Cyanobacteria (see page 24) living inside are bathed in light. Cycads seem to carefully control which bacteria can get into their roots.
3	**SAGO FLOUR** The center of the "trunk" of young cycads, such as sago palms, is high in carbohydrates. It can be carefully separated from poisonous parts of the plant, ground into flour, and used to make flatbreads called dosas.
4	**MEGA PARTS** Cycads reproduce very slowly due to their long life span. Fadang are huge cycads that live in Guam and Micronesia. Male trees produce cones that can grow more than 50 cm (1.6 ft) high. Female plants also grow a huge structure, called a megastrobilus.
5	**POISON PROOF** Some cycads produce heat and strong smells to attract pollinating insects such as butterflies. They produce poisons to deter other insects, but certain insects quickly become resistant to cycad poisons, allowing them to dig in.

FLOWERING PLANTS

ANGIOSPERMS

YOU ARE HERE

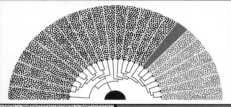

	EUKARYOTA
	ARCHAEPLASTIDA

KEY FACTS

- More than 300,000 species
- From tiny flower plants less than 2 mm (0.07 in) total to trees more than 100 m (328 ft) tall
- Found on every continent (including Antarctic islands), on land and sometimes in water

SPECIMEN

GIANT WATER LILY

Flowering plants are such show-offs! But their beauty is not for our benefit...

ALL ABOUT

The flowering plants are the largest clade of seed plants. From buttercups to apple trees, all flowering plants make flowers and fruit. Flowers are where the plant's eggs and pollen are found. A single flower may have male pollen or female eggs, or both. The eggs are protected inside a hollow ovary. Large bright petals help flowers to attract pollinators such as bees, beetles, and butterflies, which collect the pollen as food.

When a flower has been pollinated, it begins to develop into a seed, and parts of the flower around it begin to change into a fruit. The fruit protects the developing seed and often helps it find its way to a new home. Many fruits are so delicious, juicy, and rich in energy that they get eaten by a bird or mammal, ensuring that the seed is pooped out far from the parent plant!

Not all flowers are as bright as buttercups and not all fruit as large as apples. Grasses, cacti, herbs, oak trees, Venus flytraps, and palm trees are flowering plants too. There are even seagrasses that produce flowers beneath the ocean waves!

The first flowering plants were rather like today's water lilies. Over the last 130 million years, other flowering plants have evolved a vast range of sizes, shapes, colors, smells, and tastes as they adapted to live in different habitats.

SHARED FEATURES

- Special structures called flowers hold the plant's reproductive parts, including the female ovum (egg) and the male pollen
- When a fertilized egg begins to change into a seed, the flower around it begins to change into a fruit

GOOD NEIGHBORS?

Almost all the plants we use as food are in this group, including every type of fruit. People enjoy growing flowers, having flowers in their homes, and even decorating clothes and objects with pictures of flowers. We have also learned to turn different parts of flowering plants into medicines, clothes, building materials, paper, tires, and many other things.

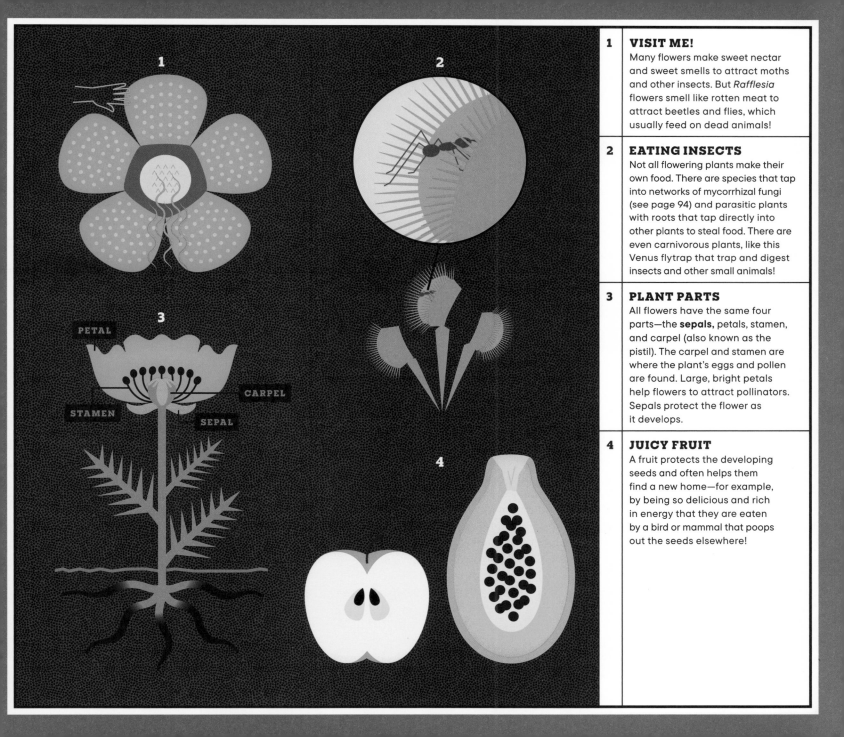

1 VISIT ME!

Many flowers make sweet nectar and sweet smells to attract moths and other insects. But *Rafflesia* flowers smell like rotten meat to attract beetles and flies, which usually feed on dead animals!

2 EATING INSECTS

Not all flowering plants make their own food. There are species that tap into networks of mycorrhizal fungi (see page 94) and parasitic plants with roots that tap directly into other plants to steal food. There are even carnivorous plants, like this Venus flytrap that trap and digest insects and other small animals!

3 PLANT PARTS

All flowers have the same four parts—the **sepals,** petals, stamen, and carpel (also known as the pistil). The carpel and stamen are where the plant's eggs and pollen are found. Large, bright petals help flowers to attract pollinators. Sepals protect the flower as it develops.

4 JUICY FRUIT

A fruit protects the developing seeds and often helps them find a new home—for example, by being so delicious and rich in energy that they are eaten by a bird or mammal that poops out the seeds elsewhere!

PETAL

CARPEL

STAMEN

SEPAL

MAGNOLIIDS

MAGNOLIIDS

This group of flowering plants are famous for their flavors. Their fruit, leaves, and even bark have been spicing up food for thousands of years.

YOU ARE HERE

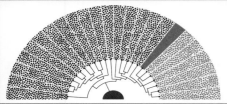

	EUKARYOTA
	ARCHAEPLASTIDA

KEY FACTS

- Around 10,000 species
- From small herbaceous plants to long vines that use other plants for support
- Found throughout the world, but especially in warm, humid habitats

SPECIMEN

MAGNOLIA

ALL ABOUT

This group is named after some of their members—the magnolias—which are famous for their large, tough flowers. Some of the oldest flowering plant fossils belong to this group, which tells us they have been around for a very long time.

Over 130 million years, many different magnoliids have evolved—from long-lived, woody evergreen trees to herbs that **germinate**, flower, and die in just one year. They include tall trees, short shrubs, and long clinging vines. They include parasitic plants that tap into the roots of other plants and steal their food.

Magnoliids share some features with monocots (see page 72) and some with eudicots (see page 78), which is a clue that they have been around longer than either of these groups. This makes them very interesting to study, as they can tell scientists how flowering plants got started and what made them so successful.

Magnoliids make two types of **alkaloid** chemicals that are rare in other plants. These help to defend the plants from attack by **microbes** and hungry herbivores. Humans have found lots of ways to use these chemicals to make medicines and to flavor foods. For example, black pepper has been one of the most widely used spices for thousands of years. Peppercorns have even been found in the nostrils of ancient Egyptian mummies!

SHARED FEATURES

- Long, wide leaves
- Large flowers
- Petals and sepals may look the same
- Produce strong chemicals called alkaloids

GOOD NEIGHBORS?

Many of the spices people use in cooking come from plants in this group, as well as popular foods such as avocados. Many only grow in tropical parts of the world, and the business of growing them and transporting them to other places (the spice trade) has played a huge role in shaping human history, culture, and politics.

1 BEETLE POWER
Many magnoliids rely on beetles to spread pollen from flower to flower. Beetles (see page 138) appeared on the planet before bees and have been pollinating flowering plants for far longer.

2 GREEN GOLD
Avocados are the fruit of a tree in the magnoliid clade. Most of the world's avocados are grown in Mexico and Central America, but eaten in Europe, North America, and Asia. Clearing land to grow thirsty avocado trees is causing environmental damage and has even disrupted the migration of the Monarch butterfly (see page 85).

3 REST ON YOUR LAURELS
The leaves of laurel trees are today used to flavor food, but in Ancient Rome they were also used to make wreaths to crown important people. We still use the world "laureate" to mean someone who has been honored for their achievements.

4 SPICE SOURCE
Many favorite spices come from plants in this clade, including peppercorns (the fruit of vines), cinnamon (the dried and rolled bark of trees), and nutmeg (the seeds of trees). The strong taste of black pepper comes from fruit oils, but the tingle comes from piperine, an alkaloid chemical made by the plants for self-defense. In ancient Rome, black pepper was so precious it was used as money and became known as "black gold."

PLANTS WITH ONE SEED LEAF

MONOCOTS

This group of flowering plants is incredibly important for humans, because it includes most of the crops that we grow on farms.

YOU ARE HERE

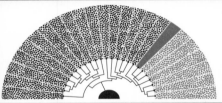

	EUKARYOTA
	ARCHAEPLASTIDA

KEY FACTS

- More than 60,000 species
- From duckweed *Wolffia*, about the size of a period, to Quindío wax palms up to 60 m (nearly 200 ft) tall
- Most monocots are tropical plants found in warm and humid parts of the world; the ones that aren't are found just about everywhere

SPECIMEN

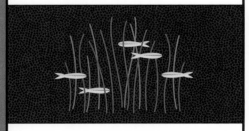

SEAGRASS

ALL ABOUT

If you've ever watched seeds begin to grow, you might have noticed that at first a new shoot has either one leaf or two. Scientists used to sort flowering plants into two groups based on this. Plants with one seed leaf were known as "monocots" and plants with two leaves as "dicots." Looking closely at genetic information revealed that the dicots are not actually closely related to each other. But most monocots do share a **common ancestor**.

Monocots have other features in common too. For example, their pollen grains each have just one dent or pore—compared to three in most other flowering plants. But you would need a microscope to check this out! Luckily, there is an easier way to figure out if a plant is a monocot or eudicot.

Next time you see a flower, count the petals, stamens, or other parts. If the number can be divided by three, it's likely to belong in this group. But if its parts come in fours or fives (for example, four petals, five carpels, or ten stamens) it's probably a eudicot (see page 78). Of course, the math won't work if some of the parts have been eaten by a hungry herbivore before you get there!

Perhaps the most visible difference of all is that monocots can't make wood or bark. This means there are no true trees in this group—although some monocots known as palms have a different way of making tall, strong "trunks."

SHARED FEATURES

- Veins run from top to bottom of leaves in parallel lines, instead of branching out in different directions like a net
- Can't make wood or bark
- First shoots have one seed leaf
- Flower parts come in threes

GOOD NEIGHBORS?

The most important crop plants in the world (the ones that feed the most people) are all monocots. They include grasses (see page 76) such as corn, wheat, rice, and barley, as well as sugarcane and bananas. We also use monocots such as bamboo and palms for building things and for making vegetable oil and fabrics.

1 PRECIOUS FLOWERS
The spice saffron is made from the stigmas (the tip of the flower's carpels) of certain crocuses. Each flower only makes three stigmas, which are picked by hand at sunrise and dried. It takes about 15,000 flowers to make around 2 pounds of the spice.

2 NO WOOD
Palms are fake trees! Palms are monocots, and just like other monocots they can't make wood or bark. Their stems can't grow outward—only up. The "trunk" of palms is really just the overlapping bases of old leaves. Cycads (see page 66) and ferns (see page 60) grow in the same way.

3 CORPSE FLOWER
The 3-meter (about 10-foot) flowering body of the titan arum is the biggest in the world. It's not actually a single flower, but a huge spike covered in small flowers. It only blooms every seven years or so, for 48 hours, and makes a smell like rotting meat to attract the beetles and flies that pollinate it.

4 ENERGY SOURCE
Agave is famous for its rosettes of thick, leathery leaves that store water (the plants grow in very dry habitats). In parts of the world, agave has been used for thousands of years to make tough fibers and sweeteners. These plants are so packed with energy, they could soon be used to make biofuel.

5 RAINBOW COLORS
Most plants that form bulbs are monocots, from onions and garlic to daffodils and tulips. More than 90% of the tulips sold around the world are grown in the Netherlands.

ORCHIDS

ORCHIDAE

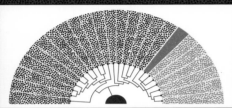

	EUKARYOTA
	ARCHAEPLASTIDA

KEY FACTS

- Around 28,000 species
- Orchid flowers can be as small as 2 mm (0.08 in) and up to 380 mm (15 in) across
- Wild orchids are found all around the world from deserts to the Arctic Circle, but especially in wet tropical areas

SPECIMEN

EPIPHYTIC ORCHID

Orchids are the Lokis of the plant world, using all kinds of tricks and disguises to lure insects to their extraordinary flowers.

ALL ABOUT

Members of this huge family of monocots are found all around the world, from tropical forests to the frozen Arctic. Their unusual flowers often have just one line of symmetry—more like an animal than a flower. In fact, many orchid flowers have evolved to look like insects! Instead of wasting energy making extra pollen and nectar, some orchids attract insects simply by looking like bees, flies, or spiders themselves.

Orchids also have unusual seeds compared to other flowering plants. Each flower produces tiny seeds, no bigger than specks of dust, which are spread on the wind. They are far too tiny to include the fuel a growing seed needs to get started. By producing millions of seeds, the orchids increase the chances that some seeds will happen to land on friendly fungi. They begin to grow on the fungi, using some of the fungi's food until the orchid has leaves to make their own food. Without that first fungi to call home, orchid seeds will not germinate!

When a young orchid is big enough, it may start feeding the fungi in return, with sugars made in its leaves. Or it may start a new, independent life.

Rather than using their roots to anchor themselves in soil, many orchids piggyback on larger plants. Orchids are most diverse in tropical cloud forests, clinging to treetops, where their leaves can soak up sunlight, and their spongy roots can soak up water from the moist air.

SHARED FEATURES

- Flowers often have just one line of symmetry, with three petals and three sepals that may look like petals
- Produce millions of tiny seeds that are spread by wind
- Roots attach to surfaces, rather than growing down into soil

GOOD NEIGHBORS?

People love to grow orchids in gardens and homes, so millions are sold around the world each year. A few species of orchids are used to get a type of natural glue, but vanilla flavoring is the only major product made from orchids. This may change as we learn more about these plants.

1	**IS IT A WORM?** Not all orchids are considered beautiful. The newly discovered "ugliest orchid" has flowers that look like slimy brown worms! They have no leaves and spend their lives buried in rotting leaves on the forest floor, getting fed by fungi!
2	**MEGA MOTH** It's not just flowers that adapt to insects. The sphinx moth, with its 25-cm (almost 10-in) "tongue," has adapted to drink from the huge trumpet of the ghost orchid's nectar, which it pollinates at the same time.
3	**VANILLA FLAVOR** Vanilla orchids coat their seeds in a sticky goo. When the pods open, the seeds stick to passing animals and get carried away from the parent plant. Humans like to use the sticky goo to flavor food!
4	**LOOK-ALIKES** Bee orchids look and smell like female bees, to ensure frequent visits from male bees. One petal is specially shaped as a landing platform. The bee doesn't get any food from the flower, but he flies off covered in pollen!
5	**ANT ARMY** Some orchids make nectar, but it's not always found in the flower. They store it in different parts of the plant to attract ants. The ants then chase away other insects that eat plants. Some orchids even grow on ants' nests to benefit from this ant army.

GRASSES, CATTAILS & SEDGES

POALES

Much of Earth's land is covered by grasses—from wild savanna to fields of rice and wheat. These plants make it possible for almost 8 billion humans to live on the planet.

YOU ARE HERE

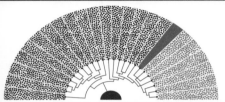

EUKARYOTA

ARCHAEPLASTIDA

KEY FACTS

- More than 18,000 species
- The largest are bamboo plants, which can grow up to 40 m (over 131 ft) tall
- Found on every continent and in all kinds of habitats, from dry deserts to soggy swamps

SPECIMEN

ROUGH MEADOW GRASS

ALL ABOUT

Most individual grass plants aren't very big, but together they take up a LOT of space on Earth's surface. They are the main plants in savannas, steppes, meadows, prairies, tundra, paddy fields, and bamboo forests.

The secret to grasses' success is the strange little bumps near the bottom of each stem. Most plants grow at the tips, but grass grows from these bumps. This means animals can nibble grass above this bump, and the grass just keeps growing! It helps grasses survive in conditions that are too tough for most plants.

For humans, grasses are the most useful plants on the planet. Grasses produce small, hard seeds called grains. They don't have juicy fruit around them, but they are packed with starch—a brilliant source of energy—as well as proteins and oils. Our ancestors began eating grasses about 3.5 million years ago. By cooking grains (grass seeds) we digest even more of its energy. One theory is that this energy boost is what allowed humans to develop such big brains for our size.

Today, up to 70% of the world's farmland is used to grow grass of different kinds. These include grass for grazing animals, and grass crops such as rice, wheat, barley, oats, and sugarcane. Cereals provide more than half of the energy needed by the world's people. Grassy lawns are popular all over the world in gardens and as soft surfaces to play sports.

SHARED FEATURES

- Thin roots that spread through the soil
- Long, narrow leaves called "blades"
- Tiny flowers hidden in groups called "spikelets"
- Pollen is spread by the wind

GOOD NEIGHBORS?

Grass is the most important family of plants for humans. Over thousands of years, we have farmed wild grasses to create the crops known as "cereals." Just 35 different food grasses are the main source of human food, and not just for vegetarians. Many of the animals we farm for meat and dairy also graze on grasses or are fed cereals.

1	**DEATH TRAP** This family of plants also includes pineapples and their relatives, the bromeliads. The leaves of tank bromeliads collect water and become habitats for animals such as tree frogs. Be warned…some tank bromeliads are carnivorous!
2	**SWEET MUSIC** Woodwind instruments such as saxophones have a reed in the mouthpiece that vibrates to make sounds. The reeds in a woodwind instrument are made from the stems of grass called *Arundo donax*. This giant grass mainly grows in the Mediterranean.
3	**VEGGIE STEEL** Bamboo is the tallest, toughest grass. Some species can grow almost a meter (over 3 feet) in a day. For its weight, bamboo is stronger than steel when stretched and stronger than concrete when squashed!
4	**ALARMING SMELLS** The smell of freshly cut grass is actually a call for help! When grass plants are damaged by nibbling insects, they release smelly chemicals that attract animals that eat insects. The same thing happens when grass is damaged by a lawnmower.
5	**SLICING BLADES** Grasses have another trick for keeping hungry herbivores at bay. Their leaves are packed with silica—the main ingredient in glass! As grazing animals chew, their teeth are worn down by the silica, which is why a cow's teeth keep growing its whole life.

EUDICOTS

EUDICOTS

YOU ARE HERE

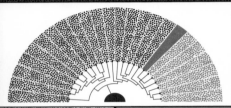

EUKARYOTA

ARCHAEPLASTIDA

KEY FACTS

- At least 190,000 species
- From tiny bellflowers just a few millimeters (about 0.01 in) tall to the tallest flowering plants, 100-m (328-ft) mountain ash trees
- Found in all kinds of different habitats, including some of the highest and driest places on Earth

SPECIMEN

BARREL CACTUS

Surprising as it seems, an ancient oak tree is more closely related to a carrot than a towering fir.

ALL ABOUT

Monocots (see page 72) may have made their mark on the planet, but the biggest group of flowering plants are the eudicots. This clade is named after the dicots—an older word to describe flowering plants that begin as a shoot with two seed leaves.

One way to tell if you are looking at a eudicot is to count the parts that make up its flowers. Many eudicot flowers have five sepals and petals, and ten stamens. Sometimes the petals and other parts of the flower are fused together to form a shape such as a bell, which helps the right insects get in and out. But if you look closely, you should be able to see the joins and count the petals. There are plenty to count, because three-quarters of flowering plants—and more than half of all plants—fall into this group!

Eudicots include most woody plants, from oak, maple, and beech, to fruit trees such as apple, plum, peach, and olive. Within this massive group, plants can be sorted into two smaller **clades** known as the rosids (see page 80) and the asterids (see page 84). The rest of this chapter explores some of the amazing adaptations that allow eudicots to live in a huge range of habitats, from crowded tropical forests to the driest deserts.

SHARED FEATURES

- Flower parts that come in fours and fives
- Leaves with branching patterns of veins
- Pollen grains have three small holes or grooves
- Roots branch off from a large taproot

GOOD NEIGHBORS?

Eudicots help to make our lives fun—and delicious! Lots of our favorite foods come from this group, including tropical fruit, berries, and chocolate. They also include legumes (see page 82) such as peas, peanuts, and soybeans. We grow them in gardens, climb them, and make clothes and paper with their fibers.

1	**TAPROOT** The taproots of carrot plants are a popular food. Wild carrots have whitish roots, but around a thousand years ago, people began breeding carrots with the bright orange, sweet-tasting roots that are sold all around the world today.
2	**PROTEAS** Some eudicots stand out as unusual, in looks, lifestyle, and even when we peer closely at their genes. They include the woody *Protea*, which can survive forest fires.
3	**LIVING STONES** Living stones are close relatives of cacti and live in similar dry habitats. They don't have spines but their pebble-like looks are enough to put animals off taking a bite!
4	**MISTLETOE** Mistletoe lives a partly parasitic life, attached to a host tree or shrub, or even another mistletoe! They get water and nutrients from the bigger plant but also make their own food. Their seeds are spread in bird droppings, or sometimes by shooting them away at nearly 50 miles per hour.
5	**GIANT RHUBARB** Coming across a giant rhubarb plant feels like wandering back in time to the Cretaceous. This is when these strange plants first evolved. They have huge leaves big enough to use as umbrellas, but the spiny stems might put you off trying one.
6	**WILDFLOWERS** The buttercup family of eudicots includes lots of wildflowers. Fast-growing wildflowers are important sources of food for insects, which in turn help to pollinate plants we depend on.

ROSES & RELATIVES

ROSIDS

Ask for a bunch of rosids, and you might just end up with a handful of cabbage, kale, or Brussels sprouts!

YOU ARE HERE

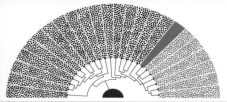

EUKARYOTA

ARCHAEPLASTIDA

KEY FACTS

- More than 90,000 species
- Yellow meranti trees, found in the tropical rain forests of Indonesia, can grow up to 90 m (nearly 300 ft) tall
- Found in a vast range of habitats around the world, but especially in tropical forests

SPECIMEN

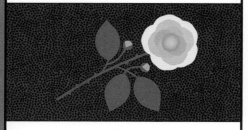

ROSE

ALL ABOUT

This huge clade of eudicots is named after roses, one of the biggest families of flowering plants. It includes all kinds of fruit trees, such as apple, plum, and nectarine trees, deciduous forest trees such as oak, birch, and hornbeam, and extraordinary mangrove trees that live in salt water. The rose family itself includes thorny shrubs such as brambles and beautiful rosebushes. Roses are famous for their beautiful, fragrant flowers. A rose's thorns are shoots that have adapted over time to be hard and spiky, to stop herbivores from taking a nibble.

Vegetables such as broccoli, Brussels sprouts, cauliflower, and kohlrabi are also close relatives of roses. In fact, all these vegetables are varieties of just one species of rosid—*Brassica oleracea*! Hundreds of years ago, *Brassica oleracea* was a small plant that grew near coasts. By picking plants with certain features to breed together, and repeating this over and over again, farmers have created dozens of different versions of this one leafy vegetable.

For some of us, this is not good news! Brassicas contain chemicals that are toxic for some insects, and have a bitter taste for bigger herbivores. Some people, known as "supertasters," can taste these bitter chemicals more than other people, which may explain why some of us hate these leafy veggies while others dig in happily!

SHARED FEATURES

- Many rosids can "fix" or get ahold of nitrogen from the air, thanks to bacteria living in **nodules** on their roots
- Many rosids have flowers where each petal stands separately, instead of being joined together with others

GOOD NEIGHBORS?

This group includes important timber trees, rubber trees, and cotton plants, as well as incredible edibles such as apples, pears, melons, okra, star fruit, pumpkins, cucumbers, almonds, walnuts, and pecans. Roses themselves are popular plants for gardens and homes, and their flowers are used to make perfumes and flavor foods.

1	**MANY GUISES** Broccoli, Brussels sprouts, kale, kohlrabi, and cauliflower are all varieties of just one species of plant—*Brassica oleracea*!
2	**CLEVER CURE** A Hawaiian chemist named Alice Ball is famous for turning oil from chaulmoogra tree seeds into an effective treatment for a devastating skin infection called Hansen's disease.
3	**STINGING "HAIRS"** Stinging nettles are covered with tiny, fragile "hairs" that break when something brushes against them. The broken tip scratches the skin and releases chemicals that cause a painful sting.
4	**MARSHMALLOW ROOT** This brown, stringy root doesn't look very tasty but was the ingredient used to make the first-ever marshmallows! A thick, gluey substance in the plant's roots was used to make the marshmallows chewy.
5	**MOUNTAIN ASH** Rowans are also known as mountain ash trees. They have inspired many stories of magic and mystery, and in some parts of the world people once planted them outside houses believing they would keep evil away. Their bright red berries are eaten by birds, which then spread the seeds in their droppings.

LEGUMES

FABACEAE

Let's zoom in to the rosids clade to take a closer look at farmers' favorite family of plants.

YOU ARE HERE

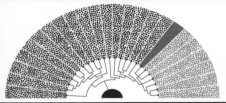

	EUKARYOTA
	ARCHAEPLASTIDA

KEY FACTS

- More than 19,000 species
- From small plants to tropical rain forest trees that can grow to 88 m (288 ft)
- Legumes are found all around the world, having been introduced to new areas more than any other type of plant

SPECIMEN

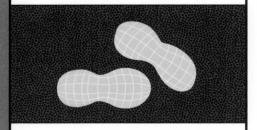

PEANUTS

ALL ABOUT

All plants need nitrogen to grow, but only plants that produce peas and beans have the power to grab nitrogen from thin air. This can then be used by other living things, supporting the whole **ecosystem**.

Plants that produce peas and beans are known as legumes. They are the third-largest family of flowering plants and a very important source of human foods and medicines. They grow almost everywhere. Only grasses (see page 76) are found in more places around the world. Legumes can even grow in very poor soil, thanks to their ability to grab nitrogen from the air.

Legumes do this with the help of nitrogen-fixing bacteria such as *Rhizobium* that live in special nodules on their roots. The bacteria soak up nitrogen from the air and turn it into a form that can be used by plants to build proteins. The nitrogen can then also be used by other living things in the ecosystem. This makes legumes a very important part of Earth's nitrogen cycle.

Legume seeds are often very tough. Certain legume seeds lie dormant until there is a forest fire! The high temperature triggers germination. This adaptation means their seeds start to grow without competition from other plants (which take longer to grow back in the burned soil).

SHARED FEATURES

- Some have flowers that grow in clusters, known as inflorescences
- Others have flowers that look like butterflies
- Fruit are often long, narrow pods with seeds arranged in a line
- Pods release their seeds by splitting open

GOOD NEIGHBORS?

The legumes are incredibly important for farming. They include many important food crops, such as peas, beans, soy, lentils, peanuts, and alfalfa. They are also used to "fix" nitrogen to make soil more fertile for other crops. Woody legumes are important sources of timber, fuel wood, useful resins, and natural dyes.

1	**ANT ARMIES** Acacia trees live closely alongside ants (see page 136). The ants discourage herbivores from eating the trees and reduce the number of harmful bacteria living on the trees' leaves. In return, the ants get nectar made by the acacia and shelter in the trees' hollow thorns.
2	**KING OF BEANS** Soybeans are known as the "king of beans" because they can be crushed to make many other things, such as vegetable oil, tofu, soy milk, and chocolate ingredients. However, clearing forests to grow so much soy is causing harm to environments and indigenous peoples around the world.
3	**LUCKY CLOVER** Have you ever hunted for a four-leaf clover? This small legume is a common sight in gardens and grasslands. It is often added to pastures on purpose because it fixes nitrogen so well.
4	**MEDICINES** More than 2,000 species of legumes are used as sources of medicines—more than any other plant family! The plants produce chemicals such as alkaloids for self-defense, but in small amounts they can be used to disrupt harmful cells or processes in our bodies.
5	**CROP ROTATION** Planting legumes can help restore soil that has lost much of its nitrogen and make it fertile again. George Washington Carver famously discovered that planting peanuts or soybeans for a year helped farmers recover lost nutrients without paying for expensive fertilizers.

ASTERIDS

ASTERIDAE

YOU ARE HERE

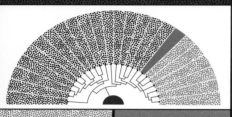

EUKARYOTA

ARCHAEPLASTIDA

KEY FACTS

- Around 100,000 species
- From plants that live their whole lives in a year, to large trees
- Found in a huge range of habitats, from rain forests to deserts, and from land to water

SPECIMEN

SUNFLOWER

Almost a third of all flowering plants belong in this clade. They include plants that are very pretty and plants that are very poisonous!

ALL ABOUT

Let's hop from the rosids "twig" of the tree of life onto a neighboring twig—the asterids. Asterids are a super-successful set of eudicots that have adapted to live in a huge range of different ways. Instead of having individual petals, the petals of most asterids are joined together to form a sort of crown. Sometimes, this crown is curved into a trumpet, tube, or bell shape. This will help you spot asterids, but when you do, proceed with caution!

Many asterids produce toxic chemicals to stop animals from munching on them, or to kill fungi that try to grow on them. Mandrake and deadly nightshade plants contain some of the most dangerous poisons in the world. Potato plants are also in this family of asterids, and if potatoes are turning green or growing sprouts, they are producing enough poisonous solanine to be toxic too. Solanine can be destroyed by frying a potato (a reason to eat more French fries?), but a better way to stay safe is to keep potatoes in the dark and avoid eating green potatoes.

Many other familiar foods belong to this group, including tomatoes, eggplant, olives, carrots, sweet potatoes, and lettuces. They also include plants that people like to grow in gardens, such as holly and honeysuckles.

The next page zooms in to take a closer look at the daisy family of asterids, which also includes dandelions and sunflowers.

SHARED FEATURES

- Petals are often fused together to form a trumpet, tube, or bell shape
- Single whorl of stamens
- In some asterids (such as sunflowers) the fused petals make the shape of petals themselves, but if you look closely, you can see the joins

GOOD NEIGHBORS?

Plants in this group include many important crops, grown as sources of food and useful chemicals. Some make defensive chemicals that can also be dangerous poisons, and getting to know them better has saved lives. Coffee has become the most popular drink in the world, with more than 2 billion cups sold every day.

1	**TOUCH-ME-NOT** You might have heard of forget-me-nots but touch-me-nots (also known as spotted jewelweeds) are even easier to remember! When their seed pods are ripe, they explode at the slightest touch, scattering their seeds far and wide!
2	**CURING CANCER** The rosy periwinkle is a pretty rain forest plant with a pretty name, but it's also the source of tough, cancer-fighting medicines. Scientists found out about the amazing powers of the periwinkle by learning how it was used by traditional Madagascan healers.
3	**FLOWER-SHAPED BILLS** Hummingbirds have evolved long, sometimes curved bills that allow them to reach in and drink nectar from specific asterids. As they do this, they also pollinate the plants.
4	**POWER GRAB** Certain insects have adapted to cope with the toxins made by asterids. Monarch butterfly caterpillars can feast on milkweeds without being harmed. They actually store the toxic chemicals in their bodies, making themselves toxic to predators such as birds!
5	**COFFEA PLANTS** Coffee beans are the pips of *Coffea* fruit. They contain high levels of an alkaloid chemical called caffeine, which is an adaptation to put animals off eating the seeds. Billions of people enjoy the bitter taste of drinks made with these seeds.

DAISIES & RELATIVES

ASTERACEAE

Daisies and dandelions have all kinds of strange secrets, making them some of the most amazing flowers of all.

YOU ARE HERE

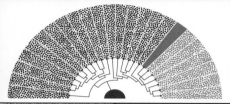

EUKARYOTA

ARCHAEPLASTIDA

KEY FACTS

- At least 24,000 species
- Flower heads can range from less than 3 mm (0.12 in) to more than 80 cm (2.6 ft) across in the giant sunflower!
- Found in almost every type of land habitat, including sand dunes, steep cliffs, and disturbed soils that are unfriendly to most other plants

SPECIMEN

DAISY

ALL ABOUT

Daisies and their closest relatives are part of the asterid clade of the tree of life. They have some unique features all of their own. Have you ever picked a daisy and counted the petals? Surprisingly, each petal is a tiny white flower itself! This crown of white flowers surrounds a cluster of even tinier yellow flowers at the center of the daisy. Together, the collection of tiny flowers is known as a "head."

The same is true for many members of the daisy family of asterids, which includes sunflowers and dandelions. The head of a sunflower is made up of hundreds of tiny flowers, or florets. They include the dark brown flowers of the main disc and the bright yellow flowers that form a crown around the outside.

Each flower forms a fruit with just one seed, and these fruit are also packed closely together. But this gives the plant a problem: seeds need to germinate as far as possible from one another in order to have enough space, water, light, and nutrients to grow. In this family of plants, the flower's sepals help with this. They transform into a ring of hairs or bristles. In dandelions, they act as tiny parachutes, helping seeds travel on the wind. In burrs, the bristles hook on to the fur of passing animals, who then carry the seeds to a new home.

This is how you see "weeds" such as dandelions and thistles appear so quickly on churned-up soil.

SHARED FEATURES

- Flower head is made up of hundreds of tiny flowers
- Each flower forms a fruit with one seed
- The flower sepals form bristles or hairs to help the seed travel far from the parent plant

GOOD NEIGHBORS?

Certain plants in the Asteraceae group cause allergies in late summer and early autumn. However, we get some very important chemicals from this family of flowering plants, including eco-friendly insecticides, dyes, and medicines that can fight tiny **parasites** that cause harm if they get inside our bodies.

1 ON THE WIND
The sepals of each dandelion flower become a ring of tiny hairs. They act as tiny parachutes, helping the seeds to drift away on the wind.

2 TREATING MALARIA
Malaria is a deadly infectious disease, caused by parasites spread by mosquito bites. After reading an ancient Chinese book that described how the sweet wormwood plant was used to treat malaria, scientist Tu Youyou set about extracting the chemical that fights the malaria-causing parasite. Since the 1980s, her work has saved millions of lives and won her the Nobel Prize.

3 ALLERGIES CULPRIT
Ragweed is one of the key culprits in causing allergies in late summer and early autumn. A single ragweed plant can release millions of pollen grains, which drift into a person's eyes and nose, causing sneezing, itching, and even asthma.

4 SEED SNACK
Sunflower seeds are popular with birds, but humans have found all kinds of ways to use them too. They are crushed to release the oils inside and used to make spreads, soap, and paint.

5 HITCHING A LIFT
In some Asteraceae, the sepals form bristles that hook on to the fur of passing animals, who then unwittingly carry the seeds to a new home. The bristly sepals of burrs were the inspiration for Velcro®, which uses tiny hooks and fuzzy "fur" as a fastener.

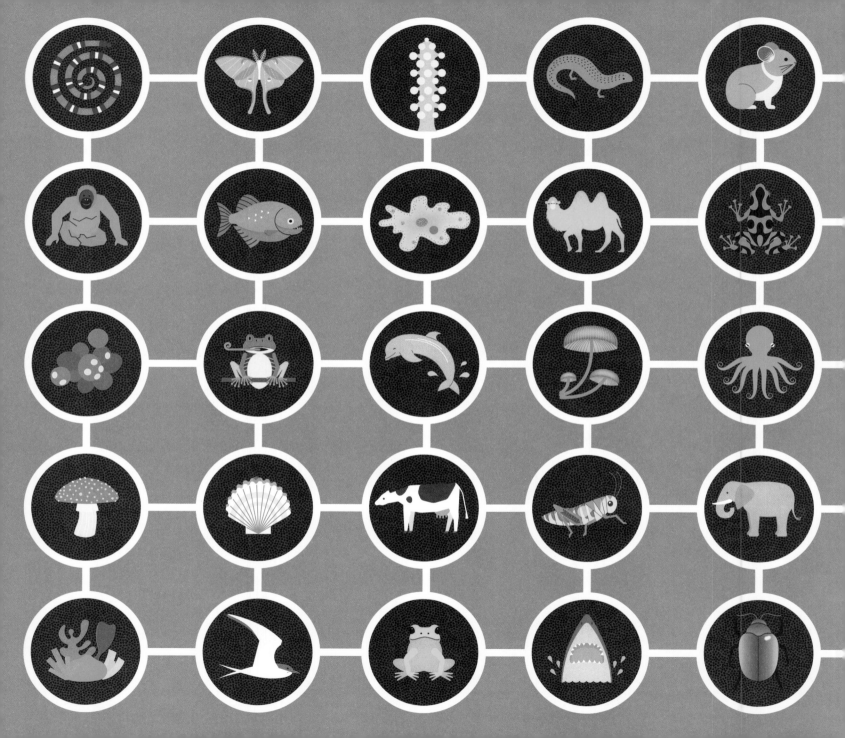

FUNGI, ANIMALS & RELATIVES
AMORPHEA

AT FIRST GLANCE, TIGERS AND TOADSTOOLS DON'T SEEM TO HAVE MUCH IN COMMON. BUT STUDYING THEIR GENES REVEALED THAT ANIMALS AND FUNGI ARE EACH OTHER'S CLOSEST RELATIVES! BOTH BELONG TO THE SAME BRANCH OF THE TREE OF LIFE, A SUPERGROUP OF CREATURES KNOWN AS AMORPHEA.

Animals probably need no introduction! They are some of the largest living things. They can move around (at least for some of their lives) and feed by eating other living things. Most animals are large enough to see without a microscope, so people have been naming and studying animals for a long time. Of the 2 million living species named so far, more than 1 million are animals.

Fungi are often less visible than animals, but are equally fascinating and important. They were once thought of as being closely related to plants, but studying fungi **genomes** and tracing their family trees has revealed that fungi are far more closely related to animals. In fact, animal and fungi cells work in such similar ways that scientists can use fungi as models to understand how human cells work. Fungi play a vital role in almost every **ecosystem**. We also use them to improve human lives in many different ways.

The "supergroup" Amorphea also includes the single-celled Amoebozoa, or amoebas, few of which are large enough to see without a microscope. Like animals, Amoebozoa move around and eat organic matter. As they go about their lives they often change shape dramatically, forming large "fingers" that help them crawl around or feed.

TRUE FUNGI

FUNGI

Fungi may be the planet's least fussy eaters! Their ability to eat everything, from dung to dead wood, shapes the world as we know it.

YOU ARE HERE

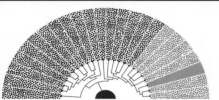

	EUKARYOTA
	AMORPHEA

KEY FACTS

- More than 140,000 species
- From microscopic single-celled species to networks of **hyphae** that spread for miles
- Found everywhere, from high in the atmosphere to Antarctic glaciers; from dry deserts to animal guts; from deep oceans to your bathroom

SPECIMEN

KING MUSHROOM

ALL ABOUT

On spotting a mushroom or toadstool on a forest floor, many people think they are looking at part of a plant. But a mushroom is more closely related to you than it is to a plant! The true fungi are nested inside the larger **clade** Amorphea, which also includes animals.

The **common ancestor** of fungi and animals may have looked rather like the first fungi: single-celled creatures with a whip-like "tail" to help them move around in watery **habitats**. There are still species of fungi that live like this, but today most fungi live on land and are made up of many **cells**.

Fungi can't make their own food like plants do, but they can't eat in the way that animals do either. Instead, they soak up **nutrients** from the surface that they are growing on. Some fungi do this on or inside living things, living as **parasites**. They may release chemicals that cause their host's cells to leak or explode so they can soak up the goo that comes out. These fungi can cause diseases in plants and animals. Some even kill their host so they can eat the whole thing very, very slowly.

However, most fungi are helpful. Many live alongside or even inside plants, helping plants to get ahold of certain nutrients in return for sugary food. Many other fungi feed on dead things, which helps with the process of **decay** and returns the building blocks of life to the environment, where they can be used by new living things.

SHARED FEATURES

- Cell walls contain chitin—the same substance that forms the **exoskeleton** of arthropods (see page 124)
- Form long, tube-shaped filaments called hyphae, which in turn form huge networks
- Some produce fruiting bodies such as mushrooms, which release spores to help the fungus reproduce

GOOD NEIGHBORS?

Although few fungi can infect humans, they can cause big problems for people by spoiling stored food or infecting crops or farm animals. But we also use fungi in medical research and to make many important foods, drinks, and medicines. Even if you don't eat mushrooms, you probably eat foods made with the help of fungi every day!

1 FOOD

As well as eating mushrooms, we use fungi to help make many other foods and drinks, including coffee, chocolate, bread, and spreads. As certain fungi feed, they release waste products that change the food in a good way. For example, as yeast feeds on sugar, it burps out gas that makes bread rise.

2 LEARNING ABOUT GERMS

The "father of microbiology," Louis Pasteur, made a huge breakthrough when he proved that a tiny Microsporidia fungus was causing a mysterious disease in silk moths. He went on to teach the world that "germs" were the cause of infectious diseases, helping doctors and scientists find new ways to prevent and fight them.

3 TINY PATHOGENS

Some fungi are tiny creatures that are made up of just one cell. They include Microsporidia, which live inside the cells of larger living things. Some microsporidia species are **pathogens** (harmful microbes) that cause diseases in insects, fish, and mammals, including humans.

4 MAKING COPIES

Fungi often have more than one way to reproduce (make copies of themselves). Some, like these budding yeast cells, simply break or split apart, each part becoming a separate living thing. Some produce **spores** that drift on the wind until they land somewhere good to grow. Many fungi can also mate with a nearby fungus of the same species, producing a different kind of spore.

CHYTRIDS

CHYTRIDIOMYCOTA

YOU ARE HERE

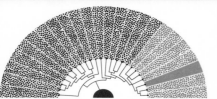

EUKARYOTA

AMORPHEA

KEY FACTS

- Around 1,000 species
- Some of the smallest fungi, usually made up of just one cell
- Found in watery habitats, from freshwater and marine habitats to soils and bogs

SPECIMEN

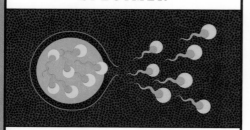

AMPHIBIAN CHYTRID FUNGUS

With tiny tails for swimming, the fungi in this group are thought to be most similar to their ancient ancestors, the very first fungi of all.

ALL ABOUT

The fungi in this group live in watery habitats and their spores even have a tiny "tail" for swimming through water. This helps the fungi to spread to new habitats or hosts when they have used up all the food in one place. Once a chytrid spore has found a good place to live, it grows lots of long "fingers" called **rhizoids** to anchor itself in place. The rhizoids release digestive **enzymes** onto the surface, then soak up the nutrient goo that results.

Some chytrids make themselves at home on or inside living algae, plants, or other fungi, and may cause harm to their host. But one creature's parasite is another's hero. Many small water animals eat chytrids. These fungi also help to bring balance to watery ecosystems, keeping algae under control and recycling nutrients.

Other chytrids live among the damp leaf litter that collects on the ground. They feed on dead plants and animals, and help to break them down. Chytrids can even break down pollen, wood, and the tough exoskeletons of arthropods (see page 124). No one knows exactly how long chytrids have been around, but one estimate is at least 1.5 billion years. Without them, the planet would be buried under dead trees and dried-out beetles.

SHARED FEATURES

- Main body called a thallus
- Long "fingers" called rhizoids anchor the fungus in place and help it soak up nutrients
- Their spores each have a tiny "tail" that whips from side to side so they can move through watery habitats in search of a good place to live
- Some chytrid cells can crawl along dryer ground

GOOD NEIGHBORS?

On land, a few chytrids infect crops such as cabbage, corn, and potatoes, causing the plants to develop "warts" or even causing them to rot away in the field. Other chytrids are helpful for meat and dairy farming, living in the guts of cattle and sheep and helping them to digest tough grass.

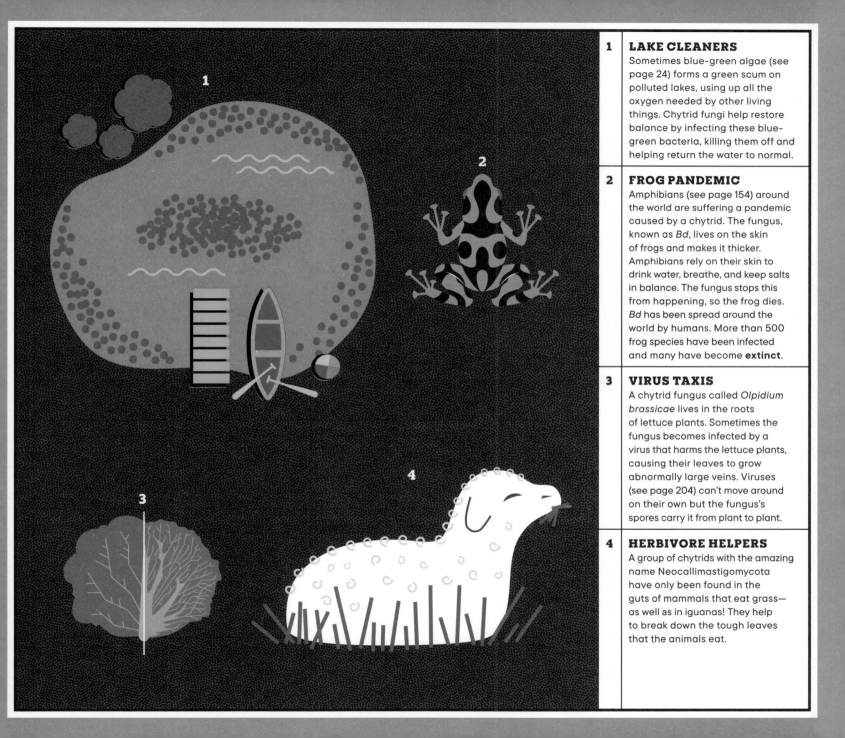

1 LAKE CLEANERS

Sometimes blue-green algae (see page 24) forms a green scum on polluted lakes, using up all the oxygen needed by other living things. Chytrid fungi help restore balance by infecting these blue-green bacteria, killing them off and helping return the water to normal.

2 FROG PANDEMIC

Amphibians (see page 154) around the world are suffering a pandemic caused by a chytrid. The fungus, known as *Bd*, lives on the skin of frogs and makes it thicker. Amphibians rely on their skin to drink water, breathe, and keep salts in balance. The fungus stops this from happening, so the frog dies. *Bd* has been spread around the world by humans. More than 500 frog species have been infected and many have become **extinct**.

3 VIRUS TAXIS

A chytrid fungus called *Olpidium brassicae* lives in the roots of lettuce plants. Sometimes the fungus becomes infected by a virus that harms the lettuce plants, causing their leaves to grow abnormally large veins. Viruses (see page 204) can't move around on their own but the fungus's spores carry it from plant to plant.

4 HERBIVORE HELPERS

A group of chytrids with the amazing name Neocallimastigomycota have only been found in the guts of mammals that eat grass— as well as in iguanas! They help to break down the tough leaves that the animals eat.

PLANT MOLDS

MUCOROMYCOTA

YOU ARE HERE

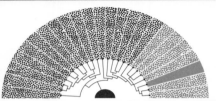

EUKARYOTA

AMORPHEA

KEY FACTS

- Around 300 species
- Clusters of hyphae are visible to our eyes, but mold spores can be as small as 3 μm
- Found throughout the world (including Antarctica), especially in soils

SPECIMEN

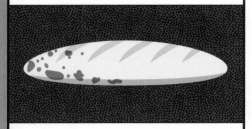

BREAD MOLD

Many of the fuzzy-looking fungi known as "molds" belong to this group. Molds have a bad reputation for spoiling food, but they also have some incredible abilities!

ALL ABOUT

Molds are fungi that grow as a cluster of wispy strands, called hyphae. The Mucoromycota are molds that like to grow on plants—dead or alive. By sending a network of filaments down through the decaying matter, they can break it down and soak up the nutrients for themselves.

If they get the chance, some of these molds will start growing on plants or other creatures that are still alive. As parasites, they can cause problems by using up the host's resources or even damaging its cells. The Mucoromycota are named after bread mold, which has been ruining people's sandwiches since ancient times and was called *mucor* in Latin.

Another group of Mucoromycota live in harmony with plants, on and inside their roots. Mycorrhizal fungi send out huge networks of hyphae that act like extra roots for the plant. These help the plant to soak up nutrients from the soil, including water, **nitrogen**, phosphorus, and calcium, boosting a plant's growth. They may even help plants to communicate with each other. In return, the fungi get some of the sugary food that the plant makes using **photosynthesis**.

Mycorrhizal fungi are an important part of Earth's **ecosystems**. In fact, some scientists think Mucoromycota allowed plants to move onto land in the first place! Before plants evolved roots, networks of fungal filaments would have helped them to collect water and nutrients from surfaces.

SHARED FEATURES

- Hyphae are made from lots of cells smooshed together, surrounded by one cell wall
- Substances such as food can travel quickly through the hyphae, over long distances, without having to cross lots of cell walls

GOOD NEIGHBORS?

Although molds can be annoying in our kitchens, Mucoromycota fungi are awesome neighbors. They are important sources of useful fats—including some that humans need to stay healthy. In fact, they are so fatty that in the future they may even be grown to make oil that can be used as biodiesel.

1 **FATTY ACIDS**
Fats make up about half the dry weight of the fungus. These include fatty acids needed by humans to help our brains and eyes develop. A fat called ARA is even harvested and used in baby formula.

2 **HAT-THROWER**
After being eaten and passed out the other end by an herbivore, the "hat thrower" pin mold grows on the animal's nutrient-rich dung. But to get its spores eaten by a new animal, it needs to get them away from the undesirable dung. To do this, it has a built-in water pistol—the "stalk" swells with water until it explodes, pinging the packet of spores up to 8 feet away!

3 **PLANT PARTNERSHIPS**
Today, about nine in every ten plants live in partnership with mycorrhizal fungi. Farmers and gardeners even add these fungi to soils to help plants grow better.

4 **CATAPULT RIDE**
Lungworms are tiny worms that infect cows. Their **larvae** are found in cow dung, but like hat-thrower fungus spores they need to get away from the dung for the best chance of being eaten by a new cow. So the worms crawl up the hat-thrower fungus stalks, sit on the "hat," and wait to be launched across the field!

5 **NOT FUSSY**
Molds are mainly found in soil, but their spores drift on the air and they can grow on many different surfaces. Some species cause strawberry rot if they happen to land on strawberry plants. They can also grow in our lungs if we breathe them in.

SAC FUNGI

ASCOMYCOTA

YOU ARE HERE

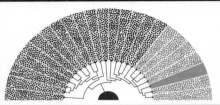

	EUKARYOTA
	AMORPHEA

KEY FACTS

- More than 57,000 species
- From small single-celled fungi to larger multicellular organisms
- Found in a huge range of habitats, including human bodies!

SPECIMEN

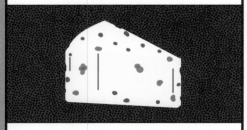

PENICILLIUM MOLD IN BLUE CHEESE

From the good (chocolate) and the bad (athlete's foot) to the terrifying (zombie ants), this group of fungi has something for everyone!

ALL ABOUT

Whatever substance you can think of, there is probably a fungus in this group that feeds on it! As a result, Ascomycota are found living everywhere from wall paint to the skin between sweaty toes! About two-thirds of the fungi we know about belong in this group. They include fungi that live alone, fungi that can only survive by living on a host, and fungi that live in harmony with plants.

They can be split into two rough groups. The first are fungi that grow as filaments and produce cup-shaped fruiting bodies big enough to see. Some species are the cause of serious disease in plants, such as Dutch elm disease. But they also play a very important role in breaking down dead plant material, so that its building blocks can be recycled by new life.

The second group is tiny, single-celled yeasts. Yeasts are a normal part of our healthy body **microbiome**. Humans have also made foods and drinks with the help of yeasts for thousands of years and yeasts have played a huge part in the history of science. Yeast cells behave like human cells in many important ways but are far easier to study. They have helped us to understand how our own cells work. A yeast was even the first eukaryote to have its genetic information read!

SHARED FEATURES

- Some grow a special structure—called an ascus— to produce spores
- An ascus is often shaped like a cup or "sac"—a bit like an upside-down mushroom! This is how the group got its name
- Yeasts reproduce in a simpler way, by budding

GOOD NEIGHBORS?

Ascomycota fungi help to turn milk into cheeses such as Camembert and Roquefort. Their filaments grow down through the cheese. As they feed and release waste products, they shape the cheese's texture and flavor. Truffles, morels, and mycoprotein (an alternative to meat) are also types of Ascomycota. *Penicillium* was the source of the world's first antibiotic medicine.

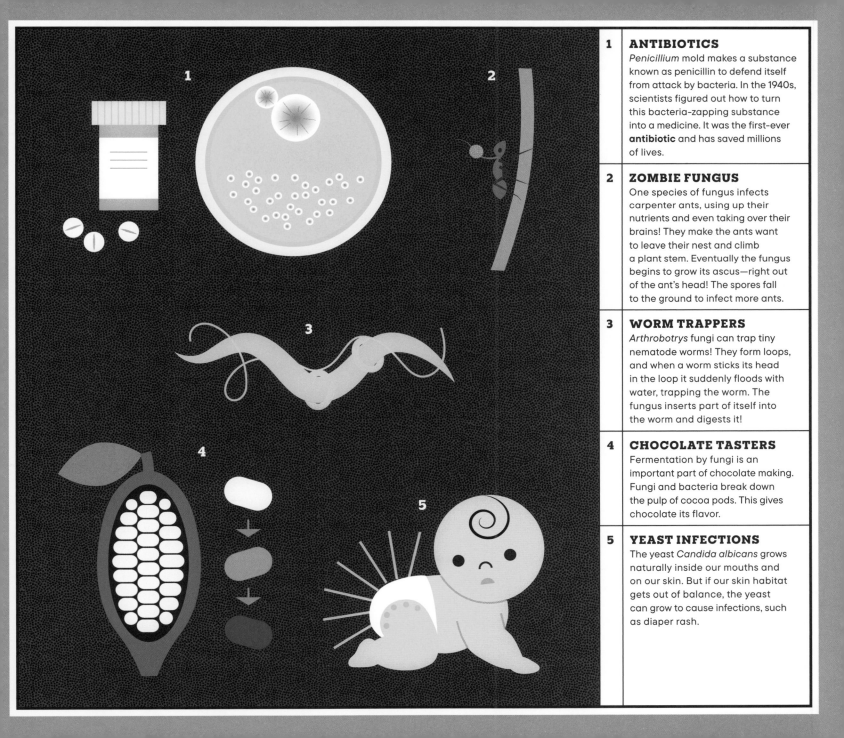

1 ANTIBIOTICS
Penicillium mold makes a substance known as penicillin to defend itself from attack by bacteria. In the 1940s, scientists figured out how to turn this bacteria-zapping substance into a medicine. It was the first-ever **antibiotic** and has saved millions of lives.

2 ZOMBIE FUNGUS
One species of fungus infects carpenter ants, using up their nutrients and even taking over their brains! They make the ants want to leave their nest and climb a plant stem. Eventually the fungus begins to grow its ascus—right out of the ant's head! The spores fall to the ground to infect more ants.

3 WORM TRAPPERS
Arthrobotrys fungi can trap tiny nematode worms! They form loops, and when a worm sticks its head in the loop it suddenly floods with water, trapping the worm. The fungus inserts part of itself into the worm and digests it!

4 CHOCOLATE TASTERS
Fermentation by fungi is an important part of chocolate making. Fungi and bacteria break down the pulp of cocoa pods. This gives chocolate its flavor.

5 YEAST INFECTIONS
The yeast *Candida albicans* grows naturally inside our mouths and on our skin. But if our skin habitat gets out of balance, the yeast can grow to cause infections, such as diaper rash.

MUSHROOMS, SMUTS & RUSTS

BASIDIOMYCOTA

Have you ever seen a tree with ears, or a log with a Jell-O on top? Welcome to the magical world of Basidiomycota—the most showstopping fungi.

YOU ARE HERE

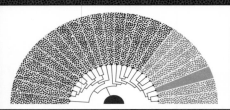

	EUKARYOTA
	AMORPHEA

KEY FACTS

- Around 40,000 species
- Certain Basidiomycota are the largest living things on the planet
- Found in all land habitats; a few species grow in water

SPECIMEN

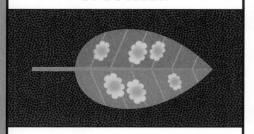

LEAF WITH RUST FUNGUS

ALL ABOUT

This large branch of the fungi family tree includes the fungi most likely to make you stop and stare! They include jelly fungi, shelf fungi, coral fungi, puffballs, stinkhorns, and fungi that form mushrooms and toadstools. They are the fungi you spot growing on tree trunks, peppering the leaves of infected plants, or popping up out of the ground overnight, as if by magic.

The parts that we see are their fruiting bodies, a bit like the apples on a tree. Most of the fungus is hidden away from us, in the form of a network of hyphae (filaments) that may spread for many feet—or even miles—through the soil. The networks that honey fungi form underground can weigh around 22,000 pounds—around the same as a blue whale! They take more than a thousand years to grow this big.

This clade also includes fungi known as rusts and smuts, which live on or inside other creatures and are infamous for causing diseases in plants. One smut fungus can cause dandruff when it lives on human scalps, feeding on the oils made by our skin.

Many Basidiomycota are able to grow and feed on dead wood, so they play a very important role in forests. They convert trapped nutrients, such as carbon, into forms that can be used by new living things. Other Basidiomycota feed on leaf litter or dung, ensuring that we are not all knee-deep in animal droppings.

SHARED FEATURES

- The fruiting body—called a basidiocarp—is where spores are made and released into the air, so that the fungus can reproduce
- If a fruiting body such as a mushroom is damaged, it won't harm the fungus itself, which is hidden away underground (or inside its host)

GOOD NEIGHBORS?

The mycorrhizal and wood-decaying fungi in this group are vital for plants to survive. They are even used for garbage composting. But the group also includes fungi that are major pests of crop plants, such as the rusts and smuts. Wheat stem rust has caused crop failures and famines for thousands of years.

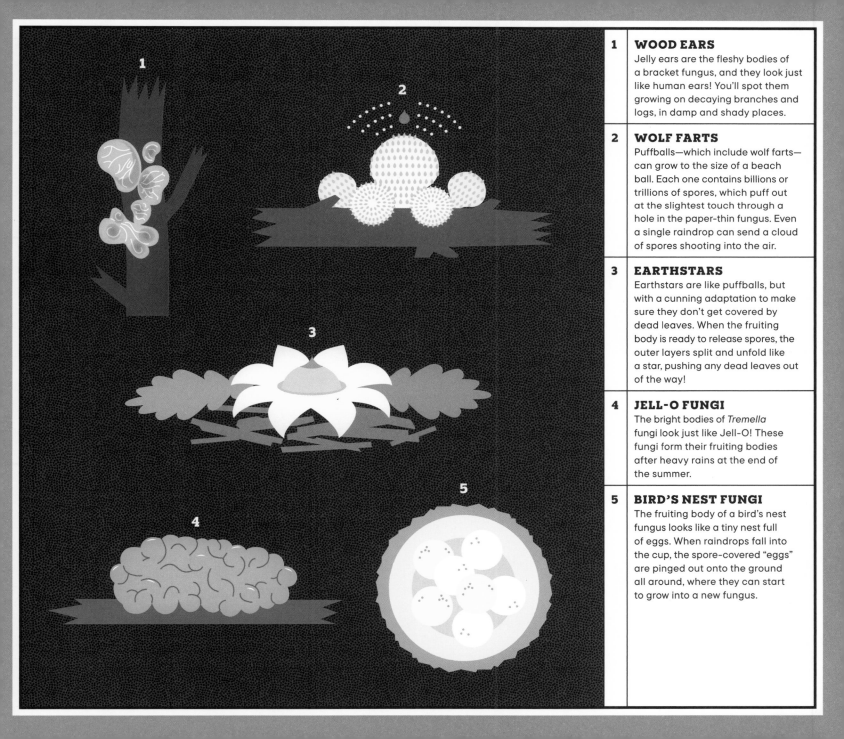

1 WOOD EARS
Jelly ears are the fleshy bodies of a bracket fungus, and they look just like human ears! You'll spot them growing on decaying branches and logs, in damp and shady places.

2 WOLF FARTS
Puffballs—which include wolf farts—can grow to the size of a beach ball. Each one contains billions or trillions of spores, which puff out at the slightest touch through a hole in the paper-thin fungus. Even a single raindrop can send a cloud of spores shooting into the air.

3 EARTHSTARS
Earthstars are like puffballs, but with a cunning adaptation to make sure they don't get covered by dead leaves. When the fruiting body is ready to release spores, the outer layers split and unfold like a star, pushing any dead leaves out of the way!

4 JELL-O FUNGI
The bright bodies of *Tremella* fungi look just like Jell-O! These fungi form their fruiting bodies after heavy rains at the end of the summer.

5 BIRD'S NEST FUNGI
The fruiting body of a bird's nest fungus looks like a tiny nest full of eggs. When raindrops fall into the cup, the spore-covered "eggs" are pinged out onto the ground all around, where they can start to grow into a new fungus.

MUSHROOM-FORMING FUNGI

AGARICOMYCETES

YOU ARE HERE

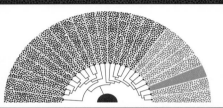

EUKARYOTA

AMORPHEA

KEY FACTS

- More than 21,000 species
- Individual mushrooms range from a few millimeters (less than an inch), to several feet wide, but the fungi they sprout from are much larger
- Found in all land habitats; a few species grow in water

SPECIMEN

FLY AGARIC TOADSTOOL

Mushrooms and fungi often appear in fairy tales, but have some real-life superpowers that are stranger than any story!

ALL ABOUT

Let's zoom into the Basidiomycota clade to take a closer look at their best-known members—fungi that form mushrooms and toadstools. These dome-shaped fruiting bodies are just small parts of a much larger fungus, hidden underground. The fungi produce mushrooms to help them spread spores aboveground.

Mushrooms form in an amazing variety of shapes and sizes, and a rainbow of colors from smooth white domes and bright pink or blue umbrellas to deep black, velvety toadstools that look as if they are dripping ink. They include slime-tipped stems that smell like rotting meat as well as mushrooms that branch like corals or fold like brains. There are even cannonball fungi that open like stars and shoot their spores several feet into the air!

Mushrooms grow on their source of food. They start off as tiny structures, which take a few days to form. Then suddenly they soak up water from their surroundings, puffing up so fast it can look like they've appeared out of nothing! The main types of mushrooms that we eat are farmed on compost made from waste, including horse manure and crushed-up corncobs.

Many wild mushrooms and toadstools grow from friendly fungi that live closely alongside tree roots, so they are signs of a happy and healthy forest.

SHARED FEATURES

- Many mushrooms are domed caps on a stalk
- Underneath the cap, the spores are made on gills or "teeth"
- A single mushroom may produce trillions of spores
- A toadstool is just another name for a mushroom

GOOD NEIGHBORS?

Mushrooms have been used in traditional medicines for thousands of years. Today, chemicals made by mushrooms are being turned into medicines to fight bacteria, stop blood clots forming, and even to treat cancer. Around 25 species are used as food, because they are rich in nutrients. However, many types are very poisonous and only experts can tell them apart.

1	**GLOW IN THE DARK** A very few fungi produce chemicals that allow them to make their own light! These glowing, green mushrooms grow in just two places in the wild—Japan and Brazil.
2	**FAIRY RINGS** Sometimes you can detect how far a fungus has spread underground because mushrooms pop up all around the edges! This is known as a fairy ring. It gets bigger each year, as the fungus spreads through the soil.
3	**BLEEDING TOOTH FUNGUS** Some mushrooms look more like something from a horror story than a fairy tale. The mushroom of the bleeding tooth fungus oozes drops of sticky red sap that looks like blood.
4	**BIGGER THAN A BLUE WHALE** Honey fungi are officially the largest, heaviest living things on Earth! The mushrooms themselves are not massive, but the network of fungi underground is enormous and can weigh around 22,000 pounds—around the same as a blue whale.
5	**STINKY STARFISH** Not all mushrooms look like mushrooms! The starfish stinkhorn is one of the rarest fungi. Its fruiting body unfolds like pink tentacles at the top of a white stem. The top is covered with stinky brown slime, which attracts flies. The flies then spread the mushroom's spores.

ANIMALS

METAZOA

YOU ARE HERE

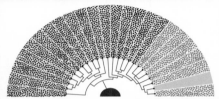

| EUKARYOTA |
| AMORPHEA |

KEY FACTS

- Around 1.2 million species
- From jellyfish so tiny that five could line up across a human hair, to the bootlace worm that can grow over 55 m (180 ft) long
- Found in all habitats, from land to water, from the highest mountains to the deepest oceans and deserts

SPECIMEN

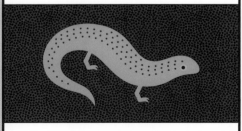

RED SALAMANDER

What makes animals different from their closest cousins on the tree of life, the fungi? For starters, a mouse can move a lot faster than a mushroom...

ALL ABOUT

Welcome to one of the biggest branches of the tree of life. The **clade** Metazoa includes all of the world's animals—more than a million different creatures and counting! Although fungi are their closest relatives on the tree of life, there are some big differences.

The animal life cycle is also more consistent than that of other living things. Most animals, from sea cucumbers and stick insects to sheep and humans, have males that make sperm cells and females that make egg cells. Each sperm and egg cell only has half the instructions needed to grow into another animal—which happens when they meet, and a sperm cell fertilizes an egg cell. There are exceptions to this **sexual reproduction**, but not as often as in plants and fungi.

Animals also tend to move around more than fungi. Some animals, such as whales and migrating birds, have lifestyles that take them all the way around the world and back. One particularly inquisitive animal (the human) has even left Earth and traveled all the way to the Moon!

We think of animals as extra special life forms—probably because we are animals too. But in evolutionary terms they are just another branch of the tree of life.

SHARED FEATURES

- Feed by eating other living things
- Some can build very tough substances, such as enamel and shell
- Often move a lot compared to plants and fungi

GOOD NEIGHBORS?

Animals are some of our most loved neighbors and are also some of the most exploited by humans. People have been farming and domesticating different animals for thousands of years and hunted them for food and skins long before that.

1	**COMB JELLIES** Comb jellies are transparent animals that move around in the sea. Although they look like jellyfish (see page 106) they are very different and don't make stinging cells (although one species has adapted to eat jellyfish and keep their stinging cells to use themselves!).
2	**MIRROR LINE** Most animals have one line of symmetry. These **Bilateria** have a left side and right side that mirror each other. They can be grouped into Protostomia (see page 108) and Deuterostomia (see page 140).
3	**WAYS TO BE A WORM** If you look at the big groups of animals, you'll notice that many of them are worms! There are lots of different ways to be a worm, from giant tube worms and roundworms to hammerhead worms just like this one.
4	**CONSUMERS** Animals can't make their own food like plants do, and they can't stay in one place and soak up food from that surface like many fungi do. Instead, animals must eat other living things.
5	**TOUGH SHELLS** The special **proteins** that sit between animal cells can collect **minerals** and turn themselves into rigid "scaffolding"—allowing animals to build tough body parts, such as bones and shells.
6	**ANCIENT ANCESTORS** It's difficult to figure out what the first animals were like, as their soft squishy parts didn't leave many fossils behind. Many scientists think the evidence points toward sponges (see page 104).

SPONGES

PORIFERA

YOU ARE HERE

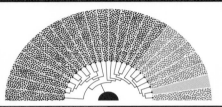

	EUKARYOTA
	AMORPHEA

KEY FACTS

- More than 8,000 species
- From a few millimeters (less than an inch) to several feet wide
- Found in watery habitats around the world, especially oceans

SPECIMEN

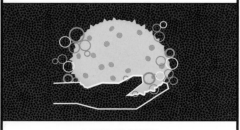

BATH SPONGE

These unusual animals can regrow their entire bodies from a single cell! This allows some sponges to live for hundreds or even thousands of years.

ALL ABOUT

At first, people thought that sponges might be plants. Their bodies seem far simpler than those of other animals and they lack organs to do different jobs. But looking closely at their cells reveals that sponges are more closely related to us than to a shrub or tree. For example, their springy skeletons are made from **collagen**—the same protein that forms many parts of your body!

Sponges start their lives as larvae, then settle in one place. They get by perfectly fine without organs because their cells can simply get what they need (food and oxygen) straight from the water, often with the help of small creatures that live alongside them. By getting a current of water flowing through their bodies, they can filter out enough tiny plankton to feed on. Some deep-water sponges eat small animals as well as plankton.

This branch of the tree of life is thought to separate into three or four smaller branches. Glass sponges and calcareous sponges are only found in seas and oceans, where they can get the minerals they need to toughen up their skeletons. Demospongiae, the biggest subgroup, are found in both saltwater and freshwater habitats. Although all types of sponges live in a similar way, scientists are not yet certain that they all share a **common ancestor**.

SHARED FEATURES

- No distinct **tissues** or organs
- Bodies have no lines of symmetry
- Can grow back missing pieces, which not many animals can do

GOOD NEIGHBORS?

Humans have used sponges for thousands of years for bathing, cleaning, and applying paint. As they are fixed in one place and can't escape, many sponges make chemical **toxins** to protect themselves from predators. Medical scientists are studying these unusual chemicals to see if they can help humans.

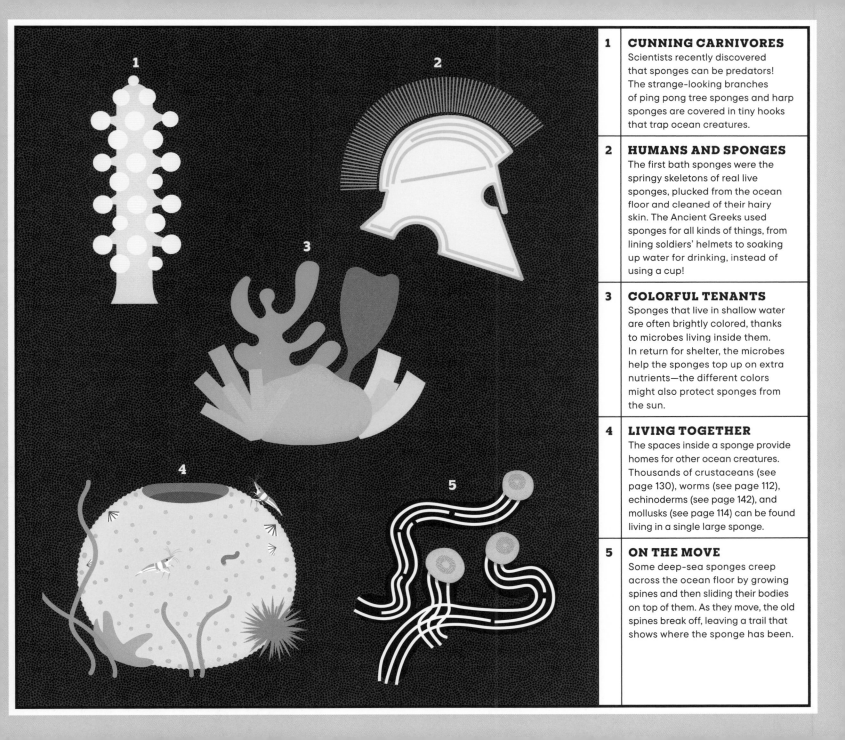

1 CUNNING CARNIVORES
Scientists recently discovered that sponges can be predators! The strange-looking branches of ping pong tree sponges and harp sponges are covered in tiny hooks that trap ocean creatures.

2 HUMANS AND SPONGES
The first bath sponges were the springy skeletons of real live sponges, plucked from the ocean floor and cleaned of their hairy skin. The Ancient Greeks used sponges for all kinds of things, from lining soldiers' helmets to soaking up water for drinking, instead of using a cup!

3 COLORFUL TENANTS
Sponges that live in shallow water are often brightly colored, thanks to microbes living inside them. In return for shelter, the microbes help the sponges top up on extra nutrients—the different colors might also protect sponges from the sun.

4 LIVING TOGETHER
The spaces inside a sponge provide homes for other ocean creatures. Thousands of crustaceans (see page 130), worms (see page 112), echinoderms (see page 142), and mollusks (see page 114) can be found living in a single large sponge.

5 ON THE MOVE
Some deep-sea sponges creep across the ocean floor by growing spines and then sliding their bodies on top of them. As they move, the old spines break off, leaving a trail that shows where the sponge has been.

JELLYFISH & RELATIVES

CNIDARIA

The animals in this group are often beautiful to look at, but don't touch . . . they are all armed with stinging cells!

YOU ARE HERE

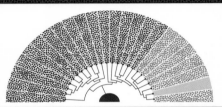

	EUKARYOTA
	AMORPHEA

KEY FACTS

- Around 9,000 species
- From the world's smallest animals, 9 μm Myxozoans, to jellyfish with 30-m (about 100-ft) tentacles
- Found in oceans worldwide, especially along coastlines and in shallow tropical seas; a few species are found in fresh water

SPECIMEN

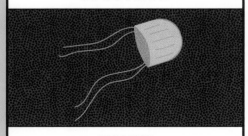

SEA WASP

ALL ABOUT

The cnidarians include jellyfish and their equally blobby relatives, the corals, sea anemones, and hydrozoans. Sea anemones, corals, and jellyfish look very different from a distance—but look closely and you'll see that they all share the same body features. Each one is basically a bag with one opening, which is surrounded by tentacles. In polyps, such as corals and sea anemones, the tentacles and mouth point up. In **medusa**, such as jellyfish, they point down.

Remember not to get too close! The strange name "Cnidaria" comes from an Ancient Greek word for stinging nettle. If you accidentally brush against one, you will understand why. All cnidarians are armed with special stinging cells for self-defense and to capture prey. When they sense vibrations in the water, they eject a tiny harpoon tipped with venom. This is used to paralyze prey.

Not all cnidarians rely on catching prey. Myxozoans are all parasites of larger animals. Coral polyps get energy from tiny algae that live inside their cells. The algae make their own food using sunlight energy, and the coral gets some of this in return for providing a home. Not all corals depend on a live-in algae for food, but those that do can only live in shallow water where they can be bathed in sunlight.

SHARED FEATURES

- Simple, jelly-like bodies with no blood, brain, or heart
- Larger cnidarians have a nervous system that can sense light, vibrations, and chemicals in the water
- Many lines of symmetry (known as radial symmetry)
- Some jellyfish glow with a green or blue light when they are touched, to startle predators

GOOD NEIGHBORS?

Around 150 million people are stung by jellyfish and hydrozoans each year, but in small amounts the chemicals in cnidarian stings can be used to make medicines. Biologists have turned these glowing jellyfish proteins into useful lab tools.

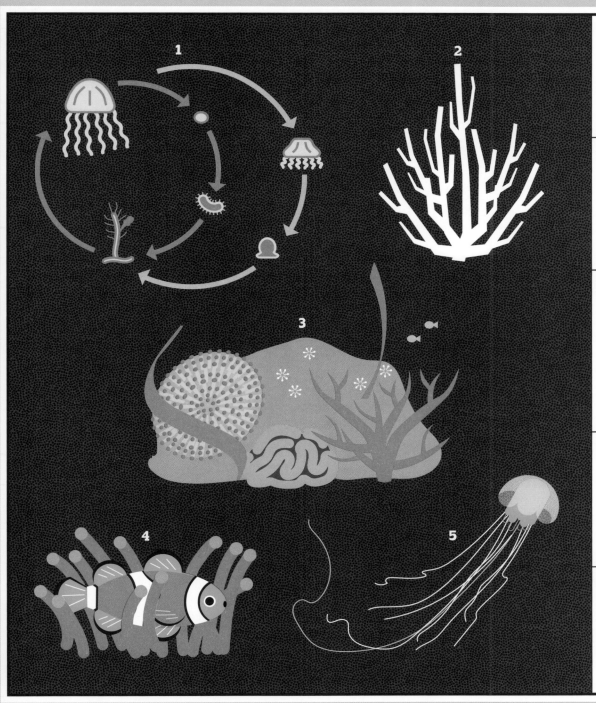

1 IMMORTAL?
Many cnidarians spend part of their lives as an "upside-down" polyp, and part as a free-swimming medusa. Scientists were amazed to find that some have the power to reverse their life cycle—like a butterfly turning back into a caterpillar!

2 CORAL BLEACHING
Global warming is harming corals. When the water gets too warm, the corals kick out the algae that live inside them and become totally white. This is known as coral bleaching. The coral is not dead, but it is more easily harmed by things like disease.

3 CORAL REEFS
Coral polyps are tiny but live in colonies of millions. They eat plankton with calcium carbonate shells, then use the calcium carbonate to build themselves a skeleton they can pop in and out of. When a coral polyp dies, its hard skeleton is left behind. New polyps build their homes on top and the reef slowly grows.

4 SEA ANEMONES
Clownfish are immune to the stings of sea anemones. They lay their eggs among the anemone's tentacles, where they are protected from predators. In return, the bright clownfish lure other fish into the sea anemone—where they get stung and then digested!

5 LION'S MANE
The lion's mane jellyfish is the world's largest cnidarian. Its tentacles can grow more than 30 meters (nearly 100 feet) long, making them longer than a blue whale (see page 174).

PROTOSTOMES

PROTOSTOMIA

This enormous branch of the tree of life includes most creepy-crawlies, from insects and crabs to earthworms and mollusks.

YOU ARE HERE

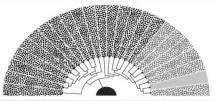

EUKARYOTA

AMORPHEA

KEY FACTS

- The largest group of animals, with more than a million species
- From microscopic zooids to medium-sized creatures such as worms and mollusks
- Found in all environments, on land and in oceans

SPECIMEN

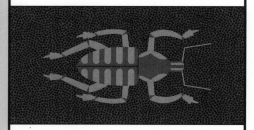

EUPHOLUS LINNEI

ALL ABOUT

While sponges and cnidarians can have many lines of symmetry (or none at all!), most animals have one line of symmetry. Their bodies have a clear left and right side, and a digestive tract with two different ends—a mouth where food goes in, and an anus where food comes out. Animals like this are known as Bilateria and they form two enormous branches of the animal family tree—the Protostomia (or protostomes) on this page and the Deuterostomia, which you'll discover more about on page 140.

The protostomes include most (but not all) of the animals traditionally known as **invertebrates**, such as flatworms (see page 110), segmented worms (see page 112), and mollusks (see page 114) as well as arthropods (see page 124), and nematode worms (see page 122).

They might look totally different as adults, but protostomes develop in a distinct way right from the start of their lives. For many, their mouth is the first end of their digestive system to develop. It's a big clue that they all share a common ancestor that also developed "mouth first."

None of these animals have a skeleton on the inside, but some have an outer **cuticle** for protection and support. To grow bigger, they must shed their hard cuticle each time they get too big for it. Some have adapted to change their entire bodies at the same time, so they look very different from their young larvae. This type of development is called **metamorphosis**.

SHARED FEATURES

- Body has one line of symmetry
- Because of this, they have a left and right side
- No skeleton inside their bodies

GOOD NEIGHBORS?

From soft and squishy worms, slugs, and snails, to scuttling scorpions and biting insects, most animals that we might think of as "creepy-crawlies" belong to this group. We might not always welcome them into our homes, but they include some of the most important animals on the planet.

1	**ROTIFERS**
	Rotifers are tiny—measuring less than 2 millimeters (a fraction of an inch)—but they pack a foot, a mouth, and a crown of 'hairs' into their miniscule bodies. The foot glues the rotifer to a surface, while the hairs waft tiny microbes into their mouths.
2	**WATER BEARS**
	There are at least 1,300 species of "tardigrades," also known as water bears. Their cute looks are only visible under a microscope! Tardigrades are super survivors known to live anywhere from the Arctic to hot springs.
3	**VELVET WORMS**
	Velvet worms live under rotting plants on the floor of tropical forests. They trap small insects by tangling them in strands of sticky saliva they shoot up to 15 centimeters (almost 6 inches) from their bodies.
4	**SOFT AND SQUISHY**
	Some protostomes include close relatives of flatworms (see page 110), segmented worms (see page 112), and mollusks (see page 114).
5	**PARTY ANIMALS**
	Bryozoans are tiny sea creatures that live in huge colonies. Each individual animal—known as a zooid—is less than a millimeter (a fraction of an inch) big, but together a colony looks a bit like coral, seaweed, or moss. They filter food from the water using tiny tentacles.
6	**AWESOME ARTHROPODS**
	Arthropods form a very hard **cuticle** known as an exoskeleton. Most famous of all are the insects (see page 134).

FLATWORMS

PLATYHELMINTHES

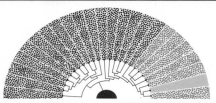

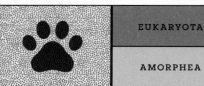

EUKARYOTA

AMORPHEA

KEY FACTS

- More than 20,000 species
- From 1 mm (0.03 in) to 15 m (about 50 feet) long
- Found in watery environments, including seas and oceans, fresh water, and the bodies of larger animals

SPECIMEN

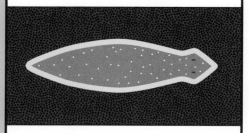

FLATWORM

Flatworms might look like they've just been squashed, but they are super survivors, able to regenerate themselves from the tiniest fragment.

ALL ABOUT

Of all the animals with one line of symmetry, flatworms are some of the simplest. Unlike your body, with its separate spaces for food, air, blood, and so on, flatworms have nothing but a gut with one opening. Food enters and waste leaves through this opening—so a flatworm's mouth is also its backside!

Their simple bodies don't mean flatworms are less evolved than their relatives. They have just landed on a lifestyle that works so well they can do away with many of the "extras" that other animals need to survive.

Flatworms do have a head, and in that head is a very simple "brain"—basically just a gathering of nerve cells. Luckily, they don't have to do much thinking. Most (about 80%) of flatworms are parasites, which live on or inside other animals and steal their food. For this reason, they are often found hanging out in animal intestines, including the intestines of unlucky humans. Some have suckers or hooks to attach themselves to their hosts. Once they are firmly fixed in place they just eat—and grow!

Many parasitic flatworms have very complicated life cycles. Understanding them is the first step in working out how to stop people from getting infected.

Free-living flatworms are found in the oceans and on land in moist soils, where they hunt other animals for food. Their long, flat bodies often have a triangle-shaped head, and eyes for sensing light.

SHARED FEATURES

- A flattened shape
- No **circulatory system** to carry oxygen and food around their body
- Their flat body means that each cell is close enough to the outside to soak up oxygen and close enough to the gut to soak up food!
- Unsegmented bodies

GOOD NEIGHBORS?

The flatworms include parasites in humans and in animals that humans eat, such as cattle and pigs. Cooking meat well helps to stop tapeworm and fluke parasites from spreading to humans. But flatworms that spread in other ways are a serious health problem in many parts of the world.

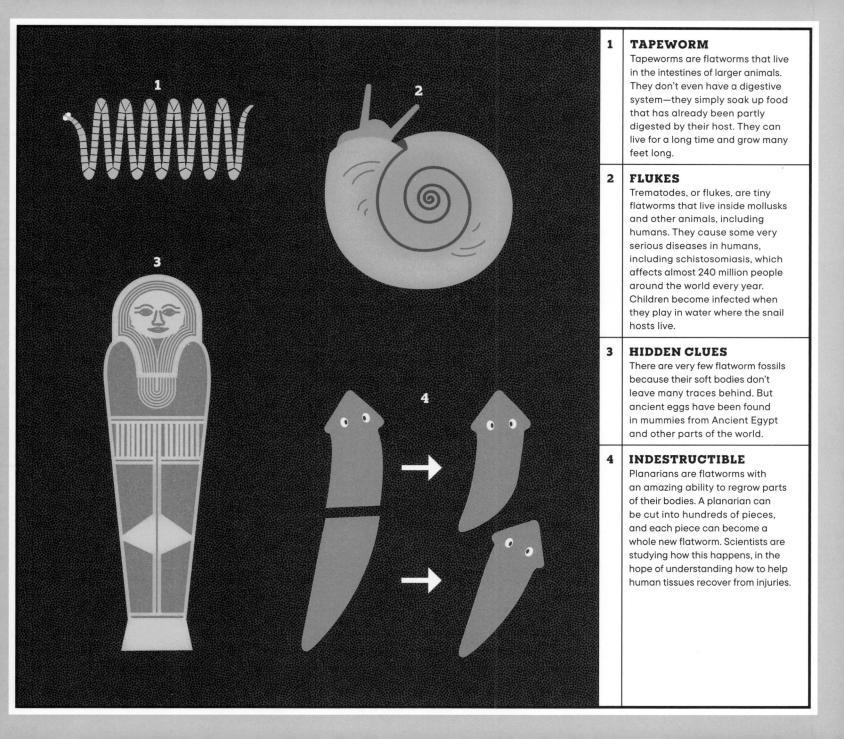

1 TAPEWORM

Tapeworms are flatworms that live in the intestines of larger animals. They don't even have a digestive system—they simply soak up food that has already been partly digested by their host. They can live for a long time and grow many feet long.

2 FLUKES

Trematodes, or flukes, are tiny flatworms that live inside mollusks and other animals, including humans. They cause some very serious diseases in humans, including schistosomiasis, which affects almost 240 million people around the world every year. Children become infected when they play in water where the snail hosts live.

3 HIDDEN CLUES

There are very few flatworm fossils because their soft bodies don't leave many traces behind. But ancient eggs have been found in mummies from Ancient Egypt and other parts of the world.

4 INDESTRUCTIBLE

Planarians are flatworms with an amazing ability to regrow parts of their bodies. A planarian can be cut into hundreds of pieces, and each piece can become a whole new flatworm. Scientists are studying how this happens, in the hope of understanding how to help human tissues recover from injuries.

SEGMENTED WORMS

ANNELIDA

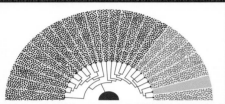

	EUKARYOTA
	AMORPHEA

KEY FACTS

- More than 14,000 species
- From 0.5 mm (0.2 in) to several feet long. The largest earthworm ever found measured 6.7 m (about 22 ft) and was 20 cm (7.8 in) thick!
- Found in marine, freshwater, and land habitats, almost everywhere except Antarctica

SPECIMEN

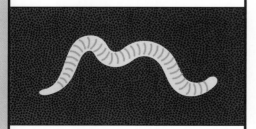

EARTHWORM

Some segmented worms are beautiful, but it's the plain and drab earthworms that are the real superstars!

ALL ABOUT

If you've ever made a bead necklace, you'll have a good idea how an annelid works! Its body is made up of identical segments arranged in a line, to form a long, cylinder-shaped worm. New segments are only added at one end, so the rings toward the back are younger than the rings at the front.

Only the first and last segments differ. In some species it's hard to tell which is which, but some annelids have a head with eyes. The head also has the mouth and sometimes teeth or mandibles for breaking up food. Although these worms have a simple circulatory system for moving blood around their body, they don't have lungs. Instead, they breathe through their skin. Earthworms come closer to the surface of the soil when it rains so they don't drown.

Segmented worms are found all around the world, from the deepest **sediments** under the sea to the soil of your back garden. Some move about freely in the water or soil, scavenging or hunting food as they go. Others spend most of their time in one spot, inside a burrow or tube. Some have tentacles to capture prey; others filter tiny particles out of the water.

There are almost 3,000 different kinds of earthworms alone. As they burrow through the ground eating decaying matter and pooping out waste, earthworms create soil and make sure that air and water get deep below the surface. No matter where they live or how they look, these superstars are vital for life as we know it!

SHARED FEATURES

- Each segment has its own tiny digestive, circulatory, and **excretory systems**
- Hairs or bristles called chaetae do several jobs, including gripping the soil to help the worm move
- Adult earthworms have a "saddle"—a special ring used to help the worms reproduce

GOOD NEIGHBORS?

For thousands of years, segmented worms have played a part in people's daily lives: they've been used as bait to help catch fish, and even used in medicines. Annelids also play a huge role in food chains and in decomposition—recycling nutrients and keeping soils healthy. Without earthworms, farming would be impossible.

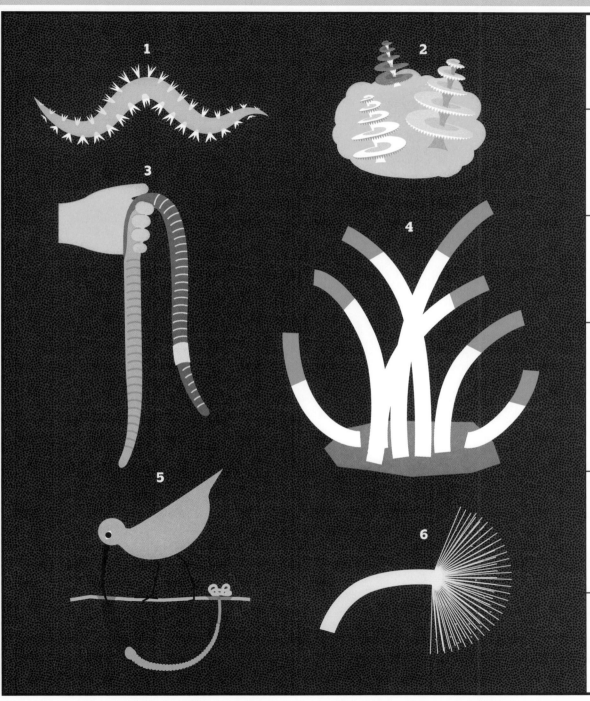

1 BRISTLE WORMS
Bristle worms look a bit like underwater millipedes. They range from tropical worms like the beautiful bearded fireworm to ragworms that live in muddy shores in the US.

2 CHRISTMAS TREE WORMS
These tube-building worms anchor themselves on coral reefs in tropical seas. Each one has two crowns of tentacles for catching plankton that drift past. If startled, they pop their tentacles back into their burrow.

3 BLOODSUCKERS
Giant Amazon leeches grow up to 45 centimeters (1.4 feet) long. These parasites attach themselves to animal skin, release saliva that stops blood from clotting, and soak up the flowing blood as food.

4 GIANT TUBE WORMS
Beard worms live in long tubes anchored to the seafloor, catching food with their feathery tentacles. The most famous are the 2-meter-(6.5-foot) long giants that live alongside hot air vents on the deep ocean floor. Their bright red plumes are packed with blood to soak up oxygen from seawater.

5 POOP PILES
The squiggles of sand that appear on beaches at low tide are piles of poop from lugworms! These bristly worms hide in the sand, in a U-shaped borrow. They eat sediment, digest what they can, and poop out the rest.

6 FAN WORMS
Fan worms build themselves a stiff, sandy tube by gluing sand grains together with mucus! They hide inside, fanning out their feathery tentacles to filter out passing food.

MOLLUSKS

MOLLUSCA

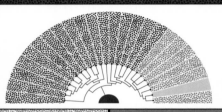

EUKARYOTA
AMORPHEA

KEY FACTS

- Around 100,000 species
- Most species are less than a centimeter (less than half an inch) long, but giant squid can grow to 20 m (65 ft) long
- Found almost anywhere there is water, except the very driest deserts

SPECIMEN

NAUTILUS

These strange, squishy animals with shells are extremely successful. They have colonized every ecosystem on Earth, from the highest mountains to the deepest seas.

ALL ABOUT

Mollusks come in more than 100,000 different shapes and sizes—from snails and slugs to octopuses, mussels, tusk shells, and chitons! Although this large branch of the animal family tree separates into so many smaller branches, under the surface they are pretty similar. Most have a soft body, with a large muscular foot that can do different jobs. An outer layer such as a shell can form a hard exoskeleton.

We know lots about the history of mollusks on Earth, because the hard shells of ancient mollusks formed fossils easily. They include beautiful, spiral-shaped ammonites, fossils of ancient creatures that were the ancestors of today's octopus and cuttlefish (see page 121).

Most of today's mollusks live in places that are wet or moist, including forest floors, damp soils, and, of course, the oceans. They are one of the most important groups of animals in seas and oceans, especially as a source of food for larger animals.

The very first mollusks probably grazed on the crust of animals, algae, and microbes that covered ocean rocks, scraping it off with thousands of tiny but tough teeth. Today there are also mollusks that eat plants, mollusks that hunt prey, mollusks that gobble corals, mollusks that filter plankton out of the water, and mollusks that scour the seabed, eating anything they find.

SHARED FEATURES

- Mouth lined with a ribbon of tiny, super-tough teeth called a radula
- Radula scrapes food off a surface and moves it into the mouth
- Some mollusks build shells of calcium carbonate
- Their body plan includes a head, foot, inner body, and mantle

GOOD NEIGHBORS?

Marine mollusks are an important source of food for fish. We eat some mollusks ourselves, including snails and shellfish, and catch others to use their shells as tools or decorations. Of all the extinctions recorded since the Middle Ages, more than 40% are mollusks. Scientists aren't yet sure why, but it could be because mollusks are easily harmed by polluted water.

1 CEPHALOPODS
Squids, octopuses, nautiluses, and their relatives are the largest mollusks, and some of the world's most remarkable animals. Find out more about these cephalopods on page 120.

2 STING-PROOF
Not all mollusks have shells. Solenogasters look a bit like furry slugs. They can gobble up tiny cnidarians (see page 106) without being stung to death, then poop out the stinging cells!

3 TUSK SHELLS
These long, narrow marine mollusks have cone-shaped shells that look like an elephant tusk. They burrow into the seabed and capture tiny prey.

4 BIVALVES
Unlike other mollusks, scallops, clams, mussels, and their relatives stay symmetrical as they grow. The two-sided shells of these bivalves (see page 118) can open to let food and water in, or clamp tightly shut to keep them safe.

5 GASTROPODS
The gastropods (see page 116) are a huge and amazingly diverse group of mollusks found in oceans, fresh water, and on land. They include slugs, snails, and limpets.

6 SUPER SCRAPERS
Chitons creep along shores, scraping algae off rocks. If disturbed they can roll up into a ball to be protected by their tough outer plates. They can also cling to rocks so tightly it's almost impossible to prize them off. This stops them from being washed away by crashing waves or drying out when the tide falls.

GASTROPODS

GASTROPODA

YOU ARE HERE

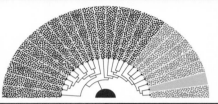

	EUKARYOTA
	AMORPHEA

KEY FACTS

- Around 65,000 species
- From 0.5 mm (0.02 in) to 91 cm (about 3 ft)
- Found in seas and oceans, fresh water, and on land, including extreme environments such as polar oceans, **hydrothermal vents,** and dry deserts

SPECIMEN

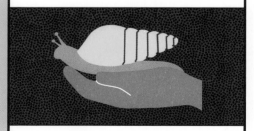

GIANT AFRICAN SNAIL

This huge group of mollusks are famous for their feet! They include slugs, snails, and some of the most beautiful creatures on the planet.

ALL ABOUT

Gastropods are the biggest group of mollusks, both in water and on land. They look different from other mollusks thanks to a strange process that happens as they grow. Their bodies twist to one side, meaning that their backside ends up above their head and most of the right side of their body disappears!

Most gastropods have a spiral- or cone-shaped shell that is rolled up to one side in a twisted spiral. The largest shells, belonging to the Australian trumpet sea snails, are about 3 feet long. The smallest belong to tiny Maitai Cave snails, as small as a grain of sugar. In each case, the body of the snail pokes out of its shell. Most of it is a huge muscular foot that the mollusk uses to creep along the ground. Some "fly" through water instead, helped by a coating of strange mucus that can act like a solid and a liquid.

While some gastropods use their feet to clamp themselves in one place, most move around in search of food. Some graze as they go, shredding plants or scraping up algae and other food. Others eat small animals or **scavenge** on decaying plants or marine "snow." Some are parasites. Others use deadly venom to kill prey. Many gastropods drill holes in the shells of other animals and suck out their insides!

SHARED FEATURES

- Gastropods twist as they develop and grow, ending up asymmetrical inside and out
- One muscly foot
- Eyes
- Tentacles
- Radula (lots of tiny teeth) for feeding
- Many have a shell

GOOD NEIGHBORS?

From whelks to snails, humans have been gathering gastropods to eat for thousands of years. In the past, their shells were used as tools, ornaments, and as money. Ancient peoples even used sea snails to make the world's first purple dyes.

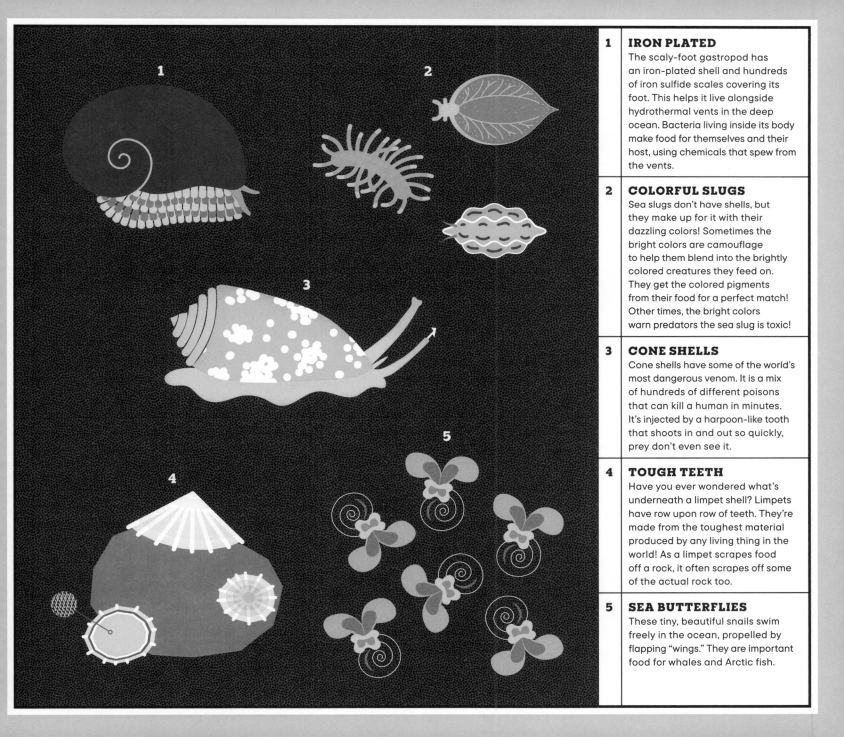

1 IRON PLATED

The scaly-foot gastropod has an iron-plated shell and hundreds of iron sulfide scales covering its foot. This helps it live alongside hydrothermal vents in the deep ocean. Bacteria living inside its body make food for themselves and their host, using chemicals that spew from the vents.

2 COLORFUL SLUGS

Sea slugs don't have shells, but they make up for it with their dazzling colors! Sometimes the bright colors are camouflage to help them blend into the brightly colored creatures they feed on. They get the colored pigments from their food for a perfect match! Other times, the bright colors warn predators the sea slug is toxic!

3 CONE SHELLS

Cone shells have some of the world's most dangerous venom. It is a mix of hundreds of different poisons that can kill a human in minutes. It's injected by a harpoon-like tooth that shoots in and out so quickly, prey don't even see it.

4 TOUGH TEETH

Have you ever wondered what's underneath a limpet shell? Limpets have row upon row of teeth. They're made from the toughest material produced by any living thing in the world! As a limpet scrapes food off a rock, it often scrapes off some of the actual rock too.

5 SEA BUTTERFLIES

These tiny, beautiful snails swim freely in the ocean, propelled by flapping "wings." They are important food for whales and Arctic fish.

BIVALVES
BIVALVIA

Scallops, clams, mussels, and their relatives all have a shell with two halves that open like a treasure chest. This shell gives this group of mollusks their name: the bivalves.

YOU ARE HERE

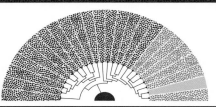

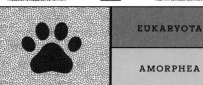

EUKARYOTA

AMORPHEA

KEY FACTS

- At least 10,000 species
- From 2-mm (0.08-in) little ones to 1.5-m (4.9-ft) giant clams
- Found in almost all ocean habitats, including **hydrothermal** vents, as well as freshwater rivers and lakes

SPECIMEN

QUEEN SCALLOP

ALL ABOUT

You'll find bivalves—or sometimes just their shells—on rocky shores, sandy beaches, mudflats, and mangrove swamps. Some burrow into the soft ground and hide away from predators. Others use tough threads of protein to attach themselves to rocks or coral reefs, making it hard for predators to prize them away!

Each one has a shell in two parts, which are hinged together. They can be opened to let water and food in but closed quickly to keep predators at bay. Some bivalves—such as scallops—can even move through water by opening their shell and snapping it shut again!

The shape and color of bivalve shells varies widely, from ridged, heart-shaped cockles to long, brown, shiny razor clams. The creatures inside, however, are similar! They are pale mollusks with no heads. Instead, the important parts of the mollusk are arranged around the edges of the shell, including sense organs such as eyes and little "hairs" called **cilia.**

The cilia vibrate to bring water in and out of the shell, so the mollusk's gills can soak up oxygen and filter out tiny particles of food. By filtering the water in this way, bivalves play an important role in keeping oceans and fresh water clean.

SHARED FEATURES

- Two-part shells, linked by a tough hinge
- Gills to soak up oxygen and filter out food
- Some have a long, flexible "foot" for digging burrows
- A siphon acts like a snorkel for breathing

GOOD NEIGHBORS?

Many bivalves are collected to be eaten by humans and some are even farmed. They include giant scallops, mussels, oysters, and clams. Oysters are also used to produce pearls for jewelry. The shimmering nacre or "mother of pearl" that coats the insides of bivalve shells is also used to decorate things.

1 PERFECT PEARLS
Pearls are popular for making jewelry, but oysters actually make them in self-defense! When a parasite or other object gets inside, the oyster's **immune system** stops it from doing harm by coating it in layers of shell!

2 GIANT CLAMS
The largest bivalves are over 3-foot-wide giant clams that live on coral reefs. Their bodies are home to colorful dinoflagellates (see page 192), which provide some of their food in return for a place to live. Scientists think that a typical giant clam grows to be more than 100 years old. The oldest ever found was estimated to be more than 500 years old and still going strong!

3 SINKING SHIPS
Shipworms use their tiny shells to bore holes in rotting wood that has fallen into the ocean. They live hidden inside the hole they have made. When humans began making wooden ships, shipworms bored holes in those too, which is how they got their name!

4 UNDER THREAT
The ocean is becoming more acidic due to the extra **carbon dioxide** that humans have released into the atmosphere. This makes it harder for bivalves to form their calcium carbonate shells. Mussels are anchored in one place for most of their lives, which means they can't adapt easily to changes in their environment. In some parts of the world mussels are going extinct, and communities that rely on farming mussels for food are under threat.

CEPHALOPODS

CEPHALOPODA

Their terrific tentacles make cephalopods some of the most amazing and recognizable creatures on the planet.

YOU ARE HERE

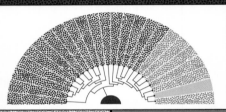

EUKARYOTA

AMORPHEA

KEY FACTS

- More than 700 species
- From 5-mm (0.2-in) pygmy squid to giant squid as long as buses
- Found in all seas and oceans, except the Black Sea, which isn't salty enough for them. Most common in warm, salty seas such as the Mediterranean

SPECIMEN

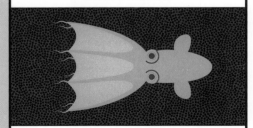

VAMPIRE SQUID

ALL ABOUT

The name cephalopod means "head-foot" and these mollusks do indeed have their foot joined to their head! The foot is divided into tentacles, which make them some of the strangest-looking creatures on the planet.

The first ever cephalopods probably had a shell for protection, similar to the fossilized ammonites (see page 114). Many of today's cephalopods, such as squid and octopuses, don't have shells. Instead, they rely on cunning camouflage, big brains (for a mollusk), and incredible tentacles. Cephalopods also have much longer bodies than other mollusks. Some giant squid can grow to be longer than a bus!

All cephalopods live in salt water and are predators. Some are so small they can only eat plankton, but the biggest can catch fish, crustaceans, and other mollusks. Giant squid may even eat each other when food is hard to find! A cephalopod's mouth is found at the very center of its tentacles and often has beak-like jaws as well as the radula ring of teeth typical of mollusks.

Predators can become prey themselves, and the soft bodies of cephalopods are popular with whales, sharks, fish, seals, and all sorts of seabirds. Some make a quick getaway by shooting out a jet of water to swim backward and even a cloud of black "ink" to cover their tracks. The ink contains melanin, the same **pigment** that gives human skin and hair its color.

SHARED FEATURES

- Front end of the foot is split into tentacles that can be used to grab things
- Hard, beak-like jaws
- Many have an ink sac to startle predators
- Foot joined to head

GOOD NEIGHBORS?

Many species of cephalopods are eaten by humans. Even their defensive ink has been used for thousands of years in different ways: to make medicines, as ink to write and paint with, as makeup, and to flavor foods. In the future, its **antimicrobial** properties might be used as a natural way to kill microbes and **sterilize** food.

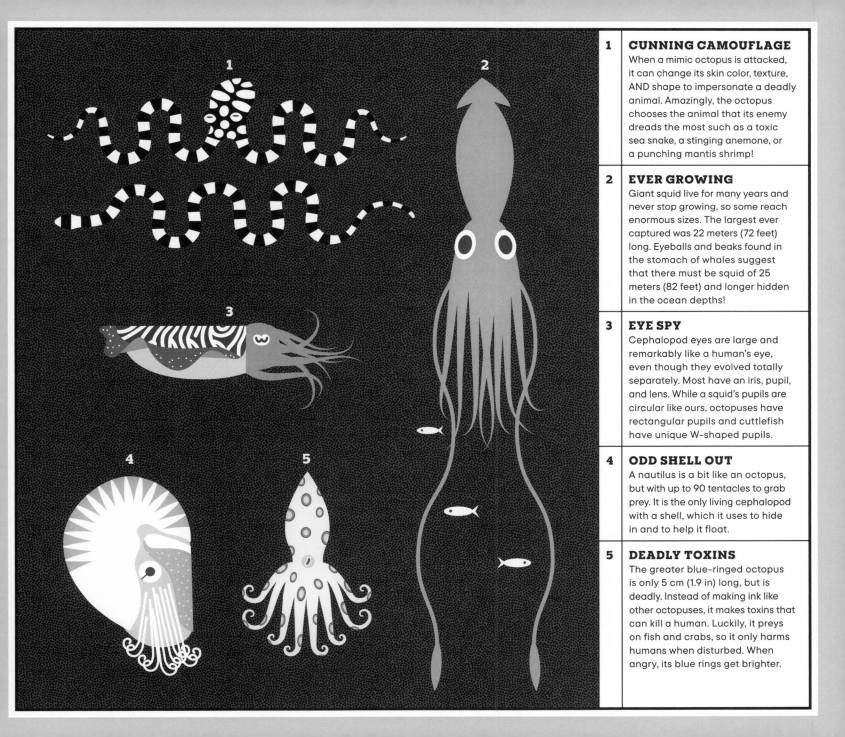

1 CUNNING CAMOUFLAGE
When a mimic octopus is attacked, it can change its skin color, texture, AND shape to impersonate a deadly animal. Amazingly, the octopus chooses the animal that its enemy dreads the most such as a toxic sea snake, a stinging anemone, or a punching mantis shrimp!

2 EVER GROWING
Giant squid live for many years and never stop growing, so some reach enormous sizes. The largest ever captured was 22 meters (72 feet) long. Eyeballs and beaks found in the stomach of whales suggest that there must be squid of 25 meters (82 feet) and longer hidden in the ocean depths!

3 EYE SPY
Cephalopod eyes are large and remarkably like a human's eye, even though they evolved totally separately. Most have an iris, pupil, and lens. While a squid's pupils are circular like ours, octopuses have rectangular pupils and cuttlefish have unique W-shaped pupils.

4 ODD SHELL OUT
A nautilus is a bit like an octopus, but with up to 90 tentacles to grab prey. It is the only living cephalopod with a shell, which it uses to hide in and to help it float.

5 DEADLY TOXINS
The greater blue-ringed octopus is only 5 cm (1.9 in) long, but is deadly. Instead of making ink like other octopuses, it makes toxins that can kill a human. Luckily, it preys on fish and crabs, so it only harms humans when disturbed. When angry, its blue rings get brighter.

ROUNDWORMS

NEMATODA

YOU ARE HERE

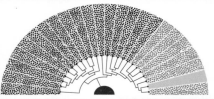

EUKARYOTA
AMORPHEA

KEY FACTS

- At least 25,000 species, although the true number is likely to be millions
- Most are microscopic, but some parasitic nematodes can grow very large
- Found in all climates, including land, water, and inside the Earth's crust

SPECIMEN

INTESTINAL ROUNDWORM

Which creatures rule the planet? When it comes to numbers, it's the nematodes! There are more of these roundworms than any other group of animals on Earth.

ALL ABOUT

Let's leap on to another large branch of the protostome tree of life. Nematodes are everywhere. Pick up a handful of soil and you'll be holding thousands of tiny roundworms, from hundreds of different species. A rotting apple can be home to 90,000. A bath-full of lake water (and the sediments that settle beneath them) might have a million or more.

In fact, if you counted every individual animal on Earth, four in every five would be a nematode. But most of the time we don't notice these worms living all around us. Most species of nematodes are transparent and microscopic—growing to no more than 1 millimeter (0.04 inches) long. They also tend to hide away, burrowing into sediment, or living inside plants and animals, including people.

What is the secret to their success? It's not their moves. With muscles running from head to tail, roundworms can only bend their bodies from side to side. They often look like they are wiggling around without getting anywhere! They can, however, lay massive numbers of eggs—up to 200,000 per day in some species! These eggs can last ten years or more, surviving terrible conditions, then hatching into larvae when the time is right.

Nematode parasites can cause diseases in crops and animals, but most nematodes are extremely helpful. They feed on dead matter and microbes, creating soil, recycling nutrients, and helping to keep ecosystems in balance.

SHARED FEATURES

- Smooth, rounded bodies that are pointed at each end
- Covered in a thick cuticle made of flexible protein, which supports their body
- Very simple inside—they are basically just a long digestive tube!

GOOD NEIGHBORS?

Most nematodes live freely in soil and water, where they are crucial decomposers and controllers of microbes. Parasitic nematodes can cause harm to plants, animals, and humans—around a sixth of crop losses each year can be blamed on nematodes. However, nematodes are also of great value as model organisms and natural pest controls.

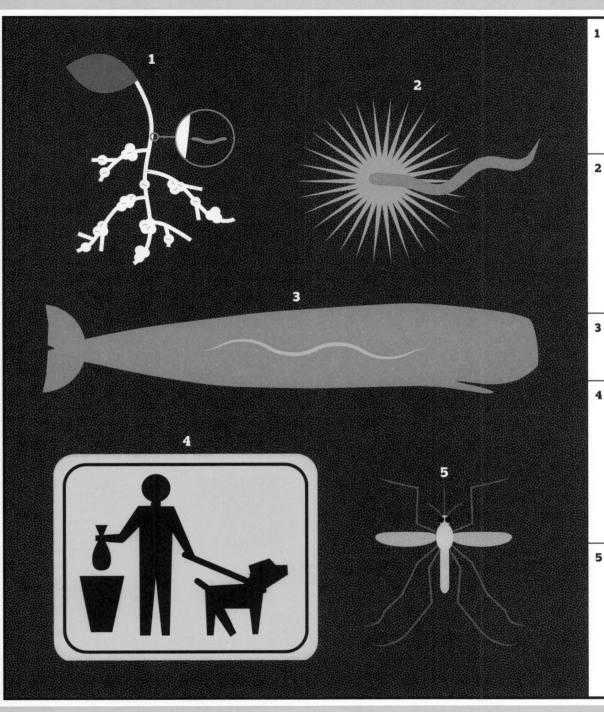

1 PLANT PARASITES

Nematodes that are parasites of plants are armed with a sharp, needle-like weapon called a stylet, which they use to pierce plant cells and suck out the contents. They can do this in the leaves, or fruit, but most damaging of all are the ones that live in plant roots.

2 SCIENCE STAR

The nematode *Caenorhabditis elegans* has been used by scientists in labs all around the world as a **model organism**. It was the first multicellular creature to have its entire genetic code sequenced, leading to amazing discoveries in biology and medicine, and helping scientists to win Nobel Prizes. It has even been sent into space!

3 FOOD FOR FUNGI

An 8.5 meter (28 foot) roundworm was once found living inside a sperm whale.

4 SCOOP THAT POOP

The pet dogs in just one UK city were found to poop out more than 7 billion roundworm eggs every two days. These roundworms don't usually cause symptoms in dogs, but if they accidentally get into a human body, their larvae may get lost and start growing in places where they cause damage, such as the eyes, muscles, or lungs.

5 PEST CONTROL

Parasitic nematodes can be used to fight insect pests, for example by infecting the larvae of mosquitoes that spread deadly diseases. Using nematodes doesn't harm the environment like chemical pesticides.

ARTHROPODS

EUARTHROPODA

YOU ARE HERE

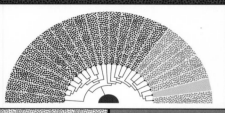

EUKARYOTA

AMORPHEA

KEY FACTS

- More than 1 million species
- Ranging from 0.1 mm (0.004 in) to more than 3 m (nearly 10 ft)
- Found in almost all land and water environments, except the polar deserts

SPECIMEN

SEA SPIDER

Arthropods have conquered every corner of Earth! They include the crustaceans of the oceans and the insects and arachnids that live everywhere on land and even in the air.

ALL ABOUT

The creatures in this huge clade are found everywhere from the deepest oceans to the highest mountains and even in the air. They include insects (see page 134), crustaceans such as crabs and barnacles (see page 130), arachnids such as scorpions and spiders (see page 126), and myriapods such as millipedes and centipedes (see page 128). Arthropods play vital roles in all ecosystems—as food for other animals, as decomposers, and as pollinators of flowering plants (see page 68).

Because of their hard exoskeleton, arthropods can't grow gradually like we do. Instead, they must molt (shed their exoskeleton) several times as they grow, replacing it with a larger one each time. Young arthropod larvae often look very different from their adult forms. Some insect larvae look just like their crustacean cousins (see page 130) and there is a good reason. Recently, scientists found that insects may be crustaceans that conquered land!

More than 84% of the living things that we know about belong in this group, and scientists think there are millions more to discover. Their incredible **biodiversity** shows that arthropods have been amazing at adapting to different habitats and lifestyles—and it is adaptation over time that leads to new species.

SHARED FEATURES

- Segmented body
- Legs with joints (the name arthropod means "jointed foot")
- Hard exoskeleton, which protects their bodies, stops them from drying out, and can give arthropods incredible strength for their size

GOOD NEIGHBORS?

Many arthropods live closely alongside humans and even on our bodies, as parasites. Some can be an important source of food for humans, and we also rely on arthropods to pollinate most of the plants we eat and use. Some arthropods, however, spread microbes that cause serious diseases that affect millions of people every year.

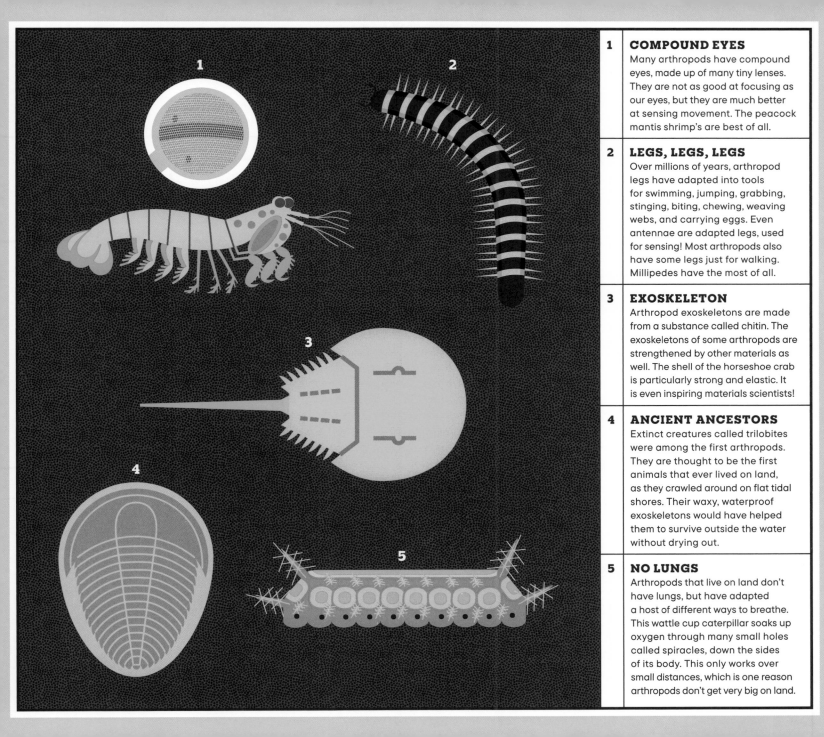

1 COMPOUND EYES
Many arthropods have compound eyes, made up of many tiny lenses. They are not as good at focusing as our eyes, but they are much better at sensing movement. The peacock mantis shrimp's are best of all.

2 LEGS, LEGS, LEGS
Over millions of years, arthropod legs have adapted into tools for swimming, jumping, grabbing, stinging, biting, chewing, weaving webs, and carrying eggs. Even antennae are adapted legs, used for sensing! Most arthropods also have some legs just for walking. Millipedes have the most of all.

3 EXOSKELETON
Arthropod exoskeletons are made from a substance called chitin. The exoskeletons of some arthropods are strengthened by other materials as well. The shell of the horseshoe crab is particularly strong and elastic. It is even inspiring materials scientists!

4 ANCIENT ANCESTORS
Extinct creatures called trilobites were among the first arthropods. They are thought to be the first animals that ever lived on land, as they crawled around on flat tidal shores. Their waxy, waterproof exoskeletons would have helped them to survive outside the water without drying out.

5 NO LUNGS
Arthropods that live on land don't have lungs, but have adapted a host of different ways to breathe. This wattle cup caterpillar soaks up oxygen through many small holes called spiracles, down the sides of its body. This only works over small distances, which is one reason arthropods don't get very big on land.

ARACHNIDS

ARACHNIDA

From giant bird-eating spiders to microscopic mites, arachnids lurk almost everywhere on Earth's surface.

YOU ARE HERE

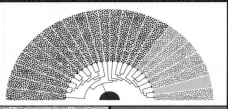

	EUKARYOTA
	AMORPHEA

KEY FACTS

- More than 60,000 species
- From microscopic mites measuring less than 0.1 mm (0.004 in) to spiders with a 30-cm (nearly a foot) leg span
- Almost all arachnids live in land-based habitats, from mountains to deserts and even on the bodies of larger animals

SPECIMEN

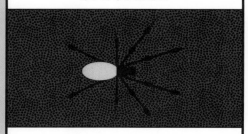

ORB-WEAVER SPIDER

ALL ABOUT

Spiders and scorpions are the best-known arachnids, but this group also includes much tinier ticks and mites, as well as weird and wonderful creepy-crawlies such as fake scorpions, whip scorpions, sun spiders, and harvestmen.

Arachnids are found everywhere on land, from cool, dark caves to hot dry deserts. Some spiders and mites are even adapted to live in water. But members of this clade are hard to spot, as they like to stay hidden, lying in wait for prey. Most scorpions and spiders are predators. They have grasping mouthparts but no jaws for chewing, so can only feast on fluids. Some solve this problem by injecting juices that digest their prey before they slurp it up.

Mites and ticks are more diverse in the way they live and feed. Many are predators but others have mouthparts specially shaped to pierce skin or plants, and suck blood or sap. A few arachnids even eat small particles, scavenging for pollen or even the dust that lies around your home.

Arachnids were some of the very first land animals, and today's spiders, scorpions, ticks, and mites look very similar to their ancient ancestors. They are tough survivors that lived through many extinction events—including the one that saw off the dinosaurs.

SHARED FEATURES

- Adults have four pairs of walking legs with joints
- Two pairs of **appendages**, such as pincers to hold, cut, or crush food, or even inject venom
- Very simple eyes, though there may be lots of them (some scorpions have 12 eyes)
- Tiny hairs so sensitive to vibrations that a spider can hear you talking from across the room

GOOD NEIGHBORS?

Many people shudder at the thought of spiders and scorpions, but these predators help us by preying on insect pests. It's parasitic ticks and mites—such as the human itch mite—that cause irritation and even spread diseases. However, some mites are also very important decomposers, breaking down dead plant matter so that new life can grow.

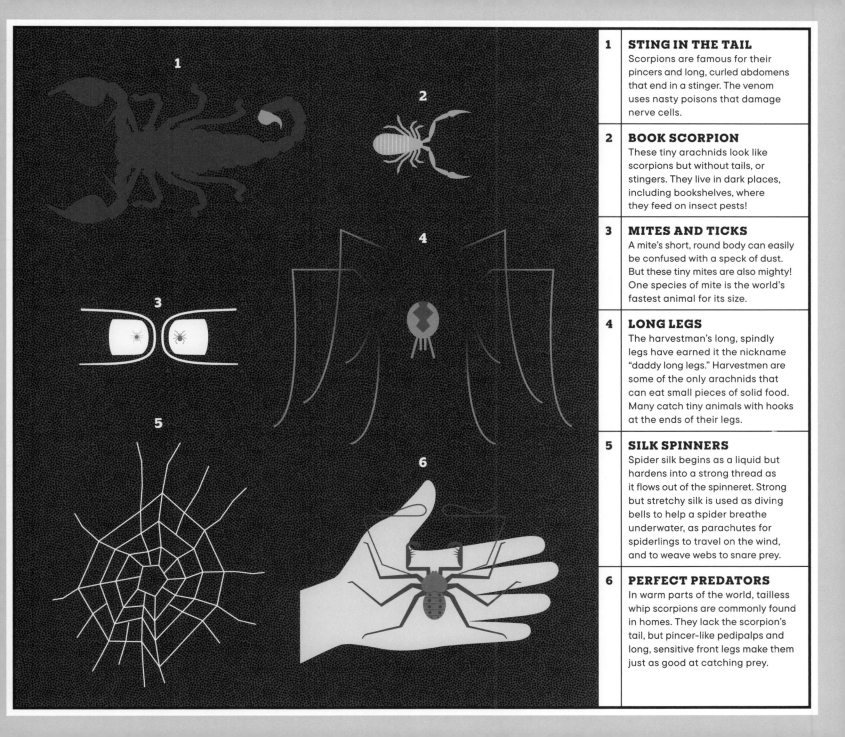

1	**STING IN THE TAIL** Scorpions are famous for their pincers and long, curled abdomens that end in a stinger. The venom uses nasty poisons that damage nerve cells.
2	**BOOK SCORPION** These tiny arachnids look like scorpions but without tails, or stingers. They live in dark places, including bookshelves, where they feed on insect pests!
3	**MITES AND TICKS** A mite's short, round body can easily be confused with a speck of dust. But these tiny mites are also mighty! One species of mite is the world's fastest animal for its size.
4	**LONG LEGS** The harvestman's long, spindly legs have earned it the nickname "daddy long legs." Harvestmen are some of the only arachnids that can eat small pieces of solid food. Many catch tiny animals with hooks at the ends of their legs.
5	**SILK SPINNERS** Spider silk begins as a liquid but hardens into a strong thread as it flows out of the spinneret. Strong but stretchy silk is used as diving bells to help a spider breathe underwater, as parachutes for spiderlings to travel on the wind, and to weave webs to snare prey.
6	**PERFECT PREDATORS** In warm parts of the world, tailless whip scorpions are commonly found in homes. They lack the scorpion's tail, but pincer-like pedipalps and long, sensitive front legs make them just as good at catching prey.

MILLIPEDES & CENTIPEDES

MYRIAPODA

YOU ARE HERE

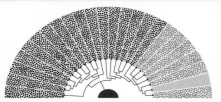

EUKARYOTA

AMORPHEA

KEY FACTS

- Around 13,000 species (roughly 10,000 millipedes and 3,000 centipedes)
- From millipedes shorter than a grain of rice to centipedes longer than an adult's forearm!
- Mainly found in damp soils, especially among the leaf litter on forest floors

SPECIMEN

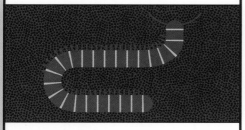

GIANT AFRICAN MILLIPEDE

Myriapods means "many legged"—and millipedes and centipedes certainly live up to their name!

ALL ABOUT

The myriapods are a group of arthropods with bodies divided into many segments. Each segment has a pair of legs attached (although millipede segments are joined together in pairs, so millipedes appear to have two pairs of legs per segment).

Each time they molt (shed an exoskeleton that has become too small), millipedes and centipedes add new segments—and new legs—to their bodies. But although "millipede" means "thousand feet," no one found a true millipede with a thousand legs until *Eumillipes persephone* was discovered deep underground in Australia, in 2021.

Myriapods like dark and damp habitats, so they lurk under rocks, in leaf litter, and in moss. Centipedes are carnivores that hunt and kill prey using venom-filled claws called forcipules. They like to eat other arthropods or small mammals but can also give humans a nasty nip.

The other myriapods, including millipedes, are almost all **detritivores**, living off the dead leaves and wood that collect on forest floors. This doesn't mean they are friendlier than centipedes though. Some have **glands** that squirt toxic chemicals at their enemies.

There is still lots to learn about these amazing animals—just be careful as you do it!

SHARED FEATURES

- First five or six segments are the head
- Usually have a pair of mandibles and two pairs of jaws
- Compound eyes
- Antennae
- Unusual sense organs, whose function is not yet known!

GOOD NEIGHBORS?

Millipedes are needed by forests around the world. They chomp away at dead leaves that gather on the forest floor, breaking them down so that all the nutrients trapped inside can be recycled and used by new living things. However, some suck fluid from living plants and are thought of as pests.

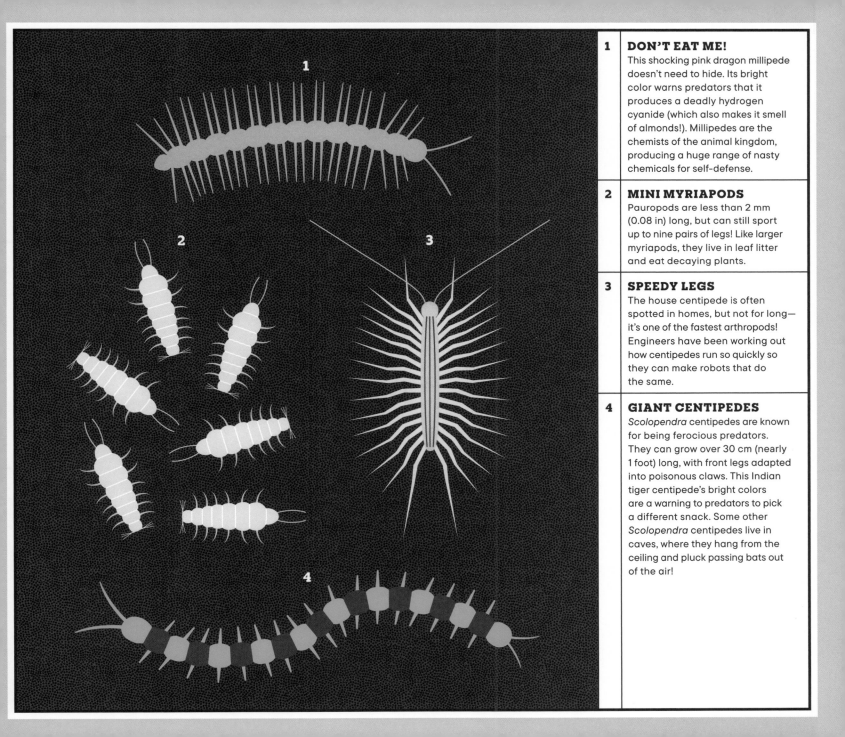

1 DON'T EAT ME!
This shocking pink dragon millipede doesn't need to hide. Its bright color warns predators that it produces a deadly hydrogen cyanide (which also makes it smell of almonds!). Millipedes are the chemists of the animal kingdom, producing a huge range of nasty chemicals for self-defense.

2 MINI MYRIAPODS
Pauropods are less than 2 mm (0.08 in) long, but can still sport up to nine pairs of legs! Like larger myriapods, they live in leaf litter and eat decaying plants.

3 SPEEDY LEGS
The house centipede is often spotted in homes, but not for long—it's one of the fastest arthropods! Engineers have been working out how centipedes run so quickly so they can make robots that do the same.

4 GIANT CENTIPEDES
Scolopendra centipedes are known for being ferocious predators. They can grow over 30 cm (nearly 1 foot) long, with front legs adapted into poisonous claws. This Indian tiger centipede's bright colors are a warning to predators to pick a different snack. Some other *Scolopendra* centipedes live in caves, where they hang from the ceiling and pluck passing bats out of the air!

TRUE CRUSTACEANS

VERICRUSTACEA

YOU ARE HERE

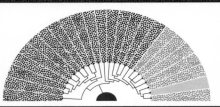

EUKARYOTA

AMORPHEA

KEY FACTS

- More than 60,000 species
- From tiny zooplankton to spider crabs with leg spans of almost 4 m (13 ft)
- Found in all watery habitats, from the seabed to the open ocean. Some species such as woodlice, live their whole lives on land

SPECIMEN

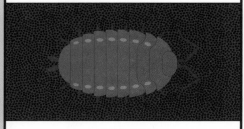

WOODLOUSE

Crabs and lobsters are the most famous members of this clade, but when it comes to supporting the planet, smaller crustaceans such as krill steal the show.

ALL ABOUT

Crustaceans are a huge group of arthropods that include crabs, lobsters, shrimp, and crayfish, but also smaller creatures such as krill, copepods, and barnacles. Recently scientists have begun to call this group the "true crustaceans" to distinguish them from insects, which are sort of crustaceans too!

Crustaceans are an important part of all ecosystems. In the oceans, krill, copepods, and the larvae of larger crustaceans gobble up many tons of phytoplankton (see page 51) and algae and are then eaten by animals higher up the food chain.

Barnacles are crustaceans that live in seas and oceans. Their larvae look like tiny shrimp, but you'll never glimpse a whole adult barnacle. Barnacles cement their head to a hard surface—from rocks and ships to the skin of a whale or the shell of a turtle. Once they are attached, barnacles form a hard "shell" and hide inside for the rest of their lives. Only their legs stick out, to sweep passing food into their mouths.

There are also crustaceans that are parasites, living their whole lives in the mouth of a fish, or in the nose of a reindeer! There are even crustaceans that live in our gardens. Next time you see a woodlouse (pill bug), take a moment to marvel at the fact that you are looking at the close cousin of a crab!

SHARED FEATURES

- Hard exoskeleton called a carapace
- More than four pairs of jointed legs
- Some pairs of legs may be adapted for grabbing food
- Eyes are usually on stalks
- Gills for breathing

GOOD NEIGHBORS?

Crustaceans are a vital part of ocean ecosystems, particularly as a food source. Some crustaceans, however, are parasites of farm animals and other animals that live in large herds.

1 **POP-UP POOLS**
This water flea is a branchiopod, a group of tiny crustaceans that also includes freshwater fairy shrimp and Triops. Their eggs can lie around for years, then hatch when they get wet. This is how these animals appear as if by magic in puddles that only last for a short time.

2 **POWERFUL PUNCH**
While all crustaceans have at least ten appendages, one or more pairs is adapted for jobs such as grabbing, sensing, feeding, or—in the case of the peacock mantis shrimp—punching! These shrimp punch their hammer-like claw fast enough to boil the surrounding water, shattering the shells of their sea snail prey.

3 **BIGGEST BRANCH**
The biggest branch of the crustacean family tree is a clade called the Malacostraca. Around half of crustacean species—including crabs and lobsters—belong to this group.

4 **STAYING PUT**
Look out for barnacles on rocks around the seashore. Most are tiny but they are fascinating. Charles Darwin spent eight years studying them and was the first to figure out that they are crustaceans.

5 **CROWDED OCEANS**
Copepods may be small—often less than 1 millimeter (0.04 inches) long—but there are lots of them—altogether they may have the largest **biomass** of any animal on Earth! Being very low in the food chain, they are vital for helping to feed life in the ocean and therefore the planet.

DECAPODS, AMPHIPODS & ISOPODS

MALACOSTRACA

YOU ARE HERE

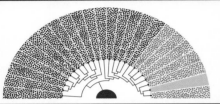

	EUKARYOTA
	AMORPHEA

KEY FACTS

- Around 30,000 species
- From less than 1 mm (0.4 in) to almost 4 m (13 ft) across
- Found in freshwater and in all areas of the ocean, including underground
- Some species, such as coconut crabs, spend their whole lives on land

SPECIMEN

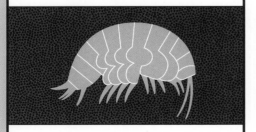

SAND FLEA

This huge group of crustaceans has taken over all possible watery habitats, from the deepest ocean floors to the splash zone around coasts.

ALL ABOUT

This large group of crustaceans includes amphipods such as sand hoppers, isopods such as woodlice, and decapods such as lobsters, crabs, and crayfish. Coastal crabs are the most familiar, often spotted as they scuttle across sand or rocks, in search of scraps to eat. Without these crab cleaners, beaches would be covered in decaying sea creatures washed up with the tide.

Much bigger crabs and lobsters lurk underwater, where the water supports some of their body weight. Giant pincers help them crack open the shells of marine mollusks. In response, many marine mollusks (see page 114) have evolved ever tougher and more elaborate armor.

Malacostracans often have super senses to help them find food, but some rely on unusual behavior instead. An isopod known as the tongue-eating louse clamps itself to a fish's tongue, causing the tongue to shrivel up and fall off. The crustacean then takes the place of the tongue, living out its life in the fish's mouth, eating mucus and blood.

Perhaps the most important malacostracans are the small krill that swim freely in the oceans, forming dense swarms near the surface. Sometimes there are more than 10,000 krill in each cubic meter (about 35 cubic feet) of water! They provide important food for fish, squid, penguins, seals, whales, and a host of other ocean animals.

SHARED FEATURES

- Head, thorax, and abdomen
- Hard carapace
- One or more pairs of compound eyes (often on stalks)
- Two pairs of antennae
- Three sets of mouthparts for chewing

GOOD NEIGHBORS?

As well as being a vital link in most ocean food chains, marine malacostracans such as shrimp, prawns, crabs, and lobsters are important foods for many human populations. There are very few crustaceans that could harm a human, but crustaceans are very vulnerable to the changes humans are causing to oceans, especially the collapse of coral reefs (see page 107).

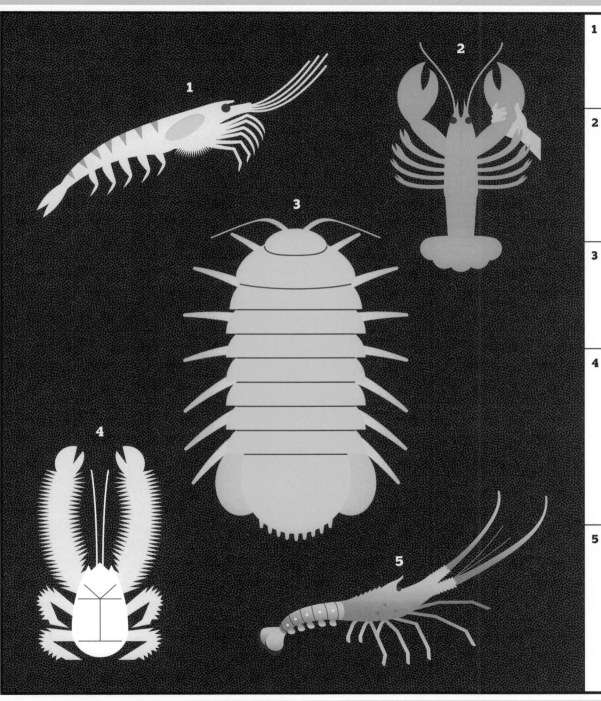

1	**WHALE SNACKS** Like copepods (see page 131), krill graze on light-harvesting microbes that float near the surface of the sea. In turn, they are eaten by fish, birds, and filter-feeding whales.
2	**HEAVYWEIGHT** American lobsters are the heaviest crustaceans, often weighing as much as a medium-sized dog. They never stop growing and can live for more than 140 years thanks to a special trick they use to protect their DNA from getting old and damaged.
3	**GIANT ISOPODS** Giant isopods look a lot like enormous woodlice. They even curl up into a ball when threatened. They are deep-sea **scavengers**, feasting on anything that drifts down from above.
4	**DEEP-SEA GARDENERS** Yeti crabs live in darkness on the world's deepest seabeds and have no eyes. Instead of hunting for food, they grow "gardens" of bacteria on their bristly claws. These bacteria get their energy from chemicals dissolved in the water streaming from hydrothermal vents. When the crabs feel like a snack, they simply scrape some bacteria off their claws.
5	**LOBSTER MARCH** As the seasons change, spiny lobsters line up and march in single-file groups of about 50 across the ocean floor to get to warmer water. They use Earth's magnetic field to navigate up to 186 miles at a time to find food.

INSECTS

INSECTA

YOU ARE HERE

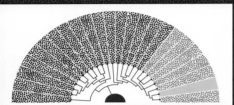

	EUKARYOTA
	AMORPHEA

KEY FACTS

- More than 1 million species
- From fairy wasps that are just 0.21 mm (0.008 in) long to giant stick insects measuring 55 cm (1.8 ft)
- Found in almost all land habitats
- Many insects start their lives in freshwater and some species remain there as adults

SPECIMEN

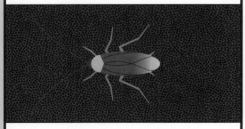

WOOD COCKROACH

If you counted all the individual leaves—or species—on the animal tree of life, most of them would be insects! How did this branch get so big?

ALL ABOUT

The first insects appeared at about the same time as plants started moving to land (see page 50). Around 400 million years later, more species of insect have been named and described than all other living things put together. Scientists think there are millions more out there.

It is hard to imagine this mind-boggling biodiversity—but if you were to collect one insect species every minute, it would take two YEARS! They creep, crawl, scuttle, swim, and fly around the planet in such great numbers that the total weight of all the insects on the planet is at least 70 times that of all the people.

One of the secrets to their success is specialization. Cockroaches, for example, can digest tough materials, such as dead wood. Wax moth caterpillars feed on the wax and honey in beehives. Each species is adapted to live in a particular place, eat a particular type of food and lead a particular kind of life. This means insects can look very different from one another. But they also have some things in common, such as their small size and the hard exoskeleton they share with other arthropods (see page 124).

Most insects also have the power of flight. Beetles, moths, butterflies, ants, bees, crickets, dragonflies, flies, and even stick insects all develop wings at some point in their life cycles.

SHARED FEATURES

- Body in three parts—a head, thorax, and abdomen
- Six legs
- Eyes and antennae for sensing
- Biting, crushing, or sucking mouthparts
- Most have two pairs of wings at some stage of their life cycle

GOOD NEIGHBORS?

Many of us only notice insects when they become pests or parasites or spread diseases. But insects are hugely important neighbors, as they support all life on planet Earth. Most of the crops that we eat are pollinated by insects. They are also good decomposers of plant and animal waste, and are an important food source for other species.

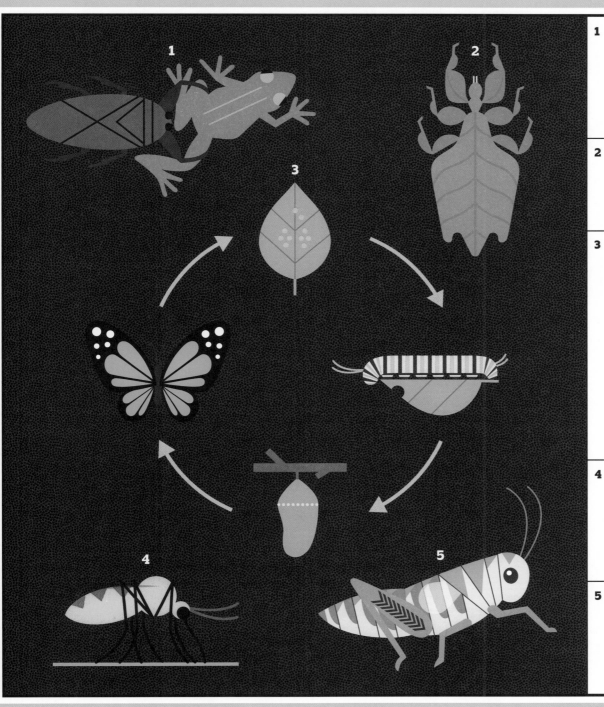

1	**WATER INSECTS** Many insects start their lives in freshwater and some remain there even when they aren't larvae anymore. Giant water bugs are large enough to catch frogs and fish with the help of their strong front legs, claws, and toxic saliva!
2	**CUNNING CAMOUFLAGE** Insects can be snack-sized, so many have evolved cunning camouflage to avoid getting eaten. Leaf insects and stick insects are most impressive of all.
3	**OUTFIT CHANGE** Like other arthropods, insects must shrug off their old exoskeleton as they grow. All insects develop in one of three ways. Some hatch from their eggs as tiny versions of their parents, known as nymphs. They get bigger each time they molt. Some nymphs change a little with each molt, for example adding wings. A third group, which includes butterflies, hatch as larvae, which look completely different from their parents. When they molt for the last time, they metamorphosize into their adult body shape.
4	**BLOOD SUCKERS** Biting insects have shaped human history by spreading diseases. Mosquitoes feed on blood. As they drink, they may unwittingly pick up or pass on microscopic parasites, such as malaria (see page 193).
5	**TOXIC CHEMICALS** Some insects don't camouflage at all. Instead, they display dazzling colors to warn predators they are not worth eating! The rainbow grasshoppers of Costa Rica taste disgusting to lizards and birds.

ANTS, BEES & WASPS

HYMENOPTERA

YOU ARE HERE

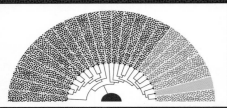

| EUKARYOTA |
| AMORPHEA |

KEY FACTS

- Around 280,000 species
- From a fifth of a millimeter (a fraction of an inch) to 5 cm (2 in) or more
- Found almost everywhere on land, in huge numbers

SPECIMEN

WALLACE'S GIANT BEE

This enormous group of insects includes hundreds of thousands of species we rarely see—as well as everyday garden friends.

ALL ABOUT

Ants, bees, wasps, and sawflies include some of the world's most important pollinators, as well as picnic-spoiling pests, and parasites with gruesome life cycles. Despite looking quite different on the outside, ants, bees, and wasps have lots in common.

Ants probably outnumber any other animal on Earth. Up to 10 quadrillion are crawling around the planet right now. Wherever ants live—from city pavements to tropical rain forests—they support ecosystems by mixing air and water into soil and breaking down nature's waste so it can be recycled into new life.

Bees are also ecosystem heroes. As they fly from flower to flower collecting nectar and pollen to eat, they pollinate flowering plants, allowing them to reproduce. Social wasps and honeybees live in huge colonies, but most types of wasps and bees live alone, or side by side in small groups. While most bees eat nectar and pollen, most wasps are predators or parasites. Some bring live prey back to their nest for their larvae to eat. Others cut or chew insects into pieces first. Most gruesome of all are parasitic wasps, which lay their eggs inside living prey, giving their larvae a hiding place and a fresh meal in one! Although we don't often spot them, tens of thousands of species of wasps live in this way.

SHARED FEATURES

- Chewing mouthparts
- Two pairs of wings
- A slender "neck" so they can turn their heads easily
- A narrow "waist" between their thorax and abdomen
- Females typically have a special ovipositor for inserting eggs into places that are otherwise inaccessible

GOOD NEIGHBORS?

Bees support humans by pollinating most of our crops. We harvest and eat the honey made by honeybees and even use their wax in cosmetics, candles, and for waxing fruit to make it look shiny and last longer. Wasps and ants are often seen as pests, but they often keep more damaging insect pests under control.

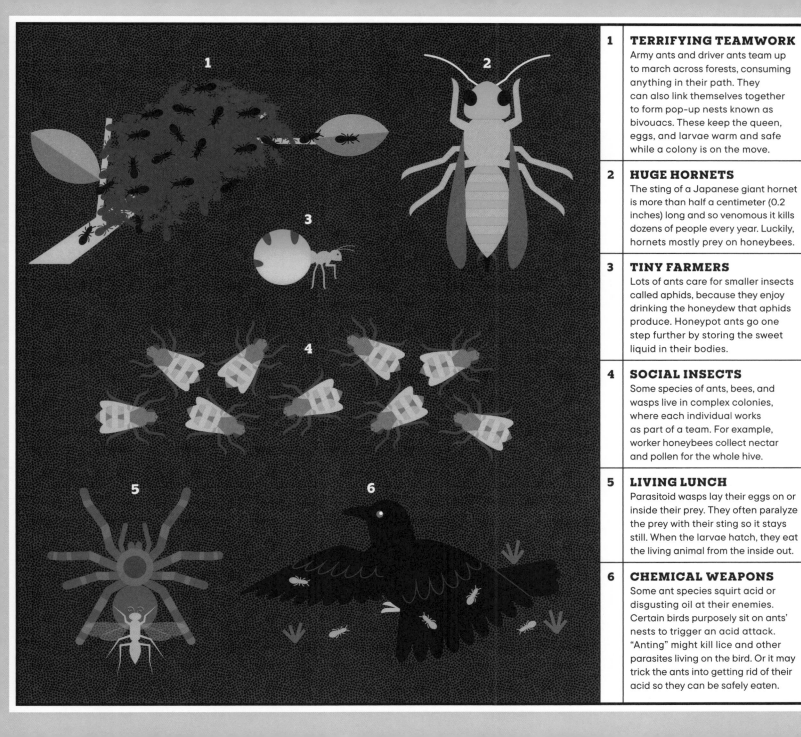

1	**TERRIFYING TEAMWORK** Army ants and driver ants team up to march across forests, consuming anything in their path. They can also link themselves together to form pop-up nests known as bivouacs. These keep the queen, eggs, and larvae warm and safe while a colony is on the move.
2	**HUGE HORNETS** The sting of a Japanese giant hornet is more than half a centimeter (0.2 inches) long and so venomous it kills dozens of people every year. Luckily, hornets mostly prey on honeybees.
3	**TINY FARMERS** Lots of ants care for smaller insects called aphids, because they enjoy drinking the honeydew that aphids produce. Honeypot ants go one step further by storing the sweet liquid in their bodies.
4	**SOCIAL INSECTS** Some species of ants, bees, and wasps live in complex colonies, where each individual works as part of a team. For example, worker honeybees collect nectar and pollen for the whole hive.
5	**LIVING LUNCH** Parasitoid wasps lay their eggs on or inside their prey. They often paralyze the prey with their sting so it stays still. When the larvae hatch, they eat the living animal from the inside out.
6	**CHEMICAL WEAPONS** Some ant species squirt acid or disgusting oil at their enemies. Certain birds purposely sit on ants' nests to trigger an acid attack. "Anting" might kill lice and other parasites living on the bird. Or it may trick the ants into getting rid of their acid so they can be safely eaten.

BEETLES
COLEOPTERA

Beetles are dazzlingly diverse thanks to their "shield wings"—tough outer wings that act as spectacular armor.

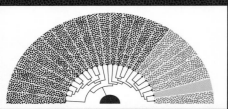

	EUKARYOTA
	AMORPHEA

KEY FACTS

- More than 300,000 species
- From 0.32 mm (a fraction of an inch) to 17 cm (over 6 in) long
- Found in almost any habitat where there are plant or animal materials to eat, including beneath the ground, in water, and in dressers, where they snack on clothing!

SPECIMEN

COCKCHAFER

ALL ABOUT

There are beetles that lurk in ponds, beetles that pretend to be bees, and beetles that can topple trees. There are beetles with rhino horns, giraffe necks, and snouts shaped like an elephant's trunk. Beetles eat fungus, furniture, and flakes of skin. Some beetles even live, breed, and feast in dung! Almost half of the insects named so far are types of beetles.

A pair of hardened shield wings makes beetles tougher than most insects, allowing them to dig tunnels, have wrestling matches, go for a swim, or squeeze into cracks without damaging the flying wings hidden underneath. They are the superheroes of the animal world.

Stag beetles use their long, spiny jaws to grab rivals and throw them off trees! Just displaying their jaws can be enough to make a smaller male back off. Titan beetles have jaws strong enough to snap a pencil in half. Goliath beetles weigh as much as an apple—making them some of the heaviest insects. But the diabolical ironclad beetle may be the toughest of all. Its outer wings are so strong, it can stand up to a crushing force 39,000 times its own weight! It's like you giving a piggyback to 39,000 of your friends!

So many different types of beetles share our planet. Altogether they are a vital part of life on Earth—as pollinators, predators, and recyclers of the building blocks of life. Together, beetles and other insects are nature's janitors, unwittingly cleaning up our planet as they eat.

SHARED FEATURES

- Hard front shell wings, known as elytra
- Large, delicate flying wings folded underneath
- Claws for gripping
- Antennae for sensing

GOOD NEIGHBORS?

Long before bees and butterflies appeared on Earth, beetles were busy pollinating plants! As they visited flowers (usually to eat them), pollen would stick to their legs and bodies and get carried from plant to plant. They are still pollinators, but beetles today are also famous for being serious plant-eating pests, damaging crops and wooden structures.

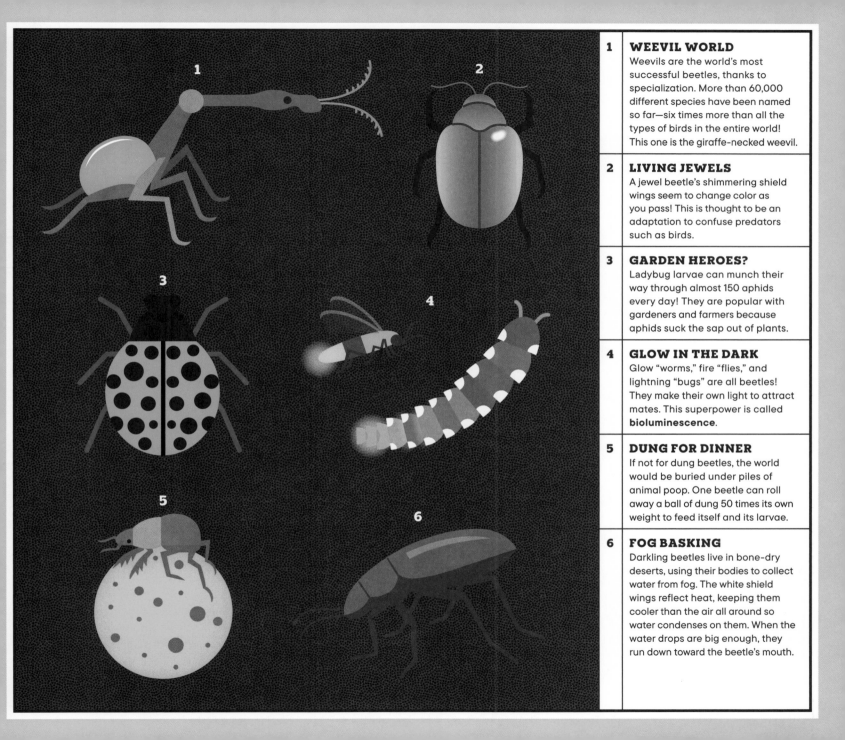

1 WEEVIL WORLD
Weevils are the world's most successful beetles, thanks to specialization. More than 60,000 different species have been named so far—six times more than all the types of birds in the entire world! This one is the giraffe-necked weevil.

2 LIVING JEWELS
A jewel beetle's shimmering shield wings seem to change color as you pass! This is thought to be an adaptation to confuse predators such as birds.

3 GARDEN HEROES?
Ladybug larvae can munch their way through almost 150 aphids every day! They are popular with gardeners and farmers because aphids suck the sap out of plants.

4 GLOW IN THE DARK
Glow "worms," fire "flies," and lightning "bugs" are all beetles! They make their own light to attract mates. This superpower is called **bioluminescence**.

5 DUNG FOR DINNER
If not for dung beetles, the world would be buried under piles of animal poop. One beetle can roll away a ball of dung 50 times its own weight to feed itself and its larvae.

6 FOG BASKING
Darkling beetles live in bone-dry deserts, using their bodies to collect water from fog. The white shield wings reflect heat, keeping them cooler than the air all around so water condenses on them. When the water drops are big enough, they run down toward the beetle's mouth.

DEUTEROSTOMES

DEUTEROSTOMIA

YOU ARE HERE

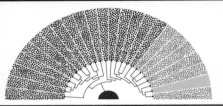

	EUKARYOTA
	AMORPHEA

KEY FACTS

- Around 60,000 species
- From sea angels less than a fraction of an inch long to blue whales, the largest animals on Earth
- Found in a huge range of water and land habitats, as well as underground and in the air

SPECIMEN

TENREC

Let's hop onto another major branch of the animal family tree, a branch that includes humans.

ALL ABOUT

From a shark to a sea star to a shrew, the animals in this group look so unalike that it's hard to believe they are closely related. But despite their very different adult bodies, most deuterostomes begin life in a very similar way.

As their bodies grow and develop, deuterostomes tend to follow a pattern opposite to protostomes (see page 108). The bottom end of their digestive tract—their anus—often forms before their mouth. More than 100 years ago, this characteristic was used to give deuterostomes their name, meaning "second mouth." Other shared body features seemed to support this grouping, such as a lack of the exoskeletons found in the protostome clade. Instead, deuterostomes have an internal skeleton, supporting their bodies from the inside.

Today, scientists know that body features are not a foolproof way to figure out how closely different creatures are related. They use different methods to unravel relationships, such as comparing DNA and other proteins, and even the instructions encoded in a creature's genes. So far, this information supports the idea that all protostomes share a common ancestor. For the deuterostomes it is less clear, and our understanding of this group will continue to change as we collect more information. For now, let's take a closer look at some of the creatures long thought to be our closest relatives.

SHARED FEATURES

- They are all Bilateria with one line of symmetry (at least on the inside)
- The "rear end" of their digestive system forms first and their mouth second
- Skeleton inside their body

GOOD NEIGHBORS?

Although there are far fewer deuterostomes than protostomes (both number of species and overall population size), the deuterostomes attract more attention. This is partly because humans are deuterostomes, so the creatures in this clade are our closest relatives on the tree of life.

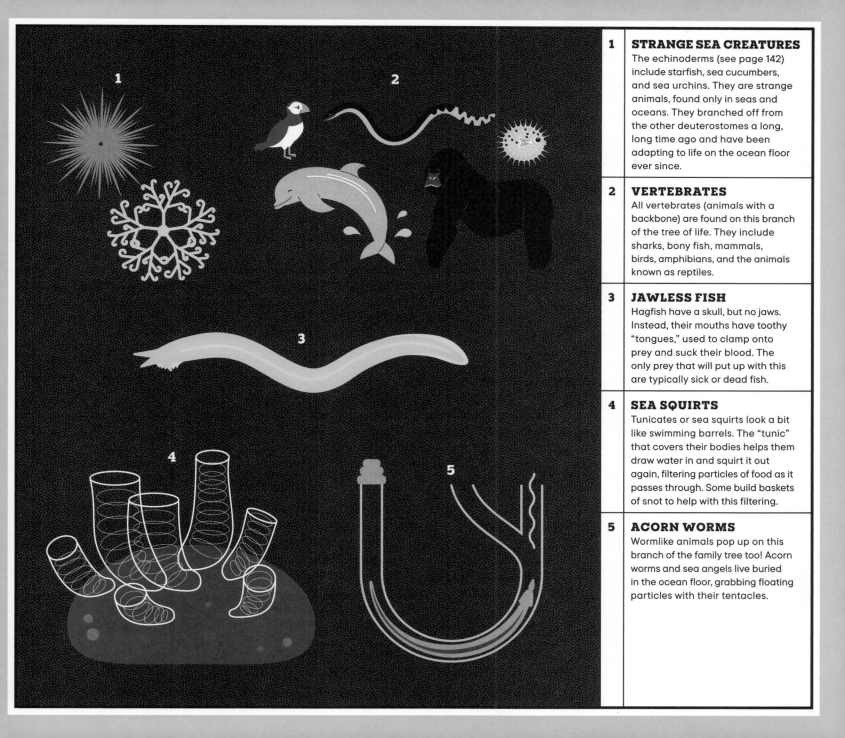

1	**STRANGE SEA CREATURES** The echinoderms (see page 142) include starfish, sea cucumbers, and sea urchins. They are strange animals, found only in seas and oceans. They branched off from the other deuterostomes a long, long time ago and have been adapting to life on the ocean floor ever since.
2	**VERTEBRATES** All vertebrates (animals with a backbone) are found on this branch of the tree of life. They include sharks, bony fish, mammals, birds, amphibians, and the animals known as reptiles.
3	**JAWLESS FISH** Hagfish have a skull, but no jaws. Instead, their mouths have toothy "tongues," used to clamp onto prey and suck their blood. The only prey that will put up with this are typically sick or dead fish.
4	**SEA SQUIRTS** Tunicates or sea squirts look a bit like swimming barrels. The "tunic" that covers their bodies helps them draw water in and squirt it out again, filtering particles of food as it passes through. Some build baskets of snot to help with this filtering.
5	**ACORN WORMS** Wormlike animals pop up on this branch of the family tree too! Acorn worms and sea angels live buried in the ocean floor, grabbing floating particles with their tentacles.

ECHINODERMS

ECHINODERMATA

YOU ARE HERE

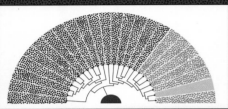

(paw print)	EUKARYOTA
	AMORPHEA

KEY FACTS

- Around 7,000 species
- Most are small, but some sea cucumbers grow up to 2 m (6.5 ft) long
- Only found in seas and oceans, all around the world

SPECIMEN

CROWN-OF-THORNS STARFISH

These strange animals are only found in seas and oceans. When it comes to body shape, they make their own rules!

ALL ABOUT

The echinoderms include sea lilies and feather stars, basket stars, sea urchins, sea cucumbers, and sea biscuits. If this all sounds pretty delicious, think again. The group is named after their rough, tough, prickly skin, which is often covered in sharp spines for protection. Even soft, squishy sea cucumbers are packed with poisonous chemicals for self-defense.

Echinoderms need this protection because they spend a lot of time sitting around on rocks and on the seabed, where they feed. Most adults can move—by pumping water in and out of their strange "tube feet"—but only slowly.

Some sea urchins, starfish, and brittle stars are predators. Their strong arms can even prize open the shells of mollusks. To eat their prey, they push their own stomach out through their mouth and into the mollusk shell, drawing it back in once the mollusk has been digested. This means sea stars can eat large prey. Others crawl over rocks, grazing on algae and other light-harvesting microbes.

Sea cucumbers are scavengers, vacuuming up the "marine snow" of dead things that drift down from the ocean above and settle on the seabed. Adult crinoids are even less active than this, attaching themselves permanently to a surface with a "stalk" and waiting for food to come to them. They filter particles and plankton from the water using tentacle-like or feather-like arms.

SHARED FEATURES

- Internal skeleton, made of calcium carbonate
- Tough skin, often covered with bumps or spines
- "Tube feet" for moving around

GOOD NEIGHBORS?

Echinoderms have been used by biologists to research the way that animals develop. They produce lots of eggs, and sea urchin eggs are sometimes eaten in sushi. Some sea urchins and sea cucumbers are eaten too.

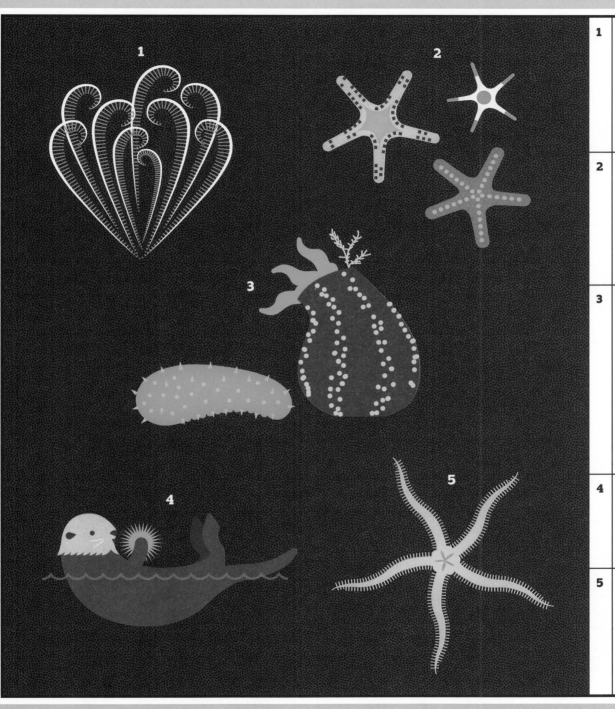

1 TUBE FEET

The feathery fronds that line the arms of crinoids are their versions of the tube feet that other echinoderms use to walk! By pumping water in and out of these tubes, sea lilies and feather stars can move the food they catch into their mouth.

2 STRANGE SYMMETRY

Like all other deuterostomes, echinoderms are Bilateria (see page 103). Their larvae begin life with just one line of symmetry. However, as they grow, many adult echinoderms develop fivefold symmetry. Most starfish have five arms, though some have more.

3 SEA CUCUMBERS

Sea cucumbers live on the dark seabed, many miles below the surface. If startled, sea cucumbers can shoot some of their inner organs out of their rear end, to scare (or disgust) an enemy! The missing organs grow back later. Most crawl across the ocean floor eating "marine snow"—a mixture of droppings and dead stuff that drifts down from above. At this depth they can't afford to be fussy eaters.

4 URCHIN CONTROL

Sea urchins have formidable spines, but many animals figure out how to eat them. Sea otters break off the spines and use rocks to crack open their tough "shells."

5 BRITTLE STARS

The arms of deep-sea brittle stars grow up to 60 centimeters (nearly 2 feet) long and are used to dance along underwater. A brittle star can grow back an arm it loses to a predator.

VERTEBRATES

VERTEBRATA

YOU ARE HERE

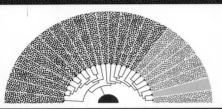

	EUKARYOTA
	AMORPHEA

KEY FACTS

- Around 69,963 species
- From tiny frogs the size of lentils, to enormous blue whales
- Found in seas and oceans, freshwater, land, and air

SPECIMEN

DOMESTIC CATTLE

You probably recognize the term "vertebrates" from school, but don't get too comfortable. This is where you learn you're really a fish!

ALL ABOUT

Members of this group all have a skeleton inside their bodies. The skeleton includes a line of vertebrae, known as a backbone, running from the front of their bodies (the mouth end) to the back. This gives this clade its name.

The very first vertebrates were fish. This means that all other vertebrates descended from them are technically fish that have adapted to live in different habitats, including on land.

Most living vertebrates have jaws, allowing them to bite and even chew food instead of just wafting or sucking it into their mouths. A long time ago, these vertebrates with jaws split into two branches that have been evolving separately ever since.

The first branch are the cartilaginous fish, with skeletons made of cartilage rather than bone. They have been hunting in the oceans for 400 million years, and today's sharks, rays, and skates are remarkably like their ancient ancestors.

The second branch contains the bony fish, whose tougher skeletons made of bone have helped them conquer the land and skies as well as the oceans. They are the ancestors of most fish and all tetrapods (animals with four limbs), including amphibians (see page 154), birds (see page 182), mammals (see page 158), and you! Humans are bony fish with bodies that are so well adapted to life on land that they can read books . . . and even write them.

SHARED FEATURES

- Inner skeleton made of cartilage and/or bone
- Parts of the skeleton called vertebrae. These protect the nerves that run through them

GOOD NEIGHBORS?

Humans have focused lots of attention on naming and studying vertebrates. This is partly because they are the largest animals on the planet and partly because we are vertebrates ourselves. By studying the bodies and behavior of other vertebrates, we can understand ourselves better.

1   TO LAY OR NOT TO LAY?

The tetrapods split into two main groups—animals who lay their eggs in water (such as amphibians—see page 154) and animals whose young grow in a special water-filled sac, called an amniotic sac. This means their eggs can be laid on land, or even develop inside the mother.

2   FOUR LIMBS

Tetrapods are animals with four limbs. These limbs might be legs for leaping, wings for flying, or even paddles for swimming, but they are always arranged in pairs— just like the fleshy fins of their lobe-finned fish ancestors.

3   FROM GILLS TO LUNGS

As well as gills, lungfish have lungs rather like ours. If their freshwater homes are low on oxygen, they stop using their gills and come to the surface to breathe air instead.

4   BLOOD SUCKERS

The lampreys are long, stretched-looking fish without pairs of fins. They also lack jaws to bite food. Instead, their mouths have a sucker so they can clamp themselves to prey and use their tooth-covered "tongue" to suck blood.

5   LARGE JAWS

Most other vertebrates have jaws in two parts, so they can bite and even chew their food. Some of the biggest bites belong to cartilaginous fish such as sharks.

6   BONY VERTEBRATES

About half of today's bony vertebrate species are fish. They include a few lobe-finned fish such as coelacanths, which have been swimming unchanged for up to 70 million years.

CARTILAGINOUS FISH

CHONDRICHTHYES

Sharks, rays, skates, and chimaeras are an ancient group of fish. They are also misunderstood. We are far more of a threat to them than they are to us.

YOU ARE HERE

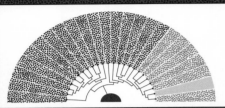

EUKARYOTA

AMORPHEA

KEY FACTS

- Almost 1,000 species
- From 10 cm (4 in) to 12 m (39 ft)
- Found in all oceans, except the deepest and coldest parts. There are also a few freshwater species

SPECIMEN

HAMMERHEAD SHARK

ALL ABOUT

Almost all sharks, rays, and their relatives are predators, which partly explains their fearsome reputation. The other factor is a mouthful of teeth that never stop growing. These teeth are the only part of their skeleton that is toughened with a thin layer of calcium-containing bone. Unusually for vertebrates, the rest of these fish's skeleton is made entirely from cartilage—the same flexible material that shapes your nose and ears!

This softer skeleton explains why we find very few complete fossils of sharks and their relatives, even though they have been prowling Earth's water for more than 455 million years. Only their teeth are tough enough to become preserved as fossils.

Sharks are excellent swimmers, but only if they keep moving. They have no swim bladder, so must swim nonstop to avoid sinking. As they bend their heads and tails from side to side, their huge tail fin propels them forward. As water flows across fins on their sides it generates an upward force called lift, just like the wings of a plane. These large pectoral fins also help them to steer. Fins on their backs and bellies stop them from rolling over in the water.

Most incredible of all is their skin, which can detect the weak electric fields generated by animals' nervous systems. Chondrichthyes use this sixth sense to find prey and may even be able to communicate with each other using electrical signals.

SHARED FEATURES

- Skeleton formed of cartilage, not bone
- Hard, tooth-like scales
- Paired fins
- Gills
- Tiny sense organs that can detect weak electric signals

GOOD NEIGHBORS?

It's common for humans to fear sharks, but only around ten people are killed by sharks each year. In comparison, 20,000 people are killed by diseases passed on by freshwater snails. We are terrible neighbors for sharks. About 100 million sharks are killed by fishing each year, and a third of shark species are on the brink of extinction.

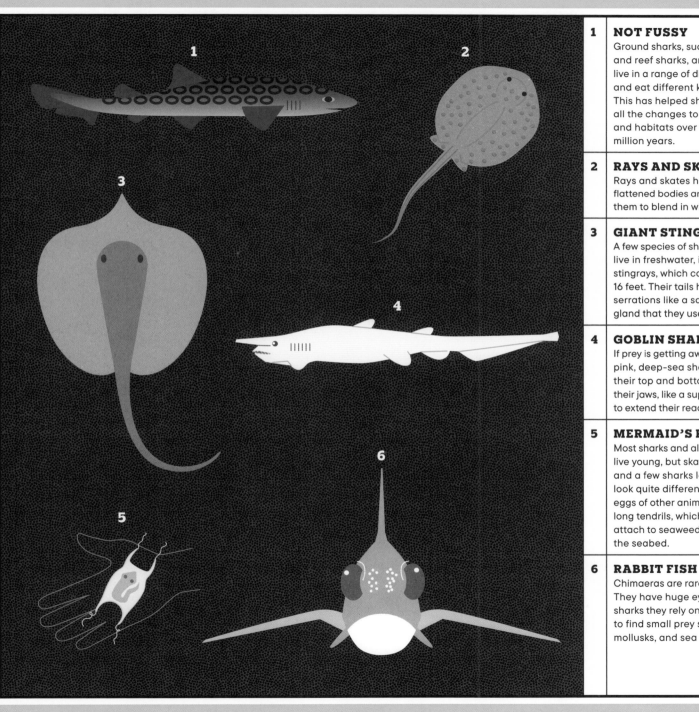

1 NOT FUSSY
Ground sharks, such as catsharks and reef sharks, are happy to live in a range of different habitats and eat different kinds of prey. This has helped sharks survive all the changes to Earth's climate and habitats over the last 400 million years.

2 RAYS AND SKATES
Rays and skates have wide, flattened bodies and skin that helps them to blend in with the sand.

3 GIANT STINGRAY
A few species of sharks and rays live in freshwater, including giant stingrays, which can grow up to 16 feet. Their tails have a spine with serrations like a saw and a venom gland that they use in self-defense.

4 GOBLIN SHARK
If prey is getting away, these strange, pink, deep-sea sharks can throw their top and bottom teeth out of their jaws, like a superfast slingshot, to extend their reach!

5 MERMAID'S PURSES
Most sharks and all rays give birth to live young, but skates, chimaeras, and a few sharks lay eggs. They look quite different from the eggs of other animals. Some have long tendrils, which help them attach to seaweed or rocks on the seabed.

6 RABBIT FISH
Chimaeras are rare deep-sea fish. They have huge eyes, but like all sharks they rely on electroreception to find small prey such as crabs, mollusks, and sea urchins.

RAY-FINNED FISH

ACTINOPTERYGII

YOU ARE HERE

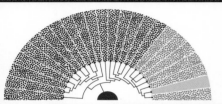

| EUKARYOTA |
| AMORPHEA |

KEY FACTS

- Around 27,000 species
- From goby fish just 17 mm (about half an inch) long to giant oarfish measuring 8 m (26 ft) or more
- Found in all watery habitats, both freshwater and marine

SPECIMEN

FLYING FISH

Half of all vertebrates are members of this group, known as the ray-finned fish. Let's delve into a colorful world that is usually hidden underwater.

ALL ABOUT

The science of fish is called ichthyology. It's a huge area of science but fish have been very hard to study compared to land animals. Until underwater technology was invented, most fish that scientists got to see were dead ones, brought up from deep in the ocean by fishers or dredgers. It was like trying to understand a rain forest based only on the stuffed animals in museums! The underwater habitats are also huge compared to land habitats.

With the help of technology, today's ichthyologists are making exciting discoveries all the time. They are still working out how all the different groups and species of ray-finned fish are related to one another.

We know that all these fish share a common ancestor, which had a single dorsal fin and diamond-shaped body scales. The ray-finned fish probably also inherited lungs from an even earlier ancestor. Over time, these lungs adapted into a swim bladder that ray-finned fish can inflate with gas or deflate, allowing them to rise or sink in the water, or remain in the same spot—something that sharks, rays, and skates can't do (see page 146)! This helps ray-finned fish save energy, which is likely to be a big part of their success.

SHARED FEATURES

- Paired fins, made from lots of small bones arranged like a fan
- Single dorsal fin
- Swim bladder

GOOD NEIGHBORS?

Fish have been an important source of food and income for humans for thousands of years. In some parts of the world, they are the main source of animal protein. Certain fish eggs are also eaten, such as the eggs of sturgeon, which are known as caviar. As a result of illegal fishing, sturgeon around the world are at risk of extinction.

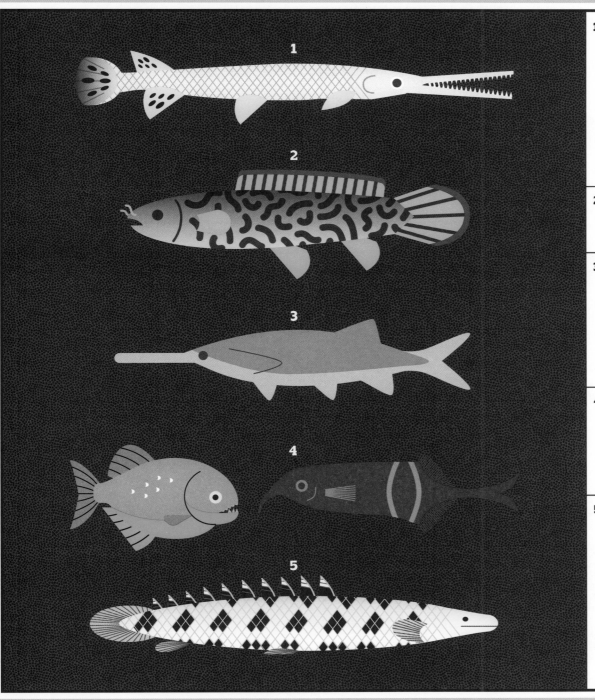

1	**ARMORED SCALES** Fossils show us that ancient ray-finned fish had very tough, bony scales. The scales of Ginglymodes or longnose gars like this one are still covered in a material like the enamel that covers your teeth. As a result, the fish shine like porcelain underwater. They hunt by hiding and waiting for other fish to pass by. Like reedfish, their swim bladders can double as lungs.
2	**BOWFIN FISH** There is just one species of bowfin, with a long dorsal fin that runs down almost its entire body.
3	**FLEXIBLE FISH** Most of today's ray-finned fish have much lighter, thinner, more flexible scales, helping them twist and turn more quickly in the water to catch prey or escape predators. Most extreme is the skin of sturgeons and paddlefish, which are almost scaleless.
4	**FOOD SLURPERS** More than 20,000 species of ray-finned fish are members of a clade called teleosts, which share the terrible table manners of slurping their food! Let's dive in and meet some of them on the next page.
5	**DRAGON FISH** Bichirs and reedfish look a bit like swimming snakes or dragons, thanks to their long bodies and dorsal fins that are separated into many different "humps." They wind through shallow, plant-filled waters in Africa. Young reedfish have gills, but the adults can use their swim bladders to breathe air and survive outside the water in the dry season.

TELEOSTS

TELEOSTEI

This group of fish are incredibly diverse but are all linked by their terrible table manners.

YOU ARE HERE

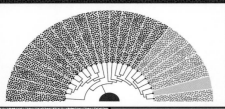

| EUKARYOTA |
| AMORPHEA |

KEY FACTS

- Around 24,000 species
- From tiny cyprinid fish measuring just 7.9 mm (0.3 in) to whopping 4-m-long (13-ft-long) sunfish
- Found in all marine and freshwater habitats, from the deepest point in the ocean to mountain streams more than 4,500 m (2.8 mi) above sea level

SPECIMEN

LANTERN FISH

ALL ABOUT

Instead of grabbing prey with snapping teeth, all teleosts slurp their food. By opening their lower jaw while raising their heads and pressing their tongues down to the bottom of their mouths, they suck water in and bring their food with it. Sometimes, they jut out their lower jaw too, creating even more space in their mouth. Try doing all of this in front of a mirror and you will see how hard it is to eat like a teleost fish. You may also end up looking like one!

This trait, inherited from the common ancestor of all teleosts, makes it easier to eat underwater. The fish don't have to lunge toward prey, which would warn it that an attack is coming.

Most living fish are teleosts and they have all sorts of strange body features, behaviors, and life cycles that allow them to survive in water, where it's hard to hide. Some collect in "schools" of thousands or even millions. They cross the open oceans together, moving in a synchronized way. This gives each fish a lower chance of being eaten!

Many deep-sea fish can produce light, using special organs called photophores. This is known as bioluminescence. The light probably attracts curious creatures that become prey.

SHARED FEATURES

- A tail fin that is split into two and is incredibly symmetrical
- A jaw that has a shape adapted to suck in water when lifted, to help the fish feed

GOOD NEIGHBORS?

Many land predators and humans rely on fish for food. As well as eating them, we use fish in many other ways such as making fertilizers. As a result of overfishing, many fish populations are under threat. This also puts other ocean wildlife that rely on fish in danger.

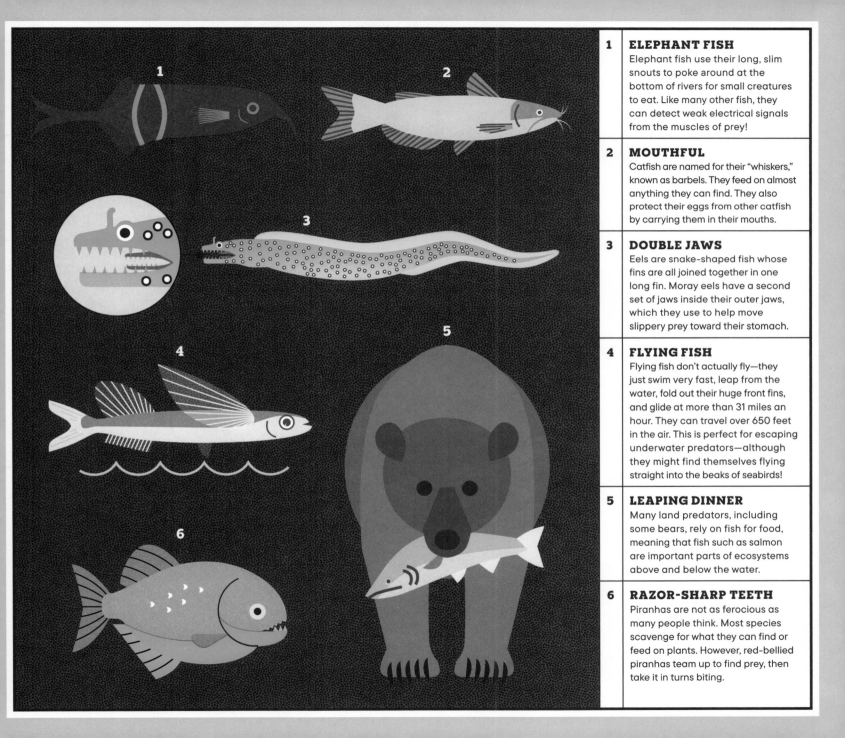

1	**ELEPHANT FISH** Elephant fish use their long, slim snouts to poke around at the bottom of rivers for small creatures to eat. Like many other fish, they can detect weak electrical signals from the muscles of prey!
2	**MOUTHFUL** Catfish are named for their "whiskers," known as barbels. They feed on almost anything they can find. They also protect their eggs from other catfish by carrying them in their mouths.
3	**DOUBLE JAWS** Eels are snake-shaped fish whose fins are all joined together in one long fin. Moray eels have a second set of jaws inside their outer jaws, which they use to help move slippery prey toward their stomach.
4	**FLYING FISH** Flying fish don't actually fly—they just swim very fast, leap from the water, fold out their huge front fins, and glide at more than 31 miles an hour. They can travel over 650 feet in the air. This is perfect for escaping underwater predators—although they might find themselves flying straight into the beaks of seabirds!
5	**LEAPING DINNER** Many land predators, including some bears, rely on fish for food, meaning that fish such as salmon are important parts of ecosystems above and below the water.
6	**RAZOR-SHARP TEETH** Piranhas are not as ferocious as many people think. Most species scavenge for what they can find or feed on plants. However, red-bellied piranhas team up to find prey, then take it in turns biting.

PERCOMORPHS

PERCOMORPHA

YOU ARE HERE

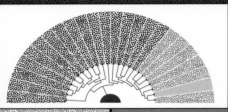

	EUKARYOTA
	AMORPHEA

KEY FACTS

- More than 14,000
- From seahorses less than 2 cm (less than 1 in) tall to giant ocean sunfish up to 4 m (13 ft) long
- Found in most watery habitats with space to swim, but especially in shallow water in the tropics

SPECIMEN

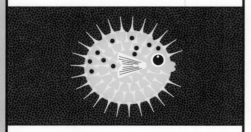

PORCUPINE FISH

Let's zoom in even more to the teleost branch of the tree of life, to a group of spiny-rayed fish with mind-boggling adaptations.

ALL ABOUT

Percomorphs are one of the biggest groups of spiny-rayed fish. They were named after the thorn-like spines that form their fins. About two-thirds of all teleosts (a third of all vertebrates!) are part of this group. They include cod, tuna, and perch as well as all kinds of exotic fish such as seahorses and pufferfish. The diversity of this group is puzzling. It's as if the tree of life stops following the "rules" when it comes to spiny-rayed fish.

In fact, scientists haven't finished understanding the percomorph family tree. We don't yet know if seahorses are more closely related to pufferfish than they are to tuna, or if a flatfish is a closer cousin of a flying fish or an anglerfish. At the moment, it's less like a family tree and more like a "bush at the top" of the teleost branch!

Studying percomorphs teaches us that the open ocean is far more complex than it first appears. One theory is that these extremely different ways of being a fish were caused by the mass extinction event that led to the death of most dinosaurs, 66 million years ago. Over time we will collect more evidence and get a better understanding of how the variety of fish in this group evolved from their common ancestor. Get involved in natural sciences and you can help figure it out!

SHARED FEATURES

- Incredibly diverse body features and behavior
- Our specimen, the porcupine fish, tries to make itself impossible to eat by inflating its body with water, making its spiny scales stand on end!

GOOD NEIGHBORS?

Many percomorph species are popular human foods, including tuna, flatfish, and even highly toxic pufferfish. Several members of this group, such as the stickleback, are model organisms. This means that biologists use them to help understand other living things.

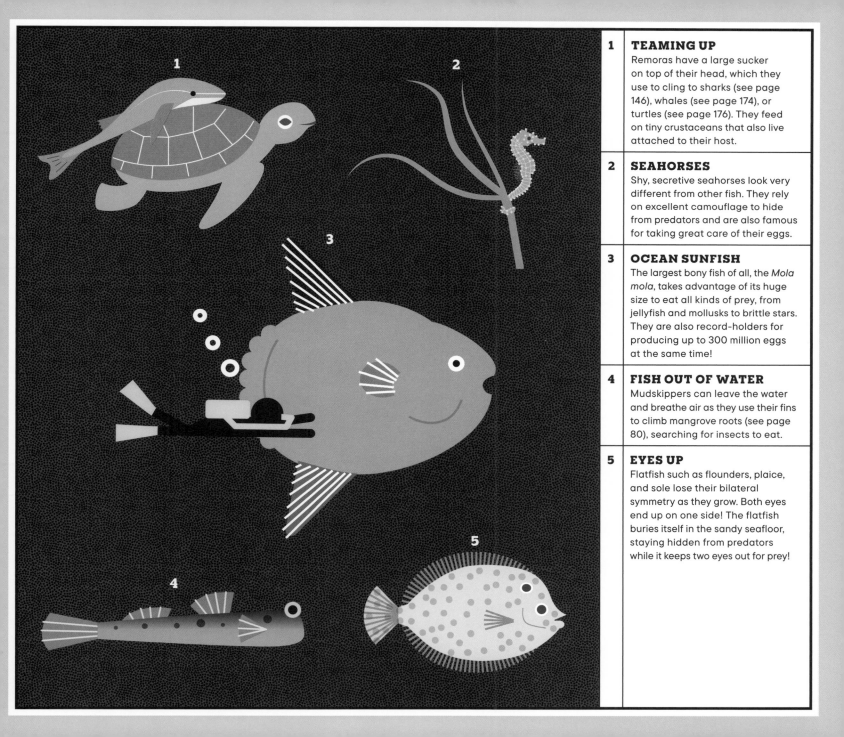

1 TEAMING UP

Remoras have a large sucker on top of their head, which they use to cling to sharks (see page 146), whales (see page 174), or turtles (see page 176). They feed on tiny crustaceans that also live attached to their host.

2 SEAHORSES

Shy, secretive seahorses look very different from other fish. They rely on excellent camouflage to hide from predators and are also famous for taking great care of their eggs.

3 OCEAN SUNFISH

The largest bony fish of all, the *Mola mola*, takes advantage of its huge size to eat all kinds of prey, from jellyfish and mollusks to brittle stars. They are also record-holders for producing up to 300 million eggs at the same time!

4 FISH OUT OF WATER

Mudskippers can leave the water and breathe air as they use their fins to climb mangrove roots (see page 80), searching for insects to eat.

5 EYES UP

Flatfish such as flounders, plaice, and sole lose their bilateral symmetry as they grow. Both eyes end up on one side! The flatfish buries itself in the sandy seafloor, staying hidden from predators while it keeps two eyes out for prey!

SMOOTH AMPHIBIANS

LISSAMPHIBIA

YOU ARE HERE

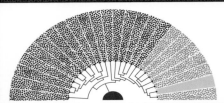

EUKARYOTA
AMORPHEA

KEY FACTS

- More than 8,000 species
- From less than 1 cm (less than half an inch) to 180 cm (5.8 feet) long
- Found worldwide except in the polar regions and in seas and oceans—they are especially common in humid and freshwater habitats, such as tropical rain forests

SPECIMEN

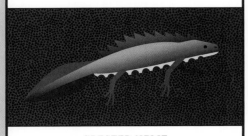

CRESTED NEWT

Frogs, toads, newts, salamanders, and caecilians all have smooth, scaleless skin adapted for multiple tasks!

ALL ABOUT

The name "amphibians" means "double life." It's a good name for animals that begin their lives in water before growing lungs to spend time on land! Lots of extinct animals lived like this too, so today's frogs, newts, and their close relatives are known as Lissamphibia ("smooth amphibians"), which helps us tell them apart from ancient amphibians.

Their smooth, scaleless skin is very different from that of other animals. Instead of being a formidable barrier, it allows gases and water to move in and out, so amphibians can breathe and drink through their skin! Mucus glands keep the skin moist and other glands secrete toxins for self-defense. Their skin is often brightly colored too, which can come in handy for camouflage, communication, or for warning other animals that amphibians don't taste good!

This amazingly adaptable skin has helped amphibians to spread to almost every type of habitat in freshwater and on land. However, it also makes amphibians very vulnerable to climate change and pollution. Recently amphibians have also been under threat from a parasitic fungus that can only grow inside their skin cells. The skin of an infected amphibian gets too thick and stops doing the jobs it normally does. This has led to falling populations of amphibians around the world and many **extinctions**.

SHARED FEATURES

- Very short ribs
- Four toes on front legs
- Five toes on back legs
- Can hear very low-pitched sounds
- Eyes can be raised out of their heads
- Often rely on breathing through their skin, but can also pump air in and out of lungs using their mouth
- Moist, smooth skin

GOOD NEIGHBORS?

Amphibians are eaten in some parts of the world. They are also valued as important predators of insects, including species that eat crops and spread diseases such as malaria. The amazing chemicals made by amphibian skin are being turned into medicines for all kinds of things that are hard to treat in other ways. Salamanders such as axolotls are popular pets.

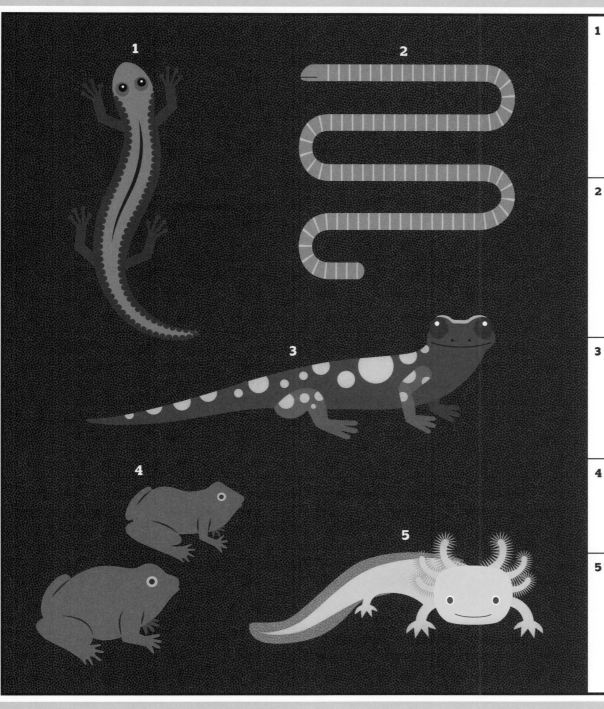

1   HEAT SEEKING
Salamanders have long bodies and tails, short heads, and very wide mouths. They live in wet habitats, where they hunt worms, insects, and other small arthropods. One type of salamander survives in the Arctic Circle. Siberian salamanders hibernate frozen in ice for winter and thaw out again in spring.

2   CAECILIANS
Caecilians look like large earthworms (see page 112), with tiny eyes and no legs. Look closely and you'll spot a strange tentacle between their eyes and nostrils, which helps them to sniff out worms and other small creatures to eat underground. They avoid getting eaten by covering their skin in toxic slime that tastes disgusting.

3   FIRE SALAMANDER
To avoid drying out, fire salamanders hunt at night and hide in cool places by day. Glands in their skin produce **alkaloids**, the bitter-tasting chemicals made by many plants (see page 70). Their bright markings warn predators that they are toxic.

4   FROGS AND TOADS
Frogs and toads look very different from other Lissamphibia, with long back legs and no tail. Find out more about this huge group (known as anurans) on page 156.

5   MEXICAN ICON
Axolotls are salamanders that live in just one place in the world—canals near Mexico City in Mexico. Most have mottled brown skin for camouflage in the water, but totally white varieties have become world-famous!

FROGS & TOADS

ANURA

Anurans are the biggest group of amphibians alive today. There are more species of frogs and toads than there are types of mammals!

YOU ARE HERE

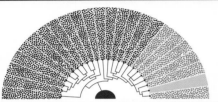

| EUKARYOTA |
| AMORPHEA |

KEY FACTS

- Around 7,000 species
- From micro frogs just 7 mm (about a quarter of an inch) long to goliath frogs more than 30 cm (nearly a foot) long
- Found all around the world except in the polar regions and in seas and oceans

SPECIMEN

GOLDEN POISON FROG

ALL ABOUT

There is no strict difference between a frog and a toad, though frogs tend to spend more time in or near water and have moist skin, while toads have drier, bumpier skin. Both have some unique body features that other amphibians don't share, including incredibly long back legs adapted for jumping and swimming. Their heads are even shorter than those of other amphibians and their eyes are even bigger. They are also much noisier, making many different sounds to communicate with each other.

Each species of frog has its own call, helping males and females to find each other when it is time to mate. These songs also help male frogs to defend their territories. Of course, these sounds would be useless if other frogs didn't have great hearing. The eardrums (tympanums) of frogs and toads are visible from the outside and are often bigger than their eyes!

Once they have mated, most frogs and toads lay eggs that develop in the water. The larvae—known as tadpoles—have gills and a tail. In a process of metamorphosis, they develop four legs and lungs to live as adults on land. Adult frogs and toads are also able to survive out of the water for longer than other amphibians, which means they are found in a wider range of habitats—and more likely to be spotted out and about during the day.

SHARED FEATURES

- Thin, breathable skin
- Adults have no tail
- Large tympanums for hearing
- Short head with large eyes and a wide mouth
- Back legs longer than front legs
- Smooth or warty-looking skin
- Most frogs and toads deter predators by oozing toxins from their skin
- Eggs develop in moist places

GOOD NEIGHBORS?

Like other amphibians, frogs and toads help keep ecosystems in balance by eating small prey. But when humans introduce them to areas where they don't have natural predators, they can become pests. As frog eggs are large and develop outside a frog's body, they have been studied by scientists working to understand how animals develop.

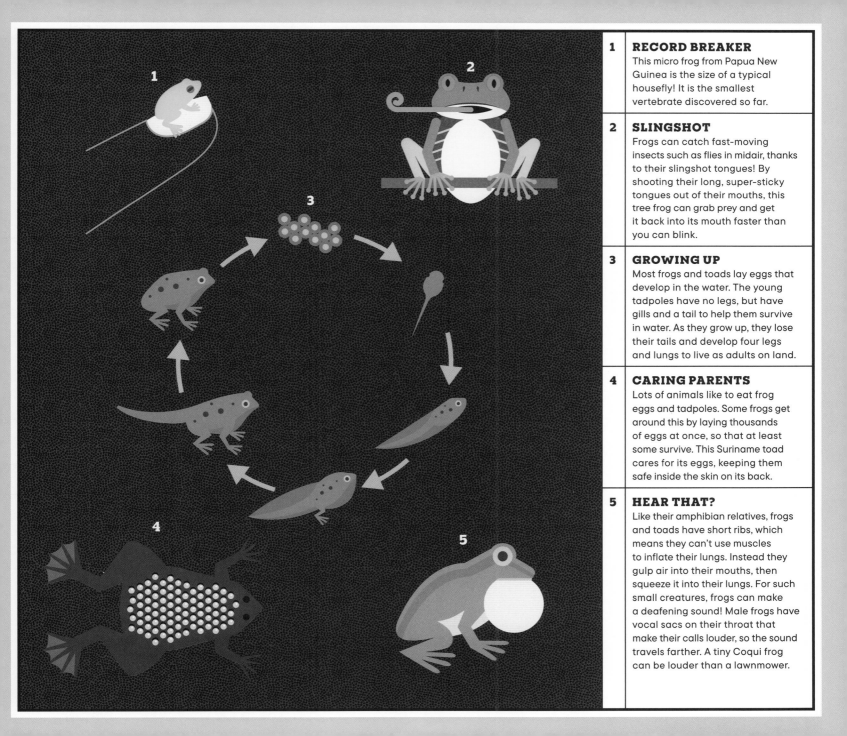

1 RECORD BREAKER
This micro frog from Papua New Guinea is the size of a typical housefly! It is the smallest vertebrate discovered so far.

2 SLINGSHOT
Frogs can catch fast-moving insects such as flies in midair, thanks to their slingshot tongues! By shooting their long, super-sticky tongues out of their mouths, this tree frog can grab prey and get it back into its mouth faster than you can blink.

3 GROWING UP
Most frogs and toads lay eggs that develop in the water. The young tadpoles have no legs, but have gills and a tail to help them survive in water. As they grow up, they lose their tails and develop four legs and lungs to live as adults on land.

4 CARING PARENTS
Lots of animals like to eat frog eggs and tadpoles. Some frogs get around this by laying thousands of eggs at once, so that at least some survive. This Suriname toad cares for its eggs, keeping them safe inside the skin on its back.

5 HEAR THAT?
Like their amphibian relatives, frogs and toads have short ribs, which means they can't use muscles to inflate their lungs. Instead they gulp air into their mouths, then squeeze it into their lungs. For such small creatures, frogs can make a deafening sound! Male frogs have vocal sacs on their throat that make their calls louder, so the sound travels farther. A tiny Coqui frog can be louder than a lawnmower.

MAMMALS

MAMMALIA

YOU ARE HERE

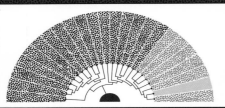

	EUKARYOTA
	AMORPHEA

KEY FACTS

- Around 6,500 species
- From bumblebee-sized bats to bus-sized blue whales
- Found everywhere in the world, from the coldest polar regions to the hottest, driest deserts, thanks to their ability to keep their body temperature steady

SPECIMEN

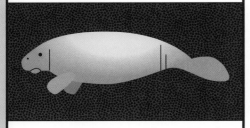

AFRICAN MANATEE

We know more about this group of animals than any other—partly because we are mammals ourselves!

ALL ABOUT

Mammals seem like some of the easiest animals to categorize, thanks to their fur (or hair) and the ability to make a special food (milk) to feed their young. These features are not shared by any other animals. However, the relationships between different mammals have been harder to figure out. As scientists learned to read and compare mammals' genomes, we have discovered unexpected surprises. For example, whales are more closely related to sheep than they are to other marine mammals, such as seals.

Another surprising finding was that mammals didn't really get started until after the dinosaurs died out around 66 million years ago—a relatively short time ago compared to the age of Earth! After an asteroid strike changed Earth's climate and wiped out the dinosaurs, mammals went on to fill every **ecosystem** niche.

Very early on in their history, three key types of mammals appeared that reproduce in three very different ways. Monotremes are mammals that lay eggs. Marsupials give birth twice (see page 160). Eutherians (placental mammals) give birth to young that are fully formed, mini versions of their parents (even if they need lots of care to start with). They are named after a special organ called a placenta, which supplies the developing baby animal with nutrients.

Today's mammals are some of the most varied animals in habitat, behavior, and size. The next few pages explore some of this incredible diversity in more detail.

SHARED FEATURES

- Can keep their body temperature steady
- Skin has hair or fur, and tiny muscles to make the hair or fur stand up!
- Sweat glands help with temperature control
- **Mammary glands** produce milk to feed young
- Big brains for their body size

GOOD NEIGHBORS?

Humans have lived closely alongside and relied upon other mammals for many thousands of years, from the dogs and cats that we keep as domestic pets to camels and horses used for transportation, as well as animals such as cattle, sheep, and goats for milk, meat, wool, and leather.

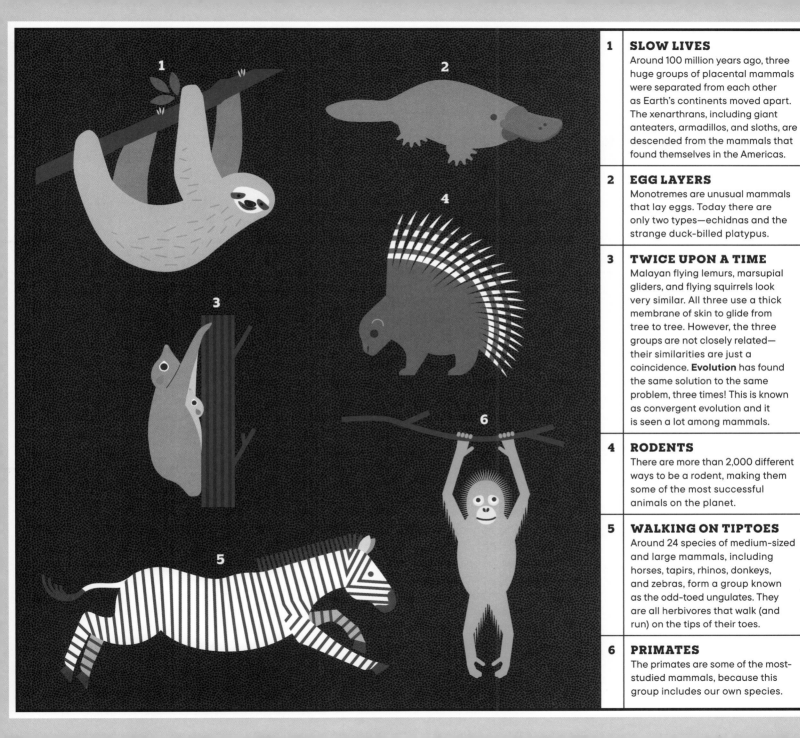

1 SLOW LIVES
Around 100 million years ago, three huge groups of placental mammals were separated from each other as Earth's continents moved apart. The xenarthrans, including giant anteaters, armadillos, and sloths, are descended from the mammals that found themselves in the Americas.

2 EGG LAYERS
Monotremes are unusual mammals that lay eggs. Today there are only two types—echidnas and the strange duck-billed platypus.

3 TWICE UPON A TIME
Malayan flying lemurs, marsupial gliders, and flying squirrels look very similar. All three use a thick membrane of skin to glide from tree to tree. However, the three groups are not closely related— their similarities are just a coincidence. **Evolution** has found the same solution to the same problem, three times! This is known as convergent evolution and it is seen a lot among mammals.

4 RODENTS
There are more than 2,000 different ways to be a rodent, making them some of the most successful animals on the planet.

5 WALKING ON TIPTOES
Around 24 species of medium-sized and large mammals, including horses, tapirs, rhinos, donkeys, and zebras, form a group known as the odd-toed ungulates. They are all herbivores that walk (and run) on the tips of their toes.

6 PRIMATES
The primates are some of the most-studied mammals, because this group includes our own species.

MARSUPIALS

MARSUPIALIA

Baby marsupials are the only animals to be born twice! After leaving their mother's womb, they continue to develop inside a special pouch in her skin.

YOU ARE HERE

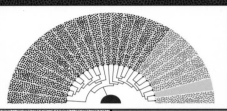

EUKARYOTA

AMORPHEA

KEY FACTS

- Around 335 species
- From tiny 10-cm (4-in) Ningbings to red kangaroos over 2 m (6.5 ft) tall
- Marsupial fossils are found all over the world, but living marsupials are only found in Australasia and the Americas

SPECIMEN

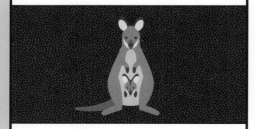

RED-NECKED WALLABY

ALL ABOUT

A developing marsupial spends a short time in their mother's womb (from 12 to 42 days) then crawls to a special pouch where they finish growing while being fed with milk. After a few months, the baby marsupial, known as a joey, is "born" a second time—by simply emerging from the pouch!

Apart from this, marsupials mirror other mammals in most ways. They include marsupial versions of moles, flying squirrels, wolves, rodents, cats, and anteaters. In the past, there were even marsupial versions of a saber-toothed tiger!

Fossils of marsupials are found all around the world, but today marsupials are only found in Australasia and the Americas. In Australia, many marsupials are threatened by animals such as foxes, cats, and rats, which were all introduced from other parts of the world. Scientists are still working out about when exactly marsupials last shared a common ancestor with other mammals—and what happened to separate them and keep them on different evolutionary paths! Marsupials probably evolved in isolation in the Southern Hemisphere for millions of years, after becoming separated by great oceans or impassable land. Meanwhile, marsupials left in the Northern Hemisphere may have been outcompeted by other types of mammals.

SHARED FEATURES

- Thick fur
- Mammary glands and nipples are hidden in a fold of skin called a pouch
- Lower body temperature than other mammals
- Born early and continue to develop in a pouch while attached to the nipples

GOOD NEIGHBORS?

In Australasia, marsupials are found at almost every link in the food chain—just like eutherian mammals in other parts of the world. Recently, scientists discovered that humans and marsupials share a feature of their genomes that could be key to understanding and treating certain human diseases.

1	**SQUIRREL GLIDER** Squirrel gliders are small possums of Australia. A large membrane of skin stretched between their legs helps them to glide from branch to branch in the forest.
2	**CONSERVATION CRISIS** A numbat's tongue is as long and thin as a pencil! It's covered in sticky snot, to collect termites as they march in and out of their nests. Numbats used to be found all over Australia, but today there are only a couple of groups left in the wild.
3	**EASTERN QUOLL** Spotted eastern quolls are nocturnal mammals with white spots. They have been extinct in mainland Australia for decades, but are now being reintroduced by conservationists.
4	**STICKING CLOSE** Joeys stay in their mother's pouch for about six months. During this time, their mouth is permanently attached to one of the mother's nipples so they can be fed milk continuously as they grow. Once joeys have been born, they still stick close to their mother. Koala joeys ride on their mother's back until they are around one year old.
5	**RED KANGAROO** Kangaroos are the largest living marsupials, up to 2 meters (6.5 feet) in height. Males grow taller than most adult humans. They are famous for the unique way they travel, by bounding on both legs, and for winning their right to mate with boxing matches.

AFRICAN MAMMALS

AFROTHERIA

YOU ARE HERE

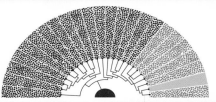

	EUKARYOTA
	AMORPHEA

KEY FACTS

- Around 80 species
- From tenrecs just 5 cm (2 in) long to 7.5-m-long (25-ft-long) elephants, the largest land animals
- Found in Africa, the Middle East, Madagascar, and Southeast Asia, and in the coastal waters of several continents

SPECIMEN

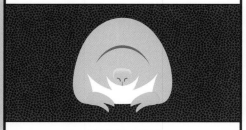

GOLDEN MOLE

Not many people expect the mammals on this page to be close relatives, but genetic information tells us otherwise.

ALL ABOUT

Tenrecs are armed with spines, much like those of a hedgehog. Golden moles share the small eyes and powerful claws of other moles. But these animals are far more closely related to each other than to their lookalikes!

By peering at their genomes, biologists have proved that elephants, hyraxes, sengis (elephant shrews), dugongs, manatees, aardvarks, tenrecs, and golden moles are all descended from a mammal ancestor that lived in Africa around 100 million years ago. This ancestor was probably a lot like an elephant shrew. At the time, Africa was cut off from other land in the northern hemisphere, so the descendants of that first lucky shrew had free reign.

Considering they are so closely related, the afrotherians are amazingly diverse. The largest are herbivores, while the smallest hunt hundreds of insects every day. Some have thick fur, while others are almost totally bald. Some live alone, while others hang out in huge family groups. There are almost too many differences to count.

Today the continents are joined once more, and hundreds of other types of other mammals live in and around Africa too. But the Afrotheria group is a very special club. It's amazing to discover that an elephant is more closely related to an aardvark than it is to a rhino! It's a very good example of how looks can be deceptive when it comes to tracing the tree of life.

SHARED FEATURES

- Afrotherians may look very diverse on the outside, but they have some striking hidden similarities, such as the number of vertebrae in their spines, features of their teeth, and of course their DNA, which shows they are closely related
- Many have long, bendy noses or snouts

GOOD NEIGHBORS?

Asian elephants were domesticated in India 2,500 years ago, for transportation and even war. The elephants that live in Africa today have never been domesticated, but they have long been hunted by humans for their tusks, which are made of a material called ivory.

1

SEA COWS
The front legs of these marine mammals are adapted into paddles for swimming, but underneath the skin and muscle they still have five digits! Hanging out in family groups of up to 100, they feast on beds of algae or seagrasses in shallow water.

2

INSECT EATERS
Elephant shrews, tenrecs, and golden moles have sensitive snouts, shaped for digging insects out of leaf litter or soil. The elephant shrews were named after their long, flexible snouts which reminded people of an elephant's trunk. No one expected them to actually be so closely related to elephants!

3

GENTLE GIANTS
With bodies up to 4 meters (13 feet) tall and over 7 meters (24 feet) long, the largest living land mammals would be remarkable even without their trunks. The elephant's elongated nose and upper lip are used for breathing, drinking, smelling, grabbing, and hugging.

4

TUBE MOUTH
Everything about an aardvark is adapted for eating termites—from the powerful claws for digging into termite mounds, to the long head and snout for reaching with the long, sticky tongue that can catch as many as possible. The aardvark then waits a week for termites to rebuild before it begins the feast again!

5

ROCK RABBITS
Hyraxes, also called rock rabbits, are herbivores that sometimes snack on crickets. They have strangely sweaty feet and stinky fur. They use scent to warn other hyraxes to stay away. If this doesn't work, they scream, stamp, grind their teeth, and poop everywhere.

PRIMATES

PRIMATES

PRIMATES

YOU ARE HERE

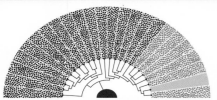

EUKARYOTA

AMORPHEA

KEY FACTS

- More than 600 species and subspecies
- From 13-cm (5-in) mouse lemurs to gorillas almost 2 m (6.5 ft) tall
- Humans live all around the world; most other primates are only found in warm areas of the world, ranging from mountain forests to grassy plains

SPECIMEN

MANDRILL

This small group of mammals is well known to humans, because we are members of this club!

ALL ABOUT

Humans belong in this group, making the other primates our closest relatives. Just like us, other primates have large heads for their body size with eyes, nose, and mouth crowded close together on relatively small faces. They share our short necks and slim limbs, often longer at the back than the front. All primates also share the ability to sit up, which frees up their hands to do all kinds of things.

A primate's hands are important. An opposable thumb and flat fingernails instead of claws allows many primates to grip and handle objects carefully. They are used for climbing, swinging, gathering and handling food, grooming, holding on to young, and even making and using tools.

Apart from humans and tarsiers, most primates have gripping feet too. Humans are the only primates that don't spend much of their time in trees, and our feet have adapted for walking and running on the ground instead. We've also lost our tails, as have other apes—the gorillas, chimpanzees, bonobos, and gibbons.

Almost all primates like to live in groups (only orangutans prefer to live alone). Group living makes communication very important. Primates use sound, gestures, facial expressions, touch, and smells to communicate. Some even communicate by changing the color of their buttocks! Human language is the most complex communication of all.

SHARED FEATURES

- Forward-facing eyes
- Large heads (and brains) for body size
- Some have flattened faces
- Some have a nose that sticks out
- Some have whiskers

GOOD NEIGHBORS?

As a species, humans are probably the worst neighbors on the planet. We have driven many species to extinction— including fellow primates—by changing the habitats of other species, taking too much from the environment, and putting things into nature that shouldn't be there. We are even causing the world's climate to change.

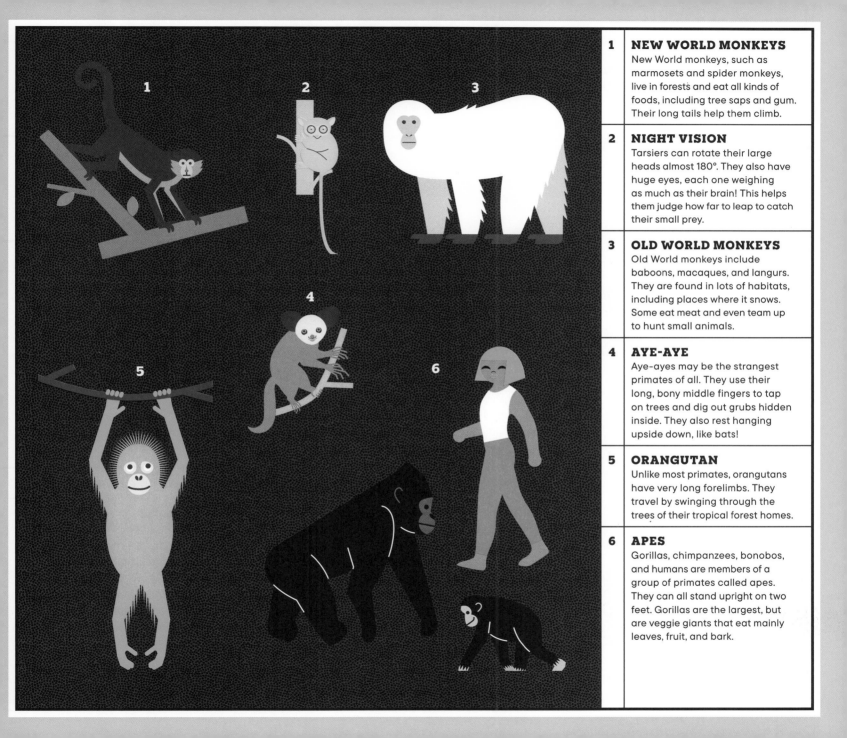

1	**NEW WORLD MONKEYS** New World monkeys, such as marmosets and spider monkeys, live in forests and eat all kinds of foods, including tree saps and gum. Their long tails help them climb.
2	**NIGHT VISION** Tarsiers can rotate their large heads almost 180°. They also have huge eyes, each one weighing as much as their brain! This helps them judge how far to leap to catch their small prey.
3	**OLD WORLD MONKEYS** Old World monkeys include baboons, macaques, and langurs. They are found in lots of habitats, including places where it snows. Some eat meat and even team up to hunt small animals.
4	**AYE-AYE** Aye-ayes may be the strangest primates of all. They use their long, bony middle fingers to tap on trees and dig out grubs hidden inside. They also rest hanging upside down, like bats!
5	**ORANGUTAN** Unlike most primates, orangutans have very long forelimbs. They travel by swinging through the trees of their tropical forest homes.
6	**APES** Gorillas, chimpanzees, bonobos, and humans are members of a group of primates called apes. They can all stand upright on two feet. Gorillas are the largest, but are veggie giants that eat mainly leaves, fruit, and bark.

RODENTS, RABBITS, PIKAS & HARES

GLIRES

From popular pets to unpopular pests, people view rodents, rabbits, and their relatives in different ways. But there is no denying they are some of the most successful creatures on the planet.

YOU ARE HERE

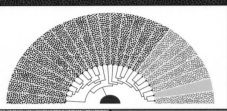

EUKARYOTA

AMORPHEA

KEY FACTS

- Around 2,000 species
- From pygmy mice with bodies just 6 cm (about 2 in) long to 70 cm (over 2ft) capybara
- Found in all biomes and climates, including places that are very tough to live in

SPECIMEN

PIKA

ALL ABOUT

Rodents are the largest group of mammals, whether you count the number of species or the number of individuals scurrying around the planet. Most rodents are small mammals, with cylinder-shaped bodies, short legs, and a long, scaly tail. They have four teeth, which never stop growing and can eventually stick out of a rodent's mouth even when it's closed. The teeth are covered with a thick layer of enamel, which allows them to chew through almost anything that catches their eye. Their front legs are very handy tools too, used for scratching, digging, climbing, holding food, and building nests.

Rodents like to live in groups, working together to protect their territory. They communicate with each other using scent, produced by glands in their skin. It's a good thing rodents like company, because they reproduce very rapidly and have huge families! A house mouse can have more than 80 babies every year.

Rodents are closely related to a group of animals called lagomorphs—this includes rabbits, hares, and pikas. They have short, bushy tails compared to rodents, and paws instead of claws. While they can't grip and climb, rabbits and hares have long, powerful hind legs for making a quick getaway. With the help of bacteria in their guts, rabbits and hares can digest the tough **cellulose** in plant cell walls, but to do so they need to eat food twice! They make soft droppings that they eat and digest again.

SHARED FEATURES

- "Stretched" skull with a long nose bone
- Tough incisor teeth that keep growing throughout their lives
- Long whiskers for sensing
- Good sense of smell
- Both rodents and lagomorphs are good at building burrows, for nesting and for hiding from predators

GOOD NEIGHBORS?

Many rodents are popular pets. Some have been hunted or bred for meat or fur for thousands of years. Rodents are also some of the most important animals used in medical and scientific research. For example, the cells of naked mole-rats are helping scientists understand how mammals can avoid getting cancer.

1	**LARGEST RODENTS** Each of a crested porcupine's spines is a giant, stiff hair. When scared, the porcupine raises and rattles the spines using the same tiny muscles that are responsible for giving you goose bumps.
2	**ARCTIC HARE** Rabbits and hares have fur that helps them to stay hidden. An Arctic hare's coat changes color with the season, turning white in winter to blend in with snow.
3	**BAD REPUTATION** Humans see many rodents as pests—especially species that like to share our homes and food. Their bad reputation became worse when scientists realized that the Black Death was caused by bacteria (see page 18) carried by the fleas that live on rats.
4	**UNSTOPPABLE** A rodent's teeth never stop growing, which means they can gnaw on very hard things. Beavers chomp their way through tree trunks and rats can chew through lead!
5	**FAMILY PETS** Guinea pigs have been domesticated for more than 6,000 years, while other rodents became pets more recently. Most of the world's pet Syrian hamsters are descendants of four hamsters found in a field in the 1930s.
6	**SOCIAL LIVES** Naked mole-rats are some of the least hairy land mammals. They live underground in warm deserts, huddling in huge groups to stay warm at night. Whiskers on their faces and tails help them sense what's around them in the dark.

MOLES & RELATIVES

EULIPOTYPHLA

YOU ARE HERE

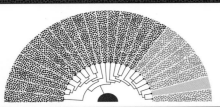

	EUKARYOTA
	AMORPHEA

KEY FACTS

- Around 450 species
- From the 4 cm (1.5 in) Etruscan shrew to solenodons with 45 cm (1.5 ft) bodies
- Found in all land habitats, except in the polar regions and in Australia. Some species spend most of their lives in freshwater

SPECIMEN

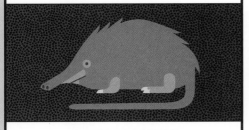

PYRENEAN DESMAN

These small animals all love the same foods— insects, earthworms, and other small crunchy and chewy invertebrates.

ALL ABOUT

This group includes the world's smallest mammals, and it is hugely interesting for scientists! The common ancestor of *all* mammals may have been a shrew-like animal and possibly even a member of this group!

The name Eulipotyphla means "truly fat and blind" in Greek. Look a little closer though and you'll see how tough shrews and their relatives turn out to be. They include the smallest diving mammals—shrews that can hunt insect larvae in freezing waters. They include shrews that survived a volcanic eruption, and shrews that can shrink their brain in winter when there is less food, and regrow it in the summer!

Other members include moles that live underground, hedgehogs with spiny coats, diving desmans that use their snouts as snorkels, voracious voles that devour plants from below, and solenodons—the only mammals with venomous saliva.

These tiny mammals need a lot of energy—the smallest of all must eat more than their own weight in food each day! Most rely on their sense of smell and hearing to dig insects and other small animals from the soil, by day or by night. Most members of this group live solitary lives, protecting the territory where they find food and only seeking each other out when it's time to mate.

SHARED FEATURES

- Long, pointed snouts
- Sharp teeth
- Small ears and eyes
- Dense fur
- Short legs with powerful claws

GOOD NEIGHBORS?

Scientists are interested in members of this group, because they could help us find out more about how the first mammals got started and became so successful.

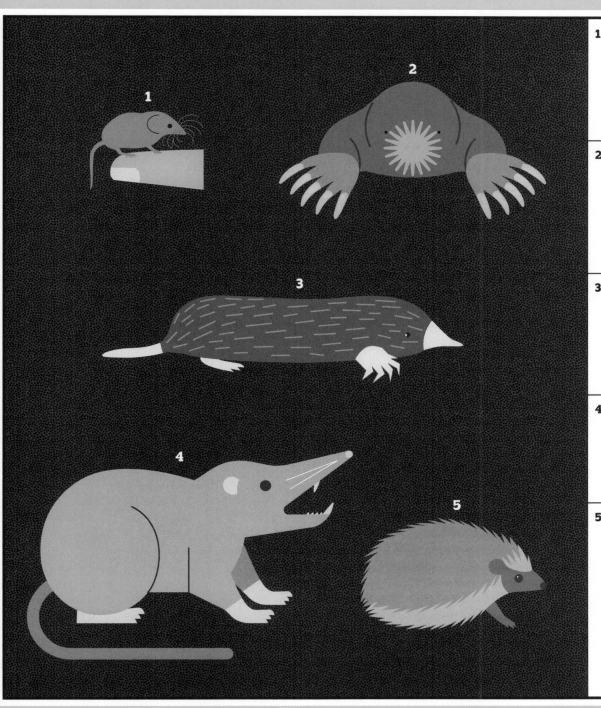

1 SMALLEST MAMMALS
There are hundreds of different species of shrews and new species are discovered all the time. Pygmy shrews have found fame as the world's smallest living mammals. They only weigh 0.07 ounces—about as much as two paper clips.

2 STAR-NOSED MOLES
Star-nosed moles can barely see anything, but because they live in darkness they rely on different senses. They use tentacles on their snouts to feel their surroundings, identifying up to a dozen objects each second to figure out which ones are edible!

3 TUNNEL DIGGERS
Moles are well adapted for digging! They have cone-shaped snouts, flattened skulls, very small eyes (often hidden by their fur), and no outer ears. Their front legs are strong and have five toes with powerful claws.

4 TOXIC BITES
Solenodons are the largest members of this group, with long legs and a stiff scaly tail. Unusually for mammals, they make venom and inject it into prey through sharp, hollow teeth, like a snake does.

5 SPINY DEFENSES
Hedgehogs are some of the best-loved members of the group, easy to identify thanks to their spines. These are made of hollow hairs that are full of keratin—the same material that makes up your fingernails. Even baby hedgehogs are born with spines hidden under their skin.

BATS

CHIROPTERA

YOU ARE HERE

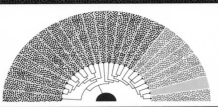

| | EUKARYOTA |
| | AMORPHEA |

KEY FACTS

- More than 1,300 species
- Bodies range from about an inch to 1.5 ft long, but the wings of some fruit bats span nearly 5 ft
- Found in a wide range of habitats, including cities, where they roost in the cracks of buildings, attics, and under bridges

SPECIMEN

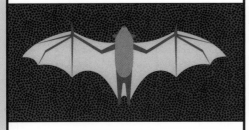

FLYING FOX

Bats are the only flying mammals and have been living by their own rules for more than 50 million years.

ALL ABOUT

Bats are the only mammals that can freely fly and their wings are powered by muscles. The wings are made from a membrane of stretchy skin between the very, very long fingers of their front limbs. This big group of mammals can be divided into two groups, the large "mega-bats," also known as flying foxes, with long, pointed snouts, and the smaller "microbats" with flatter, stranger-looking faces.

Almost all bats are nocturnal animals that hunt at night. Echolocation allows bats to "see" using sound, which makes them fantastic nocturnal hunters. The skin around a bat's nose and ears is folded into complex shapes, which helps the bat detect the echoes. These echoes come from the high-pitched chirps they send out and can be used to navigate and to hunt for prey. At night, most insect-eating birds are asleep, so bats have the air and insects to themselves. They may also hunt at night to avoid being eaten by birds!

There are more than a thousand species of bat, including bats that feed on flying insects, small animals, fruit, nectar, and even blood! Like birds, bats are sociable and often hang out (quite literally) in colonies of hundreds of thousands or even millions. Some species even migrate as the seasons change, much like birds do. Other species hibernate when it gets cold, slowing down their body processes so much they can live without food for months.

SHARED FEATURES

- Sharp claws
- Wings
- Large outer ears to help pick up sounds
- High **metabolism**, like many birds

GOOD NEIGHBORS?

Bats have a bad reputation for being the source of infectious diseases that jump from animals to humans. But bats help humans in many ways, from pollinating plants such as bananas, mangoes, avocados, and figs to eating millions of insect pests and producing mounds of droppings known as guano, which is used as fertilizer.

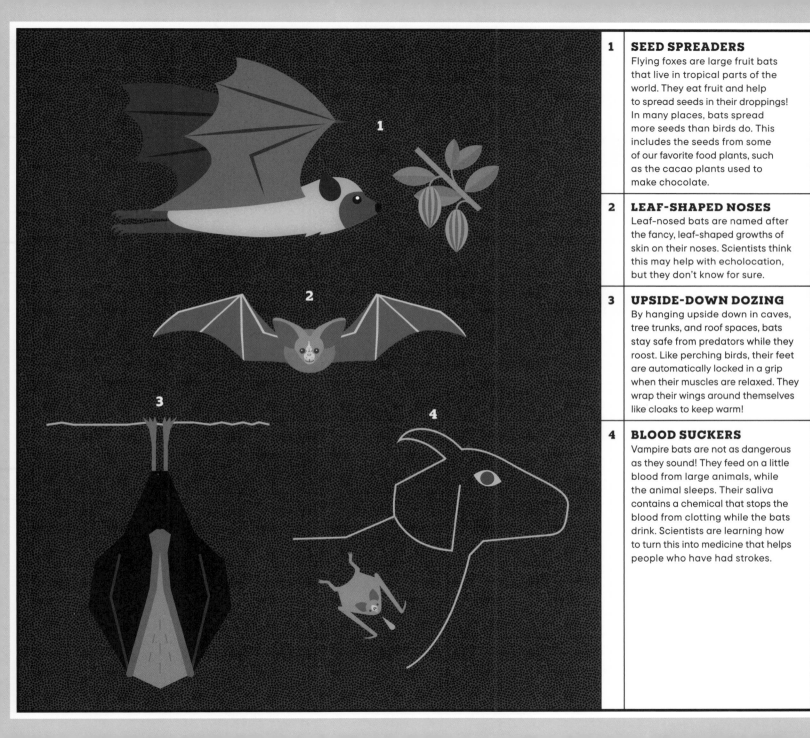

1 **SEED SPREADERS**
Flying foxes are large fruit bats that live in tropical parts of the world. They eat fruit and help to spread seeds in their droppings! In many places, bats spread more seeds than birds do. This includes the seeds from some of our favorite food plants, such as the cacao plants used to make chocolate.

2 **LEAF-SHAPED NOSES**
Leaf-nosed bats are named after the fancy, leaf-shaped growths of skin on their noses. Scientists think this may help with echolocation, but they don't know for sure.

3 **UPSIDE-DOWN DOZING**
By hanging upside down in caves, tree trunks, and roof spaces, bats stay safe from predators while they roost. Like perching birds, their feet are automatically locked in a grip when their muscles are relaxed. They wrap their wings around themselves like cloaks to keep warm!

4 **BLOOD SUCKERS**
Vampire bats are not as dangerous as they sound! They feed on a little blood from large animals, while the animal sleeps. Their saliva contains a chemical that stops the blood from clotting while the bats drink. Scientists are learning how to turn this into medicine that helps people who have had strokes.

CARNIVORES

CARNIVORA

YOU ARE HERE

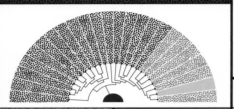

	EUKARYOTA
	AMORPHEA

KEY FACTS

- Almost 300 species
- From 13 cm- (5 in-) long least weasel up to 6 m (20 ft) elephant seals
- Found in different biomes from the poles to tropical forests; certain species hunt in seas and oceans but spend much of their time on land

SPECIMEN

COATI

These mainly meat-eating mammals can be fearsome, ferocious...and surprisingly stinky!

ALL ABOUT

Around 250 years ago, scientist Carl Linnaeus grouped together mammals that hunt prey—from bears and badgers to big cats—and named them the Ferae, or "wild beasts." Gradually, scientists figured out that many of the animals on Linnaeus's list are not close relatives after all. Today the Ferae includes carnivores such as dogs, bears, coati, seals and sea lions, cats, and mustelids, and their surprising relatives, the toothless pangolins.

Most members of Carnivora are medium or large mammals, with great senses for hunting. Apart from the vegetarian giant panda, they all eat meat of some kind. They have several different kinds of teeth, including long, pointed canines for helping to kill prey, sharp incisors for slicing through meat, and strong molars for crunching bones.

As top predators in their food chains, these carnivores are a very important part of most ecosystems. They help keep populations of herbivores under control, and their prey support insect decomposers and scavengers such as vultures (see page 186). Food chains tend to be shaped like pyramids, with fewer animals at the top. This puts carnivores at great risk of extinction when humans put their habitats under pressure.

SHARED FEATURES

- Good senses
- Five toes on their front legs
- Four toes on their back legs
- Several different kinds of teeth, including sharp canines
- Powerful jaws that only open and close—they cannot move from side to side to grind food

GOOD NEIGHBORS?

Despite their "wild" nature, members of this group have become the world's favorite pets! Dogs, cats, and even weasels have been domesticated by humans. It was thought that we domesticated wolves to help with different tasks, but scientists now think that they may have domesticated themselves, hanging around humans to get scraps of food!

1	**MARINE MAMMALS** Walruses, seals, and sea lions are known as pinnipeds. Unlike other marine mammals such as whales, or sirens such as dugongs and manatees, pinnipeds come onto land to breed, rest, and move around.
2	**CARING PARENTS** No matter how fierce and ferocious adult carnivores are, they tend to have young that are small and helpless and need lots of care. They are probably born early in their development so that their mother can keep hunting even while she is pregnant.
3	**BARELY THERE** Bears are the smallest family of carnivores, with just eight species left around the world, six of which are threatened with extinction. Giant pandas are the only vegetarians—the others are omnivores, eating meat and plants.
4	**STRONG-SMELLING** Most land carnivores are completely covered in fur, with very few sweat glands. However, their skin does produce strong-smelling oils. Carnivores rely on these for communication. Some, such as skunks, smell so strong they can even use smell as a defense.
5	**BEST FRIENDS** The ancestors of today's pet dogs are wild wolves. By selecting dogs with certain characteristics to breed together, humans have created more than 300 different breeds of dogs. But no matter how different, they are all members of the same species.

EVEN-TOED UNGULATES
CETARTIODACTYLA

YOU ARE HERE

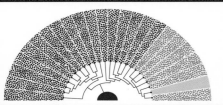

EUKARYOTA	
AMORPHEA	

KEY FACTS

- Around 300 species
- From the 45-cm (1.5-ft) mouse deer to 30-m-long (100-ft-long) blue whales
- Widespread around the world, including seas and oceans, although they were introduced by humans to Australia and New Zealand

SPECIMEN

HIPPOPOTAMUS

The close relationship between whales, dolphins, and mammals that live in the driest habitats is one of the biggest surprises on the tree of life.

ALL ABOUT

You might not expect to see whales and dolphins in a group of animals named after their toes, but their genes reveal that pigs, camels, sheep, hippos, and cetaceans (whales and dolphins) are all close relatives! All animals in this group have an even number of toes, which is different from mammals such as horses, tapirs, and rhinos, which have an odd number. However, the toes can be hard to count. In whales and dolphins, these are hidden inside their flippers. In **ruminants**, the middle toes on each foot are covered with a hoof.

All ruminants have four stomach compartments where large numbers of anaerobic bacteria and other microbes live to help break down the plants that they eat. Ruminants swallow mouthfuls of grass or other plants without chewing them properly. After the food has been broken down inside the stomach, the food is regurgitated back into their mouth and chewed again! When it is swallowed for the second time, true digestion starts. Rumination means that these animals can get maximum possible nutrition from leaves, herby plants, and grasses. They can survive in places with poor-quality food.

While ruminants can live just about anywhere, other members of this group are adapted to life at the extremes. Camels can live in the world's driest deserts, while hippos are amphibious, and cetaceans (whales and dolphins) spend their entire lives in the water!

SHARED FEATURES

- An even number of toes
- Some have hooves
- Hippos, camels, and ruminants ferment plant food in their stomachs

GOOD NEIGHBORS?

Even-toed ungulates of all kinds—from camels and reindeer to cows, sheep, and pigs—have been domesticated by humans for more than 10,000 years! These animals have also been widely hunted. Before humans began extracting crude oil from the ground, many parts of the world relied on whale oil for lighting homes and streets, and for oiling the first machines.

1 SPEEDY ESCAPES

Giraffes are the largest ruminants, and despite their supersize they are speedy sprinters, lolloping along at up to 37 miles per hour! Most ruminants, including deer and goats, are a lot smaller, so they have adapted to run from predators with great speed. Some ruminants live in large herds, for extra protection.

2 SEA ANIMALS

Cetaceans (whales and dolphins) spend their whole lives in water. They look more like fish than mammals, with their limbs adapted as fins. Their mammary glands are hidden in a pocket of skin, and a thick layer of blubber, not fur, keeps them warm. Whales and dolphins breathe air through a blowhole on top of their skull.

3 TOOTHY WEAPONS

Warthogs, wild boars, and domestic pigs have less hair than ruminants. Like their hippo cousins, some have canine teeth that never stop growing, forming tusks that they use for defense.

4 DESERT LIFE

Camels and dromedaries (a type of one-humped camel) have many adaptations that help them live in the driest, harshest conditions on the planet. This includes lips that channel snot from their noses back to their mouths so no water is wasted!

LIZARD-FACED ANIMALS

SAUROPSIDA

The animals pictured on this page are traditionally known as "reptiles"—but some of the members might surprise you!

YOU ARE HERE

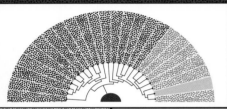

	EUKARYOTA
	AMORPHEA

KEY FACTS

- From 2-cm-long (0.75-in-long) chameleons to saltwater crocodiles more than 6 m (20 ft) long
- Everywhere on land, including the coldest, hottest, driest, and highest places on the planet. A few live in the open ocean, but none live entirely underwater

SPECIMEN

THORNY DEVIL LIZARD

ALL ABOUT

Let's leap off the mammal branch of the tree of life and onto a much bigger branch of "lizard-faced" animals. Some are known as "reptiles," but is there any such thing as a reptile? The reptiles—with their scaly skin—are not as closely related as we once thought. As scientists studied fossils and **molecules** more closely, we discovered that crocodiles and alligators are far more closely related to birds than they are to turtles, lizards, and other animals known as reptiles. This means if we want to keep using the name reptile, we must include birds too!

Because this feels a bit strange, most scientists use the name "sauropsids" instead. It may seem strange that birds belong in this group of "lizard-faced" creatures, but look closely and you'll spot many clues that all sauropsids share a common ancestor. This includes their dry, scaly skin and toes tipped with claws. Even the feathers of birds are just adapted scales.

Crocodiles and alligators are a bird's closest living relatives. They are the only living members of a group of sauropsids known as archosaurs. Millions of years ago, the archosaurs included pterosaurs and dinosaurs. Pterosaurs died out completely around 65 million years ago. Birds are thought to be the last surviving dinosaurs. There are more than 10,000 species of birds, making them the most successful reptiles on the planet! Find out more on pages 182 to 187.

SHARED FEATURES

- Small openings in their skulls just below their eyes
- Mostly reproduce by laying eggs
- Each eye has a third eyelid moved by special muscles
- Dry, scaly skin (feathers are a special type of scales)

GOOD NEIGHBORS?

Humans rely on certain birds for meat and eggs. Several species of birds, turtles, tortoises, lizards, snakes, and geckoes are popular pets. Even extinct sauropsids have a huge impact on human lives. The first dinosaur was named in 1824 and dinosaurs have been the stars of stories, toy stores, and museums ever since!

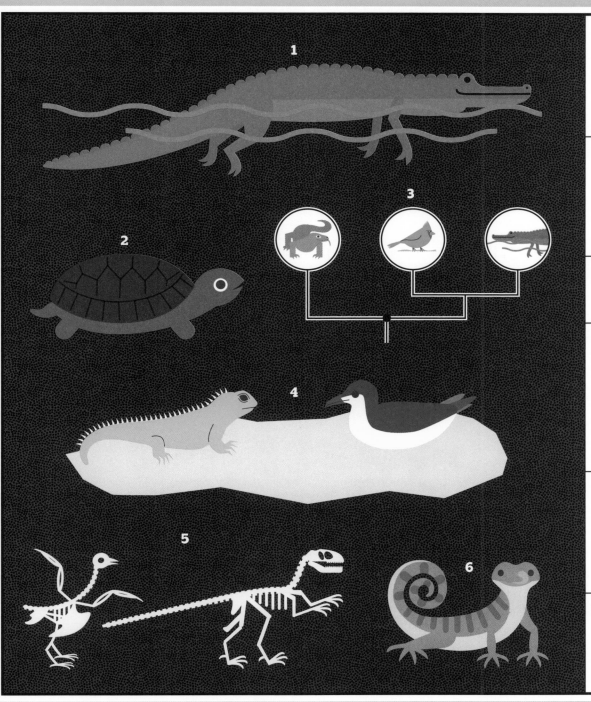

1. **KILLING MACHINES**
Crocodiles and alligators are the largest living sauropsids. They are adapted for hunting in water, with eyes and nostrils on top of their heads and enormous lungs that allow them to hold their breath for up to an hour.

2. **TOUGH SHELLS**
Turtles, terrapins, and tortoises have a two-piece shell that protects their body, and a horny beak instead of teeth. Tortoises live on land, while turtles and terrapins spend most of their time in water, returning to land to lay their eggs.

3. **WINGED WONDERS**
Comparing DNA to draw evolutionary trees reveals that birds and crocodiles are close relatives.

4. **THREE EYES**
The world's two tuatara species form a group of their own. They have some strange features that other lizards don't share, such as a third eye on top of their heads, covered with scaly skin. These big lizards are only found on islands near New Zealand, often sharing burrows with seabirds called petrels.

5. **HIDDEN CLUES**
Birds might not look much like other reptiles on the surface. But underneath, the bones of their skeletons are arranged much like those of theropod dinosaurs, and their closest relatives today— the crocodiles!

6. **LOTS OF LIZARDS**
The Lepidosauria, or "scaled lizards," include the Squamata (see page 178), a huge group of species that includes geckos, lizards, and snakes.

SCALY REPTILES

SQUAMATA

The horny scales that cover snakes, lizards, and worm lizards are the secret to their success in hot and dry places.

YOU ARE HERE

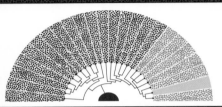

| EUKARYOTA |
| AMORPHEA |

KEY FACTS

- More than 7,000 species
- From geckoes less than 3 cm (about 1 in) long to 9-m (30-ft) anacondas
- Found on every continent except Antarctica

SPECIMEN

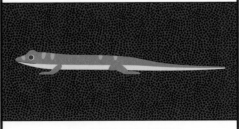

GOLD DUST DAY GECKO

ALL ABOUT

Lizards, snakes, and their closest relatives can be found digging burrows, climbing trees, swimming in salt water, gliding through the air, and even running across the surface of water! This range of movement is particularly impressive when you consider that thousands of species—the snakes and worm lizards—have no working limbs at all! They move along by bending their muscular bodies from side to side, often relying on their scales for grip.

The squamates include the longest land animals alive today—the anacondas and boas. But squamates of the past were even bigger! They include sea snakes and mosasaurs—massive sea creatures that breathed air.

"Lizard" is a name given to many different groups of animals, living everywhere from deserts and tropical forests to water. To survive in these different environments, lizards have adapted many different body features. However, they are limited by one feature of their common ancestor—they are unable to control their own body temperature from the inside, like mammals and birds can. Instead, they must control it through behavior, such as basking in sunlight or on hot rocks to warm up and sticking to the shade to cool down. Squamates that live in cooler climates often hibernate to get through the winter.

SHARED FEATURES

- Elongated bodies and tails
- Horny scales
- Forked tongue used to smell
- Most lay eggs
- Control their body temperature through behavior, using their surroundings to help warm themselves up or cool themselves down

GOOD NEIGHBORS?

Snakes are often feared for their venomous bites. Around 5.4 million people are bitten by snakes each year and up to 138,000 of those people die. However, the cocktail of chemicals found in snake venom is being used to develop medicines to help humans. The venom of the Komodo dragon, for example, could one day be used in the same way.

1	**FLYING LIZARD**
	Draco lizards have very long ribs that stick out from their sides and stretch the skin between them to form two "wings." This allows the lizards to glide as far as almost 200 feet between trees.

2	**MARINE IGUANAS**
	Marine iguanas are the only lizards to find their food at sea, nibbling red and green algae from underwater rocks. They sneeze out salt, to stop it building up in their bodies.

3	**COLOR-CHANGING**
	As well as an impressive ability to change color to show how they are feeling, chameleons have feet adapted to grip branches and a tongue that they can fling far from their mouths to grab insect prey.

4	**BLUE-TONGUED SKINK**
	Skinks are burrowing lizards that look more streamlined than geckoes. Their narrow heads, small eyes, and smooth, shiny scales are all adaptations for moving underground.

5	**KOMODO DRAGON**
	Like other squamates, Komodo dragons flick their forked tongues in and out to collect tiny traces of chemicals in the air. These are sensed by a special organ in the roof of their mouth, which boosts their sense of smell. They can even smell food buried underground!

6	**WORM LIZARDS**
	Worm lizards, such as slow worms, are even better adapted to a burrowing life than skinks. Most have lost their legs altogether and their skin is loose so they can bunch it up to help them grip the soil as they push their way through.

SNAKES

SERPENTES

Long and legless, the members of this group are easy to recognize—which is handy, because some of them have a venomous bite.

YOU ARE HERE

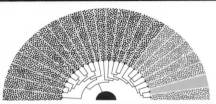

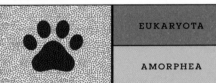

EUKARYOTA

AMORPHEA

KEY FACTS

- Around 3,400 species
- From 10-cm (4-in) threadsnakes to 10-m-long (30-ft-long) pythons
- Found in some oceans and on all areas of land except Ireland, New Zealand, certain other islands, and Antarctica

SPECIMEN

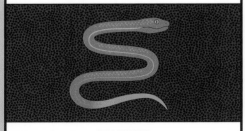

PIT VIPER

ALL ABOUT

The common ancestor of all snakes was probably a lizard with legs. The body of a snake is similar to that of a legless lizard, with one big difference. A snake's skull has a missing bar of bone, which allows them to open their jaws so wide, they can swallow prey larger than their own heads. Snakes' bodies and tails also tend to be far longer than those of most lizards.

All snakes are predators, though they hunt and catch prey in different ways. Around 600 types use venom injected using large fangs, but most are not venomous and instead overpower their prey, sometimes squeezing it to death.

Some snakes live underground; others climb trees, live in caves, and a few sea snakes even hunt fish in the ocean. They are helped by their excellent senses, which sometimes includes an extra sense—the ability to "see" heat. This helps them detect the warm bodies of their prey, even at night.

To stay safe from predators, and to sneak up on prey, snakes often have good camouflage, hide underground, and only hunt at night. Despite their lack of limbs, snakes are great at moving around quickly above and below the soil, and even through water. Some can climb rocky walls that are almost vertical while others can wind their way up trees.

SHARED FEATURES

- Lack movable eyelids
- No limbs
- No ear openings
- Super-flexible jaws and skull to swallow large prey whole
- Forked tongue for smelling
- Most snakes only have one lung
- Some snakes can "see" heat, using receptors called pit organs. This makes them very good at hunting warm-blooded animals at night

GOOD NEIGHBORS?

Snakes pose little danger to people if we respect them and keep our distance. Some people even keep them as pets. Snakes are important predators that keep ecosystems in balance. Some are "milked" for their venom to produce antidotes to snake bites, as well as medicines for high blood pressure and heart problems.

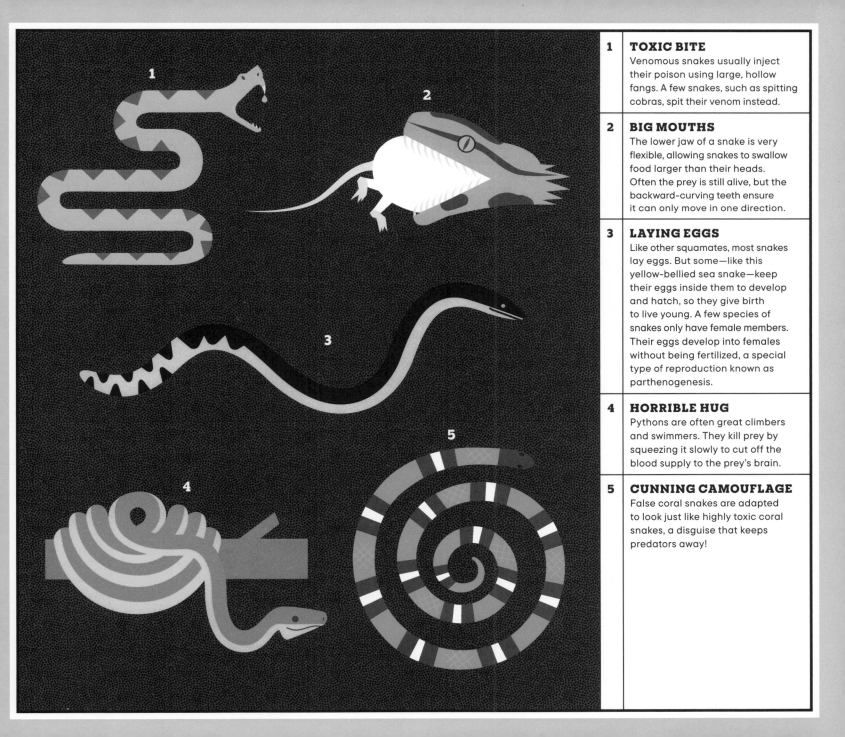

1 TOXIC BITE
Venomous snakes usually inject their poison using large, hollow fangs. A few snakes, such as spitting cobras, spit their venom instead.

2 BIG MOUTHS
The lower jaw of a snake is very flexible, allowing snakes to swallow food larger than their heads. Often the prey is still alive, but the backward-curving teeth ensure it can only move in one direction.

3 LAYING EGGS
Like other squamates, most snakes lay eggs. But some—like this yellow-bellied sea snake—keep their eggs inside them to develop and hatch, so they give birth to live young. A few species of snakes only have female members. Their eggs develop into females without being fertilized, a special type of reproduction known as parthenogenesis.

4 HORRIBLE HUG
Pythons are often great climbers and swimmers. They kill prey by squeezing it slowly to cut off the blood supply to the prey's brain.

5 CUNNING CAMOUFLAGE
False coral snakes are adapted to look just like highly toxic coral snakes, a disguise that keeps predators away!

BIRDS

AVES

Wings have helped these flying "reptiles" to conquer land, water, and air.

YOU ARE HERE

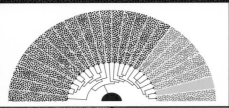

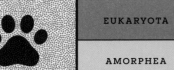

EUKARYOTA

AMORPHEA

KEY FACTS

- Around 11,000 species
- From hummingbirds just 5 cm (2 in) long to the 3.6-m (almost 12-ft) giant moa
- Wings help birds live, breed or hunt almost everywhere

SPECIMEN

PUFFIN

ALL ABOUT

Birds have four limbs like other tetrapods but their front limbs are adapted into wings. This makes most birds capable of powered flight, a superpower that has helped them to spread to all land habitats, including polluted cities, toxic salt lakes, and the frozen continent of Antarctica, where no land mammals can survive! Even the open oceans are hunting grounds for birds, such as penguins and gulls.

While marine birds focus on catching fish or crustaceans that live around the shore, other birds feed on a wide range of foods, including fruit and seeds, insects, and even mammals and reptiles. A bird's huge appetite for snack-sized prey helps to keep insect populations in balance. They also help flowering plants with pollination and seed dispersal—especially by eating fruit and pooping out the seeds. Many flowering plants (see page 68) have adapted to attract birds by producing red flowers or berries, which is a color that birds can easily see.

Birds have no teeth. Instead, they rely on a specially shaped beak or bill to help them capture their chosen food, and a gizzard to grind it up. Feathers help birds camouflage themselves and keep warm. Many birds also have bright or extravagant feathers, which can make males and females of a species look very different from one another. These are thought to help the many different species of birds to recognize their own kind and to attract a mate.

SHARED FEATURES

- Wings, most often used for flight
- Bones with air spaces to make them light
- Jaw with no teeth, covered by a horny beak
- Large stomach with a gizzard (muscular part) for "chewing" food
- Skin covered in feathers, with some scales

GOOD NEIGHBORS?

Birds are an important source of food for many predators. Chicken eggs have played an important role in the history of medicine and have been used to help make many vaccines! The droppings of seabirds have long been used as fertilizer to help crops grow. We can also thank birds for many world-shaping inventions, such as quill pens made from large flight feathers.

1 AMAZING BEAKS
A bird's beak is often very well adapted to the kind of food it eats. For example, hummingbirds have long, slender beaks for feeding on nectar, while macaws have strong, hooked beaks for breaking open nuts and seeds, and flamingos have hooked beaks lined with horny plates to filter food out of the water.

2 MASSIVE MIGRATIONS
Wings make some birds capable of huge migrations, to find the best places to eat and breed. Arctic terns travel from the Arctic to Antarctica and back every year!

3 FANCY FEATHERS
A bird's feathers are made mainly from keratin, the same tough protein that makes up the scales of snakes and lizards, and the fur, hair, claws, and nails of mammals. Feathers can make male and female birds of the same species look very different from one another—just like these peafowl.

4 FLIGHTLESS BIRDS
Although all birds have wings, inherited from their common ancestor, some birds have lost the power of flight. Flightless birds are often fantastic runners or swimmers instead. The Southern cassowary is both!

5 EGG LAYERS
Birds lay eggs with hard shells but keep them warm until they hatch. Most birds continue to care for their young, whether the chicks can walk and feed themselves or not. All birds reach their adult size in a year or less, leaving the parents free to breed again.

PERCHING BIRDS
PASSERIFORMES

YOU ARE HERE

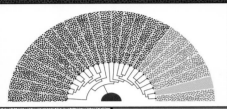

	EUKARYOTA
	AMORPHEA

More than half of all birds belong to this group. They include all the songbirds, famous for their complicated and often beautiful calls.

KEY FACTS

- Around 6,000 species
- From the 6.5-cm (2.5-in) short-tailed pygmy tyrant to ravens more than 70 cm (over 2 ft) long
- Widely scattered around the world, especially in places with trees, where they can perch

SPECIMEN

BLUE-FACED HONEYEATER

ALL ABOUT

Most of the birds we spot perched in trees, on wires, and in gardens—such as blackbirds, magpies, robins, and starlings—belong to this group. They are called "perching birds" after their special feet, with toes that automatically tighten around the branch or wire they land on and keep the bird locked on, even while they are asleep!

The perching bird's feet all work in the same way; however, this group of birds has the most variety! Their feathers, behavior, and beaks or bills are often highly adapted to suit a certain habitat and food. Some are insect eaters, with beaks that can poke into holes to dig out hidden bugs, or gape widely to catch flying insects in mid-air. Some have tough, stubby beaks for cracking open nuts and seeds. Others have long, delicate bills, for reaching nectar without damaging the flowers.

Even if you can't see them, you might hear members of this group—the songbirds that call to each other every morning as they start the day. Each species has unique songs, which are used to attract mates and to defend territories. Songbirds have some of the most complex and intelligent brains in the animal kingdom. Some can learn hundreds of different notes and difficult songs. Studies of bird brains are even helping us understand how human brains allow us to learn and use languages!

SHARED FEATURES

- Three forward-facing toes
- One backward-facing toe
- Feet grip a perch automatically
- Large brain, heart, and lungs for their size
- Use energy very quickly, so need to eat often
- Insect eaters tend to have the best eyesight

GOOD NEIGHBORS?

Studying the bodies and behaviors of perching birds is helping scientists to understand all kinds of different things about animals, from the way that our brains learn languages to the secrets of metabolism (how animals access and use energy from food).

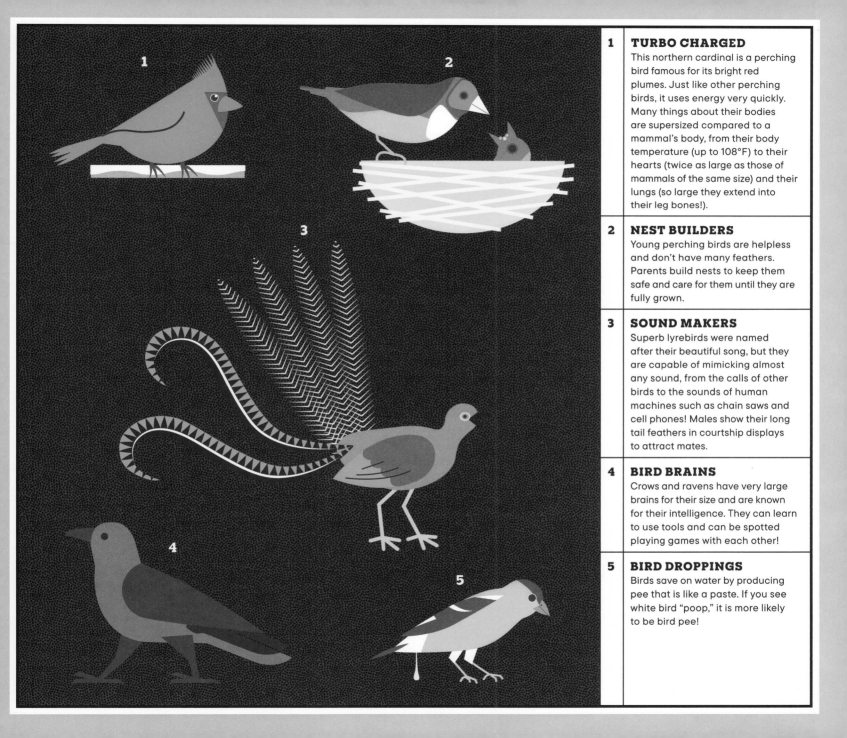

1	**TURBO CHARGED** This northern cardinal is a perching bird famous for its bright red plumes. Just like other perching birds, it uses energy very quickly. Many things about their bodies are supersized compared to a mammal's body, from their body temperature (up to 108°F) to their hearts (twice as large as those of mammals of the same size) and their lungs (so large they extend into their leg bones!).
2	**NEST BUILDERS** Young perching birds are helpless and don't have many feathers. Parents build nests to keep them safe and care for them until they are fully grown.
3	**SOUND MAKERS** Superb lyrebirds were named after their beautiful song, but they are capable of mimicking almost any sound, from the calls of other birds to the sounds of human machines such as chain saws and cell phones! Males show their long tail feathers in courtship displays to attract mates.
4	**BIRD BRAINS** Crows and ravens have very large brains for their size and are known for their intelligence. They can learn to use tools and can be spotted playing games with each other!
5	**BIRD DROPPINGS** Birds save on water by producing pee that is like a paste. If you see white bird "poop," it is more likely to be bird pee!

DAYTIME BIRDS OF PREY

ACCIPITRIFORMES

These magnificent predators hunt during the day with the help of their excellent eyesight.

YOU ARE HERE

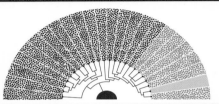

	EUKARYOTA
	AMORPHEA

KEY FACTS

- Around 250 species
- From tiny hawks with bodies just 20 cm (8 in) long to harpy eagles more than 1 m (3 ft) tall. An Andean condor's wings measure about 3 meters (about 10 ft) from tip to tip
- Found in all kinds of habitats in all parts of the world except Antarctica

SPECIMEN

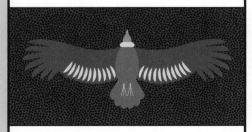

ANDEAN CONDOR

ALL ABOUT

This clade includes eagles, hawks, buzzards, kites, vultures, and most large-to-medium-sized birds of prey that hunt or scavenge during the day. These carnivores have short, hook-shaped bills and long, sharp talons for grabbing and tearing prey. They also have broad, strong wings for flying and gliding long distances, with sharp eyesight for spotting prey from high above the ground. One of the highest flyers is the Rüppell's griffon vulture. By rising on thermals (upward-moving warm air), it can soar more than two and a half miles into the sky. That's high enough to peer into the windows of a jumbo jet!

Most birds of prey build nests in trees and often pair up with the same mate for life. They don't lay many eggs at a time, so both parents often help to care for the eggs and chicks very carefully. Their chicks are not completely helpless, but even after they leave the nest it can take them a long time to learn how to hunt.

Their food ranges from insects and other small animals to fish, large mammals such as sloths and monkeys, smaller birds, and even fruit. Vultures are the odd ones out, as they typically scavenge for food that is already dead rather than killing it themselves.

When they began studying bird DNA, scientists were surprised to find that falcons are not closely related to these other birds of prey, but are actually close relatives of parrots.

SHARED FEATURES

- Hooked beaks
- Excellent eyesight
- Broad wings
- Short, strong legs
- Sharp claws, called talons
- Females are larger than males

GOOD NEIGHBORS?

Humans have been training birds of prey for thousands of years. At first, birds such as hawks were trained to help with hunting. Today they help with modern problems, such as scaring smaller birds away from airports. Many birds of prey seem to like living in urban areas, where they can catch smaller birds and mammals that also live near humans.

1 HOLD TIGHT
Ospreys dive at water feetfirst to grab fish in their talons. Sharp spines, or "spicules," under their feet stop the fish from slipping away as the osprey finds somewhere to sit and eat it.

2 VERY SLOW FOOD
Despite their shared habits of swooping down on dead food, not all vultures are close relatives. There are two groups—known as Old World and New World vultures—which seem to have evolved the same lifestyle as they adapted to fill similar niches in their habitats.

3 SLOW FOOD
Raptors' hooked beaks are shaped to bite, tear, and sometimes help kill prey. Snail kites have beaks adapted to prize snails out of their shells!

4 TERRIBLE TALONS
Eagles, hawks, and kites kill their prey by piercing it with their talons and squeezing it to death. The harpy eagle's talons are as large as the claws of a grizzly bear!

5 SECRETARY BIRD
Most birds of prey have short legs, but the secretary bird looks like it is on stilts! It uses its long legs and large feet to stamp on prey such as lizards, snakes, and large insects, while keeping its body safely out of reach.

AMOEBAS

AMOEBOZOA

Peering at amoebas through a microscope can feel like watching alien life forms! They are remarkably like the white blood cells that live in our own bodies. The tree of life reveals why: they are some of animals' closest relatives.

YOU ARE HERE

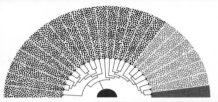

EUKARYOTA

AMOEBOZOA

KEY FACTS

- Around 2,000 species
- A single-celled amoeba can grow up to a fraction of an inch, but slime molds can cover over 30 feet!
- Found in freshwater and marine **habitats,** as well as peatlands and soils, everywhere except the most extreme environments

SPECIMEN

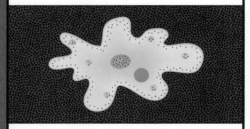

AMOEBA PROTEUS

ALL ABOUT

"Amoeba" is a common name for any blob-like protist that moves by changing the shape of its cell (instead of using little hairs or tails to swim). Most amoebas belong to one branch of the family tree, the Amoebozoa.

Amoebozoans are easy to find in nature. Pick up a handful of soil or leaf litter, or scoop up a handful of pond water, and you'll be holding hundreds of different species! Their ancestors were blobbing around the planet long before plants moved onto land. Today they are found in large numbers in all watery and moist habitats, including water tanks, sewage, contact-lens cases, cooling towers, swimming pools, and even people's noses and throats.

Instead of having different parts to do different jobs, amoebozoans rely on their shape-shifting skill. For example, they don't have little hairs or tails to help them move. Instead, they change the shape of their cells, forming "false feet" that reach out and anchor to something a little further along. Then they shift the position of their gooey insides, hauling the whole cell into a new position. Amoebozoans also change shape to wrap themselves around particles of food and engulf or "swallow" them whole.

Most amoebozoans live alone and reproduce by simply splitting in two. But some—known as slime molds—like to team up. Together they form huge slimy blobs that can move much faster than one amoebozoan on its own. Some can even form fruiting bodies like fungi (see page 90).

SHARED FEATURES

- Can form pseudopods or "false feet," which stick out like tubes or flattened lobes from the surface of the cell
- A few species build a shell called a "test" for protection
- Some form fruiting bodies and reproduce by releasing spores

GOOD NEIGHBORS?

Most amoebozoans live in soil, keeping it fertile by digesting bacteria and returning nutrients to the soil. Very few amoebozoans are parasites that cause disease. They include *Entamoeba histolytica,* which causes amoebic dysentery if it gets into a person's intestines.

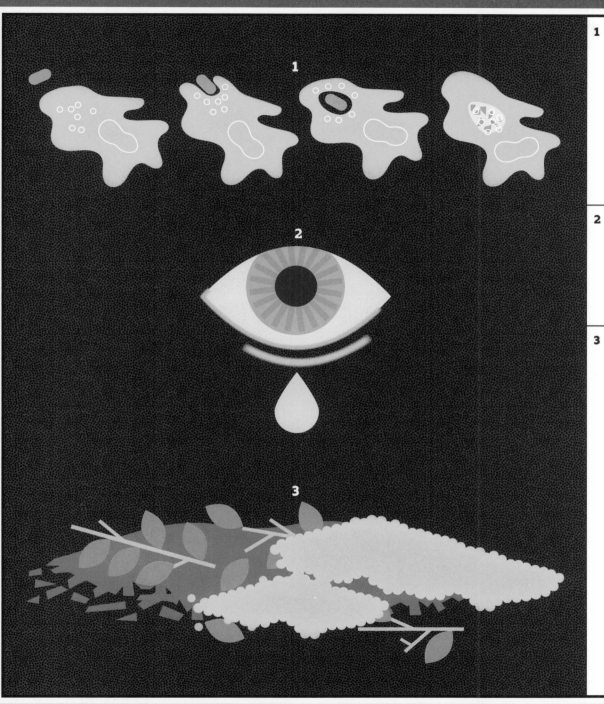

1 SOIL HEROES

Members of this group are some of the most common eukaryote **microbes** found in soils. They help to keep soils fertile for plants to grow, by gobbling up huge numbers of bacteria. This keeps bacteria under control and returns the **nutrients** collected inside the bacteria to the soil. In this sequence of images the amoeba is shown in yellow, and the bacterium it is engulfing is in pink.

2 SORE EYES

Amoebozoans that usually live harmlessly in soil or water can cause problems if they get transferred into damp parts of our bodies by mistake. Acanthamoeba species sometimes cause eye infections in people who use contact lenses.

3 SLIME MOLDS

When food is hard to find, some amoebozoans team up to form "slime molds"—huge groups of amoebas that move along the ground like a blob of slime, lifting up particles of food as they go. A single slime mold can cover an area of several feet! This one— found on forest floors—is known as "dog vomit" slime mold.

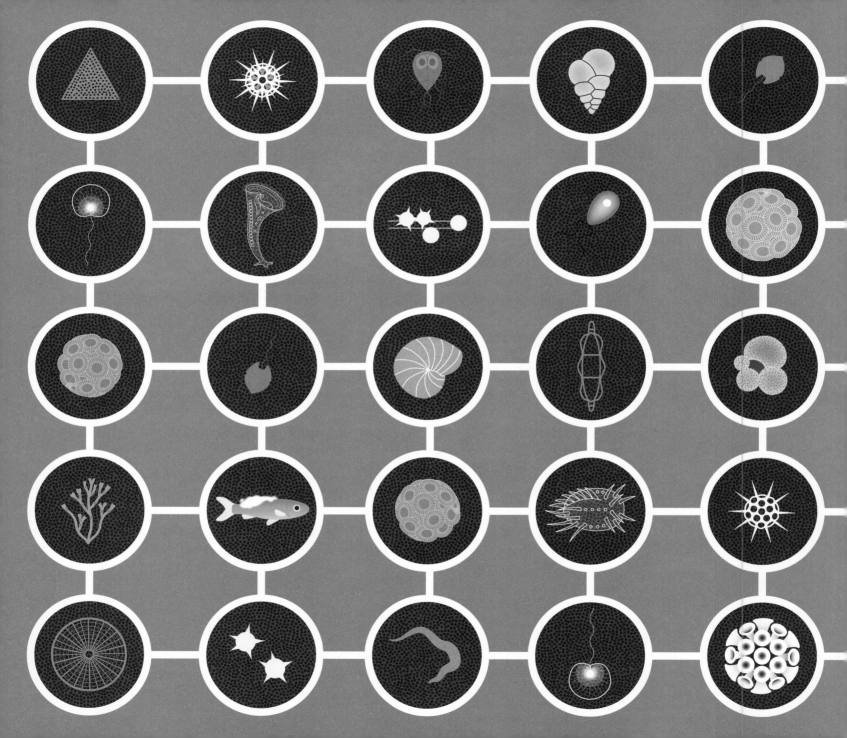

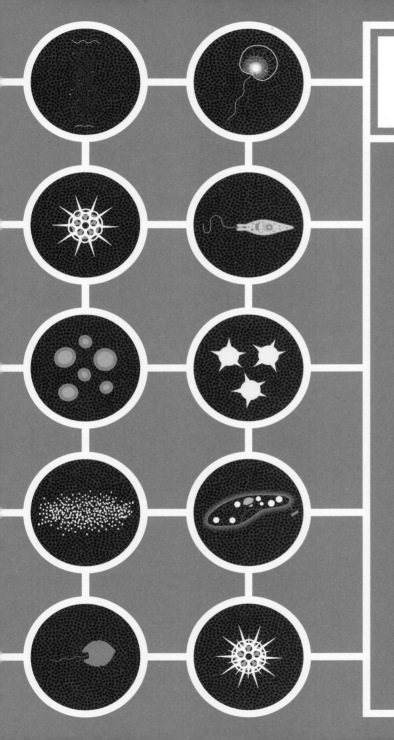

MICROSCOPIC EUKARYOTES
PROTOZOA

THIS CHAPTER GATHERS TOGETHER SOME OF THE MANY OTHER CLADES ON THE EUKARYOTE TREE OF LIFE. MOST OF THESE CREATURES ARE MICROSCOPIC, MADE UP OF JUST ONE CELL. HOWEVER, THESE CELLS ARE MORE COMPLEX AND ORGANIZED THAN THE SINGLE CELLS OF BACTERIA.

Traditionally, single-celled creatures that aren't bacteria or fungi have been known as **protists**— a "kingdom" of living things grouped together because they didn't seem to fit anywhere else. However, two protists from different branches of the tree of life are as distinct as plants and people. They range from giant seaweeds to tiny, shelled diatoms; from water molds to the five *Plasmodium* **species** that cause malaria.

Some single-celled creatures hunt even tinier prey or live as **parasites** inside plants, animals, or people. Some soak up food from their surroundings, while others are important decomposers, breaking down dead things. Several different branches include creatures that can make their own food using sunlight energy. They are part of the plankton that lie at the bottom of ocean food chains.

These eukaryotes also reproduce in very different ways. Many simply split into two or more identical cells, but others have complicated life cycles that involve moving between different hosts. The most infamous have a bad reputation for causing disease in plants, animals, and people. But on land and in oceans, their close relatives play vital roles in recycling **nutrients** and keeping the climate—and the entire planet—in balance.

ALVEOLATES
ALVEOLATA

YOU ARE HERE

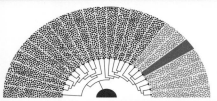

EUKARYOTA

SAR

KEY FACTS

- More than 15,000 species
- From 30 μm to around 2 mm (less than a tenth of an inch), which is large enough to see with your eyes
- Found in seas and oceans, freshwater, mosses and soils, and inside animals and other living things

SPECIMEN

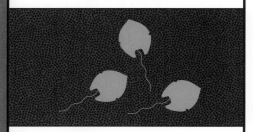

DINOFLAGELLATES

Tread carefully on this branch of the tree— it includes glittering, green plankton, but also some of the world's most ghastly parasites.

ALL ABOUT

These critters pack a lot into their single-celled bodies. Some are so good at getting around and gobbling food that the scientist who first spotted them named them "little animals." Alveolates are named after the one feature they all share—a strange water-filled cavity! Apart from this they are incredibly diverse and are grouped into three main types.

Dinoflagellates include many of the algae found floating around in seas and oceans. They can make their own food using energy from sunlight, which is known as **photosynthesis.** Many of them top up their diet by capturing tiny prey. Some produce **toxins** to help them catch prey, while others lure prey with a blue glow before trapping it with their large **flagella.**

In contrast, the large group of alveolates known as Apicomplexa are all parasites. They rely on a host for food and shelter and even have special parts to help them invade animal cells. These alveolates can live mind-bogglingly complex lives that involve moving from insect hosts to larger animals and back again!

Last, but not least, are a huge group known as ciliates, named after the fuzzy, vibrating "hairs" that cover their surface. These hairs are used for moving around and gathering food. Their food is then taken into the cell by using something that looks a lot like a mouth!

SHARED FEATURES

- A strange empty "sac" called an alveolus may help to control the amount of water moving in and out of the **cell**
- Some have many vibrating "hairs" called **cilia**
- Some have one or more "tails" called flagella, used for moving or for grabbing prey
- Simple "mouth"

GOOD NEIGHBORS?

This group includes the tiny parasites that cause malaria in humans, as well as several other major diseases. Even relatively friendly dinoflagellates can cause problems if they grow out of control (usually due to human activities, such as dumping sewage or fertilizer in the water) and cause toxic red tides.

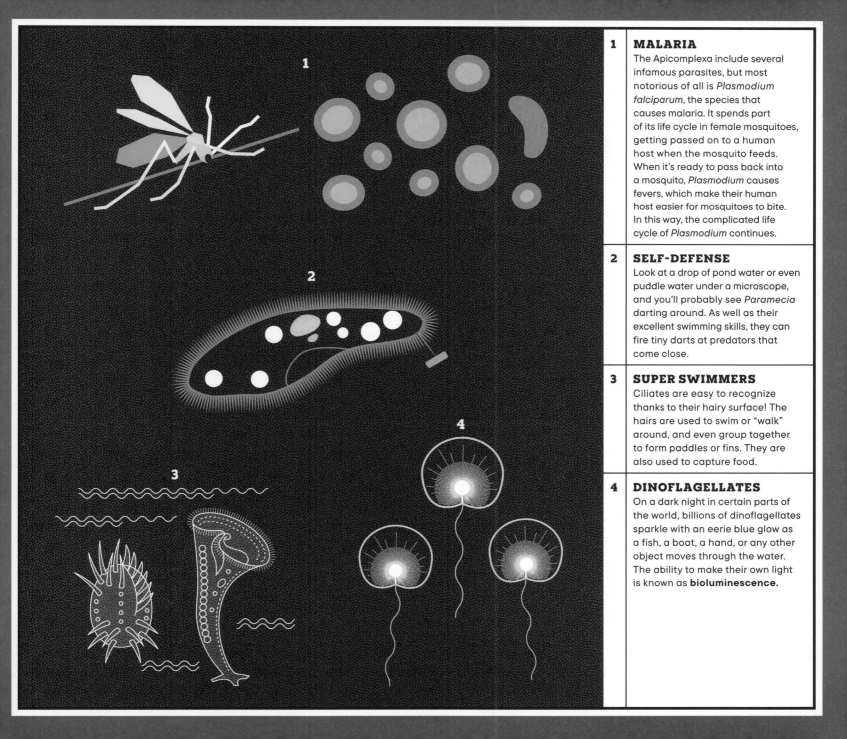

1 MALARIA

The Apicomplexa include several infamous parasites, but most notorious of all is *Plasmodium falciparum*, the species that causes malaria. It spends part of its life cycle in female mosquitoes, getting passed on to a human host when the mosquito feeds. When it's ready to pass back into a mosquito, *Plasmodium* causes fevers, which make their human host easier for mosquitoes to bite. In this way, the complicated life cycle of *Plasmodium* continues.

2 SELF-DEFENSE

Look at a drop of pond water or even puddle water under a microscope, and you'll probably see *Paramecia* darting around. As well as their excellent swimming skills, they can fire tiny darts at predators that come close.

3 SUPER SWIMMERS

Ciliates are easy to recognize thanks to their hairy surface! The hairs are used to swim or "walk" around, and even group together to form paddles or fins. They are also used to capture food.

4 DINOFLAGELLATES

On a dark night in certain parts of the world, billions of dinoflagellates sparkle with an eerie blue glow as a fish, a boat, a hand, or any other object moves through the water. The ability to make their own light is known as **bioluminescence.**

STRAMENOPILES

STRAMENOPILA

Discover a giant form of algae that forms forests under the sea and meet some of the most beautiful creatures on the planet (if you have a microscope to see them!).

YOU ARE HERE

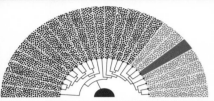

EUKARYOTA

SAR

KEY FACTS

- More than 100,000 species
- From microscopic diatoms to giant kelp more than 60 m (almost 200 ft) long
- Found in seas, oceans and fresh water, and anywhere moist on land, including soils

SPECIMEN

BLADDERWRACK

ALL ABOUT

This huge group includes the creatures known as diatoms, brown algae, golden algae, and oomycetes (water molds). Most can make their own food using sunlight, so they are an important part of ocean and freshwater food chains.

Diatoms are single-celled protists that build themselves beautiful cell walls out of silica—the same material that glass and sand are made from. When diatoms die, they sink to the bottom of the seafloor, locking away the **carbon dioxide** that they used to help build their walls. This delays the return of carbon dioxide to the atmosphere, keeping global warming at lower levels than it would otherwise be.

Brown algae are also found in seas and oceans, but unlike the diatoms, they are not all single-celled creatures. They include familiar seaweeds such as bladderwrack and giant kelp, which look and behave a bit like the plants found on land. Bladderwrack is easy to spot on rocky shores. It has lots of air-filled "bladders" that help it float upright when it's underwater. This provides hiding places and hunting grounds for smaller sea creatures.

Oomycetes send out huge networks of fluffy-looking filaments, which soak up nutrients from whatever they are sitting on. At first, oomycetes were mistaken for fungi (see page 90), leading to the name "water molds." Peering more closely at their **molecules** revealed that they belong on this branch of the tree of life.

SHARED FEATURES

- Short, stubby, hollow "hairs" cover their "tail" (flagellum)
- Many have a second flagellum without hairs

GOOD NEIGHBORS?

Diatoms are a vital part of food chains, and of the **carbon cycle** on Earth. Brown algae (seaweeds) are edible and used to make important food additives. Chemicals from brown algae are even used in the process of making batteries! However, one species of stramenopile is notorious for causing one of the worst famines in history, the Potato Famine.

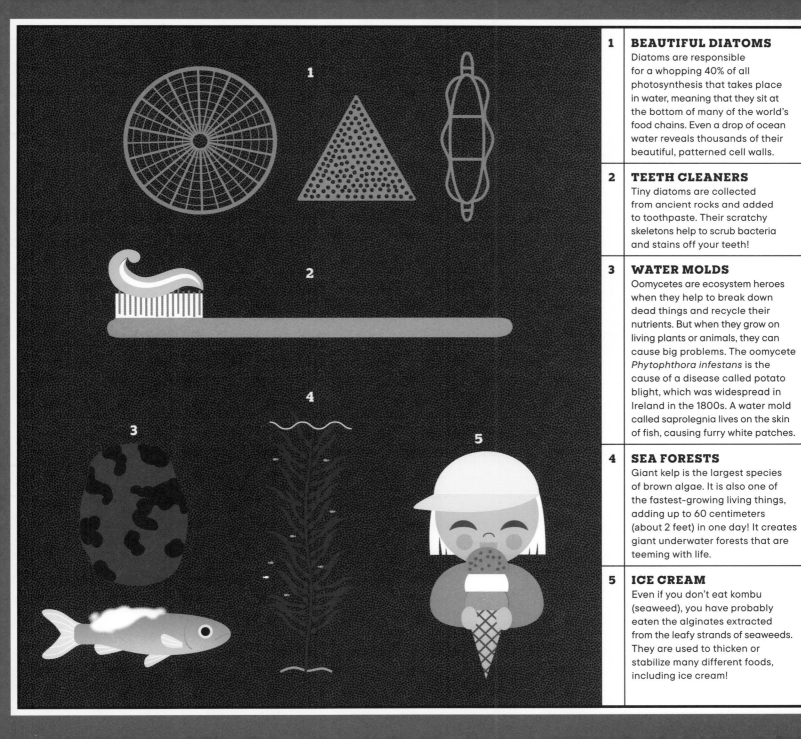

1 BEAUTIFUL DIATOMS
Diatoms are responsible for a whopping 40% of all photosynthesis that takes place in water, meaning that they sit at the bottom of many of the world's food chains. Even a drop of ocean water reveals thousands of their beautiful, patterned cell walls.

2 TEETH CLEANERS
Tiny diatoms are collected from ancient rocks and added to toothpaste. Their scratchy skeletons help to scrub bacteria and stains off your teeth!

3 WATER MOLDS
Oomycetes are ecosystem heroes when they help to break down dead things and recycle their nutrients. But when they grow on living plants or animals, they can cause big problems. The oomycete *Phytophthora infestans* is the cause of a disease called potato blight, which was widespread in Ireland in the 1800s. A water mold called saprolegnia lives on the skin of fish, causing furry white patches.

4 SEA FORESTS
Giant kelp is the largest species of brown algae. It is also one of the fastest-growing living things, adding up to 60 centimeters (about 2 feet) in one day! It creates giant underwater forests that are teeming with life.

5 ICE CREAM
Even if you don't eat kombu (seaweed), you have probably eaten the alginates extracted from the leafy strands of seaweeds. They are used to thicken or stabilize many different foods, including ice cream!

RHIZARIANS

RHIZARIA

The microscopic creatures in this group are incredible engineers and the secret strength behind the Egyptian pyramids! They also have a key role in shaping our climate.

YOU ARE HERE

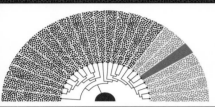

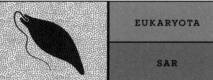

EUKARYOTA

SAR

KEY FACTS

- More than 18,000 species
- Radiolarians are typically less than a fifth of a millimeter (0.008 in), but some forams can grow shells several centimeters (about an inch) across
- Found all around the world, in watery habitats such as oceans, seas, and estuaries

SPECIMEN

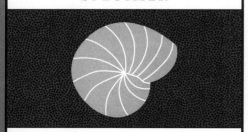

FORAM

ALL ABOUT

Rhizarians look like tiny alien spacecraft as they move around their environment searching for food. Their small size and traveling way of life make them hard to study (you have to find them first!). What we do know is that most are predators that hunt tiny plankton. Their favorite foods include the **larvae** of crustaceans (see page 130).

Radiolarians form amazing, symmetrical "skeletons" inside their cell. These delicate skeletons are often made of silica, the same material that forms glass. Parts of the cell poke out like needles, to snare food particles or grab prey.

Forams go one step further, building a shell called a "test" outside their cell wall. This can become several inches wide and include chambers where algae live and make food using sunlight energy. When the foram is feeling hungry, it can vacuum up the algae for its dinner. That's what you'd call a single-celled farmer! This strategy helps forams survive in wide, open oceans where there is nothing else to eat.

The shells of many rhizarians are made of calcium carbonate, using carbon dioxide dissolved in the ocean. When these tiny creatures die, their hard shells sink to the seabed. This locks away carbon and prevents it from being converted into carbon dioxide, which is a greenhouse gas. Locking away the carbon for over millions of years has helped to make Earth's climate cooler than it would otherwise be.

SHARED FEATURES

- Many have a hard shell or "test"
- Parts of the cell poke out through small holes in the shell, forming "false feet." Forams or "hole bearers" are named after these holes
- The "false feet" are used to trap food, soak up **minerals**, and to help with movement

GOOD NEIGHBORS?

Most rhizarians play key environmental roles as producers in food chains and in controlling the amount of carbon dioxide, **nitrogen**, and other gases in the atmosphere. Only a handful of species in this group are parasites.

1	**CLIMATE CLUES** Forams are very sensitive to pollution and changes in climate. This makes their fossils wonderful clues for working out what the world's weather patterns were like in the past.
2	**TINY TIMEKEEPERS** The glassy skeletons of dead radiolarians are also found in rocks dating back 500 million years. This amazing fossil record helps scientists to divide the past up into different periods such as the Carboniferous and Permian.
3	**GREAT PYRAMIDS** Most foram shells sink to the seabed when they die, forming a thick blanket on the ocean floor. Because they are hard, they form fossils easily. They are found in sedimentary rock, including the limestone used to build the Great Pyramids of Giza. In fact, the pyramids are *mainly* made of ancient forams!
4	**TOUGH AND TINY** Forams form hard "shells" around themselves. Parts of the cell poke out through small holes, so the foram can move about, grab food, and soak up minerals to build its shell even bigger.
5	**STAR SAND** It's not easy to take a microscope to the beach, but if you bring some sand home and put it under a microscope you might be surprised at what you see. In some parts of the world, the sand is actually made of billions of dead foram shells that have been washed up onto the shore.

HAPTOPHYTES

HAPTOPHYTA

These strange-looking, button-covered creatures play a huge role in ocean food chains and in recycling the building blocks of life on planet Earth.

YOU ARE HERE

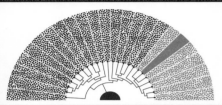

	EUKARYOTA
	HAPTISTA

KEY FACTS

- About 500 species
- Just a few millionths of a millimeter across
- Most species live in seas and oceans worldwide (except polar oceans) and a few are found in freshwater

SPECIMEN

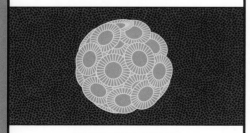

COCCOLITHOPHORE

ALL ABOUT

The creatures in this group remind scientists more of plants than animals. They grow on the ocean surface and harvest sunlight energy to make their own food. They are thought of as a type of algae, but they have some unique features. Around 300 of the 500 species build themselves a coat of tough scales. Each tiny "coccolithophore" has at least 30 of these scales clustered around it, making it more like an armored tank than a plant.

The scales are formed from calcium carbonate—a mineral made of calcium, carbon, and oxygen soaked up from the ocean. When the haptophyte dies, the scales sink to the bottom of the ocean. This locks away carbon that would otherwise be in Earth's atmosphere.

Haptophytes that lived and died millions of years ago formed the worlds' chalk rock, around the time the dinosaurs last lived on Earth. Chalk rock is an important part of many land **ecosystems**, because it can hold a lot of water. The ancient haptophyte molecules are also full of clues about what Earth's climate was like in the past.

SHARED FEATURES

- Most have a "tail" known as a flagellum
- Most have **chlorophyll** for photosynthesis
- **Exoskeleton** made of hard "scales" called coccoliths

GOOD NEIGHBORS?

Most of the world's food-producing microscopic plankton belongs to this group. They are eaten by all kinds of different sea creatures, and passed on up ocean food chains. They are also very important for locking away carbon in the world's oceans, keeping it out of the atmosphere.

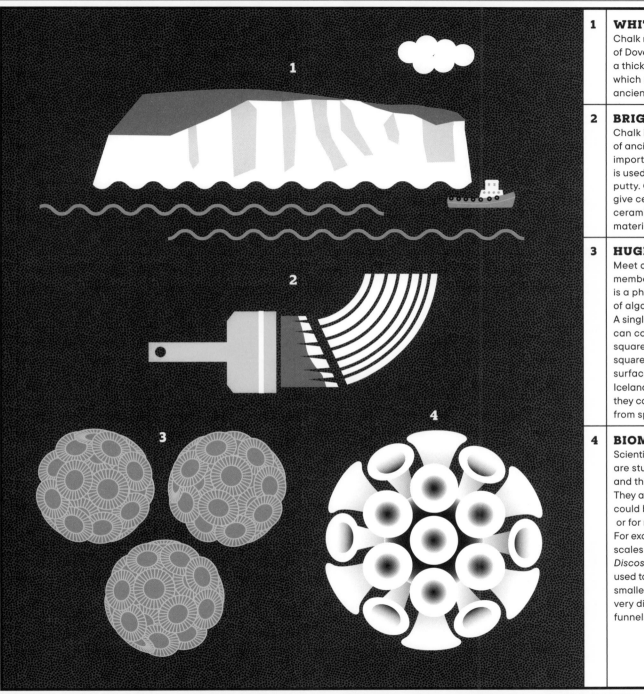

1	**WHITE CLIFFS** Chalk rocks such as the White Cliffs of Dover in England are made from a thick layer of haptophyte scales, which sank to the bottom of an ancient ocean millions of years ago.
2	**BRIGHT WHITE** Chalk is formed from the scales of ancient haptophytes. It is an important building material that is used for making cement and putty. Chalk is also used to give certain paints, cosmetics, ceramics, paper, and other materials a bright white color.
3	**HUGE BLOOMS** Meet one of the most common members of this group. A bloom is a phenomenon when a colony of algae grows out of control. A single bloom of these creatures can cover more than 100,000 square kilometers (over 38,000 square miles) of the ocean's surface, an area the size of Iceland! These blooms are so big, they can be detected by satellites from space.
4	**BIOMIMICRY** Scientists from many different fields are studying coccolithophores and the tiny structures they build. They are trying to find out how they could be used to make medicines or for nanotechnology devices. For example, the tiny funnel-shaped scales made by the coccolith *Discosphaera tubifera* could be used to control the flow of particles smaller than atoms. It would be very difficult for humans to build funnels this small!

EXCAVATES

EXCAVATA

YOU ARE HERE

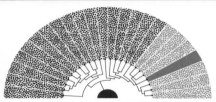

	EUKARYOTA
	EXCAVATA

KEY FACTS

- More than 2,000 species
- Most are very small, but they can grow up to half a millimeter (a 50th of an inch) long
- Found everywhere from the deep oceans to the insides of animals' intestines

SPECIMEN

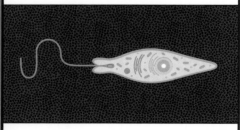

EUGLENA

Between them, the excavates are responsible for several nasty diseases and the house-destroying power of termites!

ALL ABOUT

Scientists still aren't sure if the creatures in this group share a **common ancestor.** Many scientists still group them under the name excavates, but others think of them as two separate groups of living things, known as Discoba and Metamonada. Both groups include members that cause problems for humans!

The Discoba includes protists that hunt and eat bacteria and other microbes as well as green algae that make their own food using sunlight energy. The euglenozoans are particularly unusual. They can live in the dark and soak up nutrients from their surroundings like animals but will also swim toward light. When they get there, they can make their own food using photosynthesis, like plants. Most creatures do one or the other!

Members of the second group, the Metamonada, are more animal-like than plant-like, but unusually they don't have true mitochondria (the part of eukaryote cells that generates energy). Metamonada have adapted to generate energy in an unusual way, and because of this they can thrive in environments with no oxygen, such as the digestive systems of animals. This sounds gruesome, but most Metamonada are friendly microbes. They help their hosts to break down tough plant foods such as wood in return for food and a place to live.

SHARED FEATURES

- Most have a groove on one side of their cell that looks like it has been dug out or "excavated"
- This groove is used for feeding
- Flagella for moving around (some have up to 100,000 of these!)
- Euglenozoans have very simple "eyes" known as eyespots, which allow them to sense light

GOOD NEIGHBORS?

This group includes many nasty parasites that cause different diseases in different parts of the world, such as sleeping sickness in Africa, Chagas disease in the Americas, and leishmaniasis in the tropics, subtropics, and Southern Europe. It also includes microbes that cause diarrhea, such as *Giardia lamblia.*

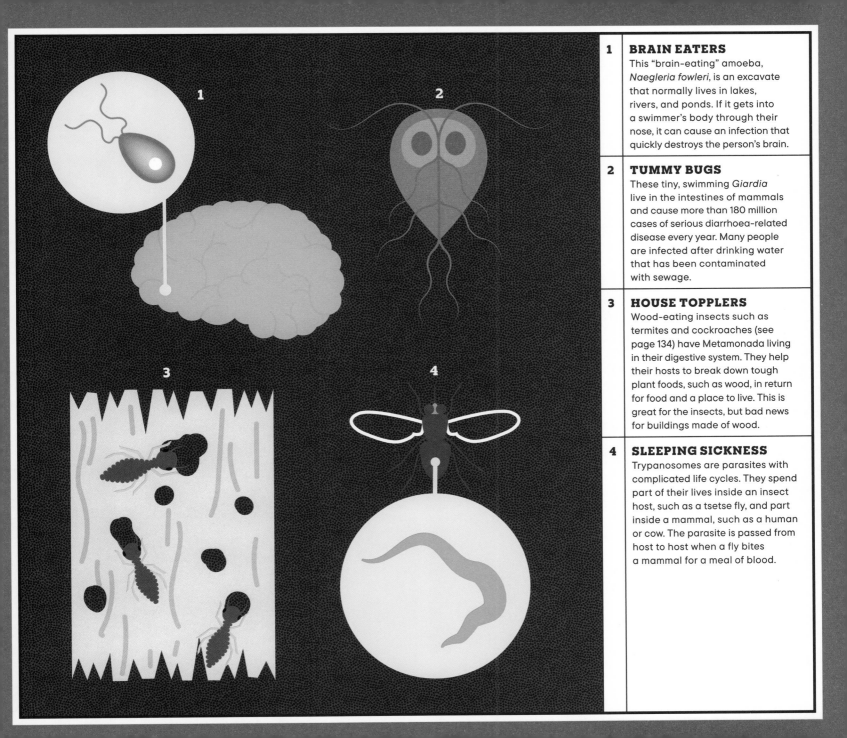

1 BRAIN EATERS

This "brain-eating" amoeba, *Naegleria fowleri*, is an excavate that normally lives in lakes, rivers, and ponds. If it gets into a swimmer's body through their nose, it can cause an infection that quickly destroys the person's brain.

2 TUMMY BUGS

These tiny, swimming *Giardia* live in the intestines of mammals and cause more than 180 million cases of serious diarrhoea-related disease every year. Many people are infected after drinking water that has been contaminated with sewage.

3 HOUSE TOPPLERS

Wood-eating insects such as termites and cockroaches (see page 134) have Metamonada living in their digestive system. They help their hosts to break down tough plant foods, such as wood, in return for food and a place to live. This is great for the insects, but bad news for buildings made of wood.

4 SLEEPING SICKNESS

Trypanosomes are parasites with complicated life cycles. They spend part of their lives inside an insect host, such as a tsetse fly, and part inside a mammal, such as a human or cow. The parasite is passed from host to host when a fly bites a mammal for a meal of blood.

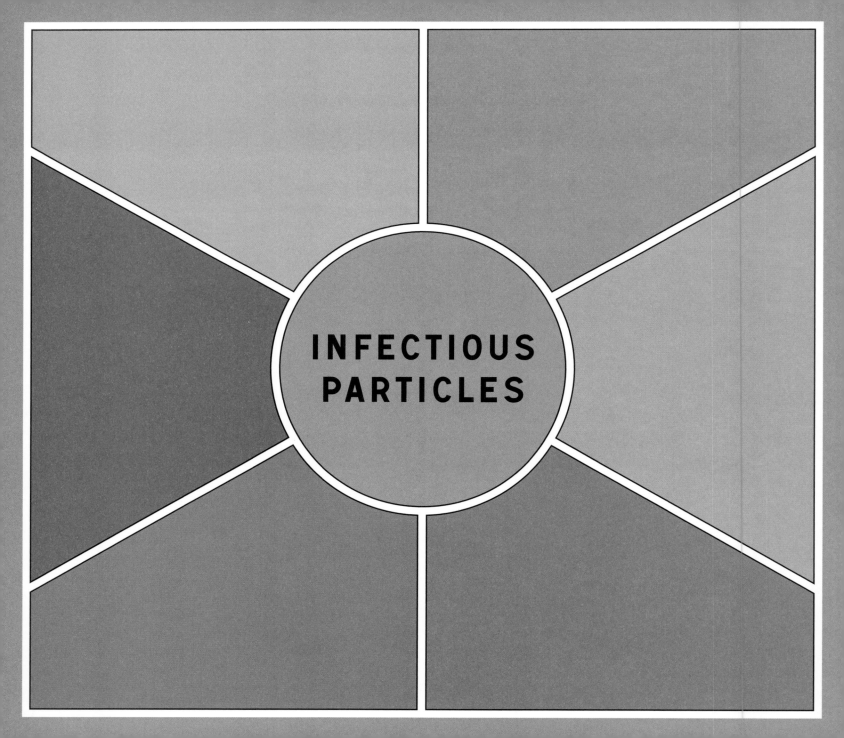

INFECTIOUS
PARTICLES

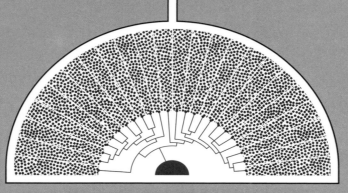

VIRUSES, VIROIDS & PRIONS

SCIENTISTS CAN'T AGREE IF VIRUSES, VIROIDS, AND PRIONS ARE ALIVE, SO YOU WILL NOT FIND THESE TINY PARTICLES ON THE TREE OF LIFE. BUT THEIR IMPACT ON EARTH'S LIVING CREATURES IS ENORMOUS.

Unlike living things, viruses are not made of **cells**. They are far smaller and simpler than even the tiniest bacterium. Viruses are just tiny packets of genetic instructions, wrapped in a protective coat. Without all the parts found inside a cell (see page 207), viruses can't feed, grow, move, breathe, or reproduce. But if a virus gets inside a living cell, it can hijack the cell's machinery to make millions of copies of itself. This can wreak havoc inside the host, causing disease.

There are several other types of infectious particles. Viroids are smaller than viruses. They are just a short, coiled-up strand of genetic instructions, with no coat. Once they get inside a plant cell, they trick it into making new viroids. Virusoids are even smaller particles, which need help from a virus to infect a host. The "helper virus" carries the virusoids inside a cell, where they get released and replicated.

Prions are the most mysterious infectious particles of all. They don't have any genetic instructions. They are animal proteins that have folded wrongly and therefore have an altered shape. Faulty **proteins** are usually quickly destroyed by an animal's **immune system**. But with prions this doesn't happen. Even worse, the prions trigger nearby healthy proteins to alter their shape too. Gradually, the prions form large clusters, damaging and destroying cells and **tissues**.

VIRUSES

VIRUSES

INFECTIOUS
PARTICLES

VIRUSES

Viruses are so small and so simple, they don't really count as living things. However, their impact on life on Earth is enormous.

KEY FACTS

- Tens of thousands of types of viruses have been identified, but there are likely to be millions or even billions
- From 20 to 500 nm wide
- Found everywhere on the planet (and inside the cells of every living thing) in unimaginable numbers

SPECIMEN

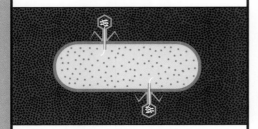

PHAGE VIRUS ON A BACTERIUM

ALL ABOUT

Viruses are far smaller than microbes such as bacteria. Viruses are not made of cells. They cannot move, feed, grow, get rid of waste, or make copies of themselves. However, viruses can trick living cells into doing these jobs for them.

A virus is basically a packet of instructions with a coat. When a virus invades a living cell, the cell can't tell the difference between its own genetic information and the instructions provided by the virus. The cell follows the new instructions, using its own energy and resources to make thousands of new viruses. The new viruses break out of the cell. The new viruses then spread to thousands of other cells. These cells become virus factories too.

No one knows how long viruses have been around. Perhaps they existed before cells did. Or perhaps they began when tiny pieces of genetic information broke free from microbes. Either way, they have been very successful. The number of viruses on Earth is mindboggling. Two pints of seawater or river water contains around 100 billion!

Do viruses count as living things? Scientists still aren't sure. But we know that without viruses, life as we know it would not exist. Every healthy plant, animal, person, and microbe is home to billions or trillions of friendly viruses. One study found 140,000 different types in the human gut alone. They are an important part of each living thing's **microbiome** in ways we don't yet understand.

SHARED FEATURES

- A virus is a strand of genetic information inside a protective coat
- The coat, called a capsid, is made of protein
- Some viruses have an extra cover, called an envelope

GOOD NEIGHBORS?

Of the millions or billions of viruses out there, just 200 or so are known to cause diseases in humans. These include Zika, HIV, smallpox, Ebola, and rabies—diseases that can be deadly because they are hard to fight. However, other viruses are a part of our healthy body microbiome that help us by activating our immune systems and destroying invading microbes.

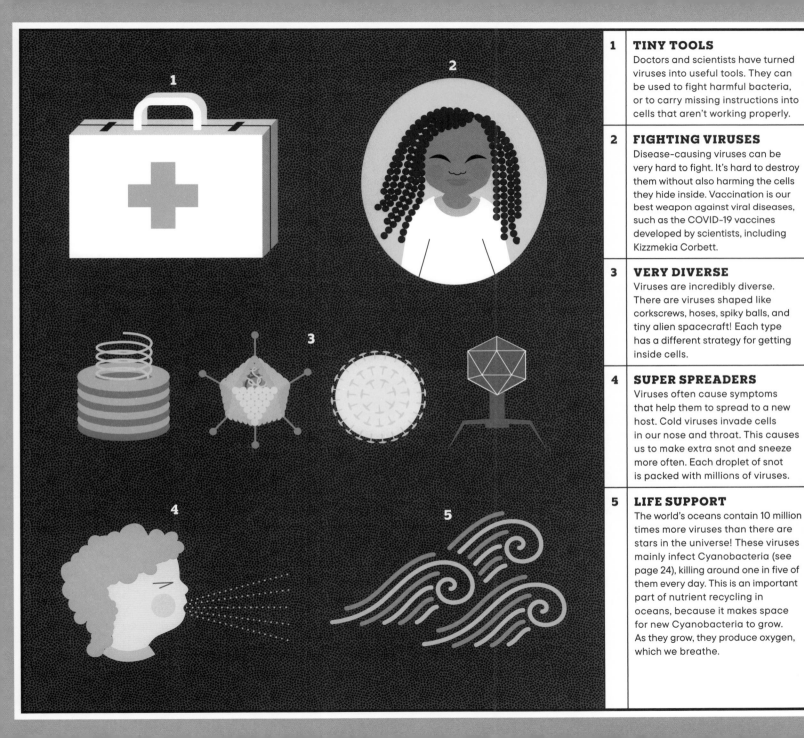

1 TINY TOOLS
Doctors and scientists have turned viruses into useful tools. They can be used to fight harmful bacteria, or to carry missing instructions into cells that aren't working properly.

2 FIGHTING VIRUSES
Disease-causing viruses can be very hard to fight. It's hard to destroy them without also harming the cells they hide inside. Vaccination is our best weapon against viral diseases, such as the COVID-19 vaccines developed by scientists, including Kizzmekia Corbett.

3 VERY DIVERSE
Viruses are incredibly diverse. There are viruses shaped like corkscrews, hoses, spiky balls, and tiny alien spacecraft! Each type has a different strategy for getting inside cells.

4 SUPER SPREADERS
Viruses often cause symptoms that help them to spread to a new host. Cold viruses invade cells in our nose and throat. This causes us to make extra snot and sneeze more often. Each droplet of snot is packed with millions of viruses.

5 LIFE SUPPORT
The world's oceans contain 10 million times more viruses than there are stars in the universe! These viruses mainly infect Cyanobacteria (see page 24), killing around one in five of them every day. This is an important part of nutrient recycling in oceans, because it makes space for new Cyanobacteria to grow. As they grow, they produce oxygen, which we breathe.

MORE ABOUT
THE TREE OF LIFE
&
OTHER
RESOURCES

LIFE ON EARTH

THIS WHIRLWIND TOUR OF THE TREE OF LIFE IS JUST THE BEGINNING. THERE ARE MANY MORE SECRETS HIDDEN IN ITS BOUGHS AND BRANCHES, WAITING TO BE EXPLORED.

Every year, thousands of new **species** are named and added to the tree. Some are discovered by scientists hunting for life in remote rain forests and deep caves. Others turn out to be living right under our noses. One team of researchers found more than a thousand new species of bacteria living in people's belly buttons. In 2019, schoolchildren from Denmark discovered ten new microbes living on fallen leaves in their parks and playgrounds. The tree of life is always growing and one day, you could make discoveries that add to it.

Why are there so many different species? Where did they come from? To answer that, we need to look more closely at life itself.

WHAT IS LIFE?

This question is not as easy as it sounds, and not all scientists agree on the answer! At school we learn that a living creature does certain things, such as feeding, growing, moving, and reproducing (making copies of itself). But as you explore the tree of life, you'll find plenty of creatures that don't follow these rules. When tiny water bears (page 108) are hibernating, they stop feeding, growing, and moving for up to a hundred years, but they are still alive. When a lion and tiger have cubs together, the male "ligers" and "tigons" cannot reproduce, but they are very much alive and could eat anyone who claimed otherwise!

To allow for these rule-breakers, biologists define life in a different way. They say that a living thing is any creature made up of one or more **cells**.

WHAT IS A CELL?

Cells are the smallest working parts of a living thing. Most cells are far too small to see with our eyes, so they were not discovered until the first microscopes were invented, around 350 years ago. When the scientist Robert Hooke popped a thin piece of cork (a type of bark) under his microscope, he was amazed to see lots of little spaces, divided by walls. He named them cells, after the tiny bedrooms used by monks at the time.

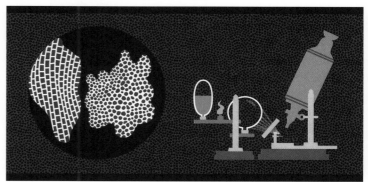

It was a good choice of name. Today we know that a cell is a bit like a tiny room, with walls that keep the insides separate from the outside world. Cells also have "doors" and "windows," that let certain things move in and out.

With the help of microscopes, scientists soon realized that every plant and animal is made up of millions of cells. They also discovered that these large living things are not alone on Earth. The planet is home to multitudes of much tinier creatures, whose entire bodies are made up of just one cell. These single-celled creatures live everywhere on Earth, from deep under the ocean to inside your body. They vastly outnumber plants and animals. How do they survive so successfully with just one cell?

HOW DO CELLS WORK?

Cells are not just jelly-filled blobs. They are as complicated as cities, with different zones and "machinery" for carrying out different tasks. Inside each cell—a speck too tiny to see with your eyes—hundreds of thousands of chemical reactions are happening at the same time. It is chemical reactions that allow a cell to take in what it needs, to store or use energy, to build and break down substances, to get rid of waste, to sense what's happening in its environment, and to move around, and to make copies of itself.

Each cell is a little compartment where conditions are perfect for the chemistry of life to happen. But how does a cell know what to do? Every living cell—no matter whether it belongs to an ant or an axolotl, a tree or a toadstool—contains a chemical called **DNA. Molecules** of DNA are incredibly long, and spend most of their time coiled up tightly so they don't get damaged. When DNA is uncoiled, it's possible to see that it's made up of smaller units called bases linked together in long chains—a bit like beads on a necklace. There are only four types of bases, but they can be linked together in an infinite number of ways.

Cells can unravel the DNA inside them and read the exact order of the bases. The sequences they find act as coded instructions that guide the work of the cell. Together, all the instructions carried on the DNA of a living thing are known as its genome.

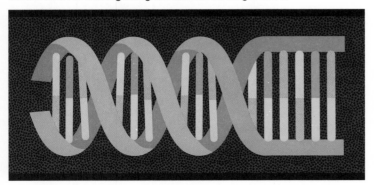

Genomes are often enormous. The human genome is made up of 6.4 billion bases. If this sequence of bases was written out on paper, it would fill at least 100 books of this size! Each of your tiny cells has a copy of your entire genome, but they don't read the whole thing and follow all the instructions at once. They only use the genes they need at the time. A gene is a short section of DNA, which tells a cell how to assemble a particular protein. Proteins are complex molecules that are the main building blocks of cells. **Proteins** also carry out jobs inside cells. For example, a protein called hemoglobin is made by your red blood cells. It can grab ahold of oxygen atoms and carry them to every part of your body in your blood.

All humans have a similar set of around 20,000 protein-coding genes. Other species have a different mix of genes. Their **genomes** may include some of the genes found in the human genome, but also lots of genes that code for unique proteins, such as the toxic proteins in a scorpion's venom, or the "antifreeze" proteins that stop the blood of Antarctic fish from freezing solid.

By guiding the work of our cells, our genes cause us to grow into humans, rather than scorpions or fish. Other creatures have a different mixture of genes in their genomes.

PASSING ON GENES

Living things get their genes from their parents and earlier ancestors. This means comparing genomes is a good way to reconstruct the family tree of life. The more genes two living things share, the more closely related they are likely to be.

For example, almost 99% of human genes are also found in the genomes of chimpanzees and bonobos, which tells us that all three species share a recent **common ancestor**. This does not mean that chimpanzees and bonobos are human ancestors. It means that if you trace the human family tree and the chimpanzee family tree back far enough (6 to 8 million years), the branches eventually merge together. The place where they join represents an animal that was the ancestor of all of today's chimps *and* all of today's humans. This ancient ancestor is now **extinct**.

The instructions carried on DNA explain why a living thing looks and acts in a certain way. But this raises another puzzling question. If living things inherit their genes from their ancestors, why are there so many different species?

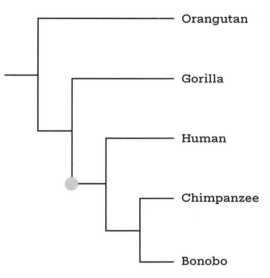

Orangutan

Gorilla

Human

Chimpanzee

Bonobo

The evolutionary tree for the great ape family of primates shows that chimpanzees and bonobos are more closely related to humans than to gorillas or orangutans. The yellow dot is the common ancestor of today's chimpanzee, bonobo, and human species.

WHY ARE THERE SO MANY DIFFERENT SPECIES?

Over time, groups of living things change as they become better suited to their surroundings. This process is known as evolution. The theory of natural selection explains how **evolution** happens and why new species appear.

HOW NATURAL SELECTION WORKS

As living things compete for the things they need, such as food, air, and water, creatures that happen to be better suited to their **habitat** are more likely to survive. When they reproduce, they pass on the features that helped them survive — so the next generation will have a slightly different mixture of genes from their parents' generation. Little by little, the typical characteristics of the population change. Over time, they may become so different from their ancestors that they count as a different species. Every living creature's genome is a mixture of genes they have inherited from ancestors, and unique genes that have arisen and been shaped in the course of millions of years of evolution.

One reason, then, for the staggering number of species on Earth is that there are so many different habitats—from vast rain forests to the underside of a single leaf, from a drop of water to the surface of your teeth. As creatures adapted to these different habitats over billions of years, millions of new species have evolved. Life continues to evolve as habitats change.

EARTH'S BIOMES

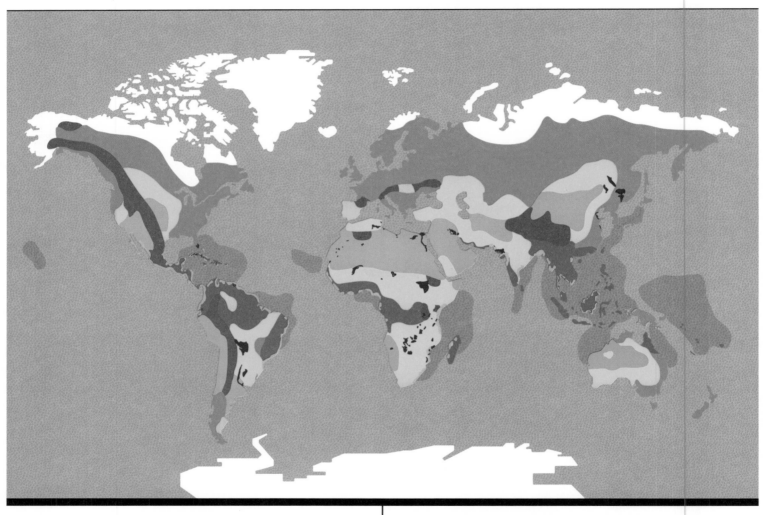

Oceans
Wetlands
Temperate forests
Tropical forests
Mountains
Grasslands
Deserts
Polar regions
Mangroves
Coral reefs

Earth is a planet of many different habitats and microhabitats. This variety of living conditions helps to explain the variety of life on Earth, as creatures have evolved different features to help them survive in very different habitats. The communities of living things found in each major habitat are known as biomes.

FROM GENES TO THE TREE OF LIFE

In the 6 to 8 million years since the common ancestor of chimpanzees and humans was alive, both human and chimpanzee DNA has continued to change, little by little, with each generation. A difference of a few percent does not sound like much, but genomes are so huge that this adds up to around 35 million differences. The same genes may also be used in different ways by the cells of humans and chimpanzees, explaining all the differences we see in our bodies, brains, and behaviors.

Scientists have also known for a long time that bacteria can cheat when it comes to the rules of inheritance by simply sharing useful genes with each other. There are even signs that certain genes have jumped from microbes to animals in the past. After a microbe's gene has inserted itself into an animal's genome, it gets inherited by all those animal's ancestors. At least 145 of our genes originally evolved in bacteria, archaea, or other microbes, and now guide our cells to do all kinds of useful things.

The genomes of today's species still carry genes inherited from the most distant ancestors. By comparing the genomes of different living things, we can find clues that help us draw the tree of life on Earth—a family tree that stretches back at least 3.7 billion years. Exploring the tree of life is the first step toward understanding **biodiversity**, the great variety of life on Earth. It is also the first step toward protecting it.

BIODIVERSITY AT RISK

Earth's dazzling **biodiversity** has taken billions of years to evolve. Sadly, it can disappear far more quickly. Species do disappear naturally as habitats change. This is why you see birds and not their dinosaur ancestors in today's parks and gardens. However, over the last 200 years, scientists have recorded far more extinctions than we would naturally expect. The most likely cause is human activities. Climate change, pollution, farming, and building are changing habitats faster than creatures can adapt. Many habitats are being destroyed altogether. Scientists have estimated that more than a million species are at risk of dying out.

Each living species is like a leaf on the tree of life. It may be a small part of the whole, but together it's the leaves that allow the tree to survive. The loss of biodiversity is a warning. It tells us that we must work harder to live in harmony with the rest of nature. Even small actions can make a big difference to Earth's living things. We are all unique. We are all important. We are all part of the same family tree.

Understanding evolution and the tree of life helps us understand why and how the natural world changes over time. It helps us understand how we got here, and our connection to every other living thing.

Look around and the planet appears crowded with life—but we can only see a fraction of its living things!

With the naked eye, we can see individual creatures bigger than half a micrometer—or half the width of a typical human hair. Most living things are far smaller than this and can only be seen with the help of a microscope. The smallest living thing found so far is Nanoarchaeum, measuring just 400 nanometers across. This is tinier than a typical speck of dust.

At the other end of the scale is the world's largest living thing—a honey fungus that has spread more than more than 5 kilometers (3 miles) through the soil. That's an amazing 12 billion times larger than Nanoarchaeum!

You can use this scale to compare the sizes of other living things in this book. It is a logarithmic scale, which means that instead of increasing in equal steps, each new measurement is ten times bigger than the last. This is the best way to fit a huge range of sizes on one chart.

1 kilometer (km) = 1,000 meters (m)
1 meter (m) = 1,000 millimeters (mm)
1 millimeter (mm) = 1,000 micrometers (μm)
1 micrometer (μm) = 1,000 nanometers
1 nanometer (nm) = 1 billionth of a meter!

1 mile (mi) = 5280 feet (ft)
1 foot (ft) = 12 inches (in)
1 inch (in) = 25400 nanometers (nm)

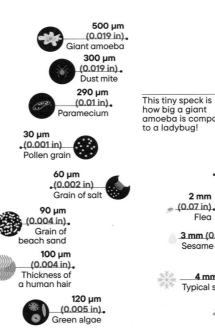
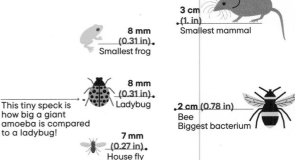
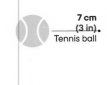

500 μm (0.019 in) Giant amoeba

300 μm (0.019 in) Dust mite

290 μm (0.01 in) Paramecium

This tiny speck is how big a giant amoeba is compared to a ladybug!

8 mm (0.31 in) Smallest frog

8 mm (0.31 in) Ladybug

7 mm (0.27 in) House fly

3 cm (1. in) Smallest mammal

2 cm (0.78 in) Bee Biggest bacterium

10 μm (0.000 4in) Human red blood cells Drops of snot when someone sneezes

500 nm Speck of dust

400 nm Nanoarchaeum (smallest living thing)

9 μm (0.0003 in) Myxozoans (smallest known animals)

30 μm (0.001 in) Pollen grain

60 μm (0.002 in) Grain of salt

90 μm (0.004 in) Grain of beach sand

2 mm (0.07 in) Wolffia (smallest flowering plant)

2 mm (0.07 in) Flea

7 cm (3 in) Tennis ball

10 nm Prion

.2 nm Width of DNA strand

100 nm Flu virus Corona virus

2.5 μm E. coli bacterium

100 μm (0.004 in) Thickness of a human hair

3 mm (0.11 in) Sesame seed

4 mm (0.15 in) Ant

10 cm (4 in) Apple

1 nm Fingernails grow 1nm per second!

45 nm Zika virus

5 μm (0.0001 in) Yeast

120 μm (0.005 in) Green algae

4 mm (0.15 in) Typical snowflake

5 mm (0.2 in) Mosquito

1 nanometer (nm)　10 nm　100 nm　1 micrometer (μm) (1,000 nm)　10 μm　100 μm　1 millimeter (mm) (1,000 μm)　10 mm (1 cm)　1 inch　100 (10

need an electron microscope to see

can be seen (better) with a light microscope

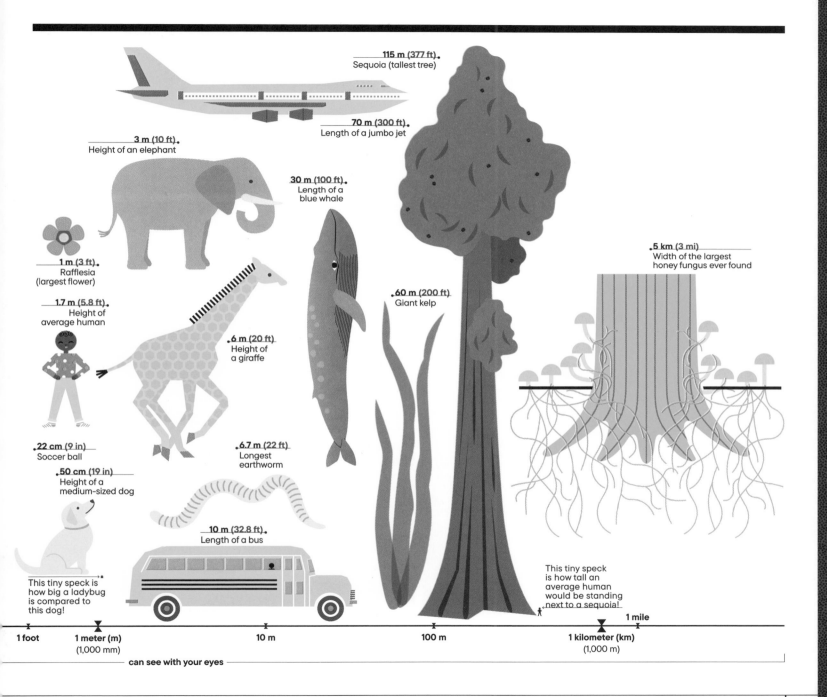

115 m (377 ft)
Sequoia (tallest tree)

70 m (300 ft)
Length of a jumbo jet

3 m (10 ft)
Height of an elephant

30 m (100 ft)
Length of a
blue whale

1 m (3 ft)
Rafflesia
(largest flower)

5 km (3 mi)
Width of the largest
honey fungus ever found

1.7 m (5.8 ft)
Height of
average human

60 m (200 ft)
Giant kelp

6 m (20 ft)
Height of
a giraffe

22 cm (9 in)
Soccer ball

6.7 m (22 ft)
Longest
earthworm

50 cm (19 in)
Height of a
medium-sized dog

10 m (32.8 ft)
Length of a bus

This tiny speck is
how big a ladybug
is compared to
this dog!

This tiny speck
is how tall an
average human
would be standing
next to a sequoia!

1 mile

1 foot	1 meter (m)	10 m	100 m	1 kilometer (km)
	(1,000 mm)			(1,000 m)

can see with your eyes

Fossils helped scientists realize that all life on Earth is part of one big family tree. They noticed that the fossils of extinct creatures shared some features of today's living things. This was important evidence for evolution, the process by which species change over time, some becoming extinct, while others appear.

Today's biologists use all kinds of different evidence to build accurate trees of life, but fossils are still important for working out which extinct creatures belong in each **clade**, and when and how different branches on the tree split from one another. We can only see the leaves of the tree, the species that are alive today, but fossils help us peer back in time to glimpse the boughs, branches, and trunk.

This timeline shows the age of the oldest fossil from some of the groups of living things featured in this book. Fossils help scientists figure out roughly how long members of each group have been roaming Earth. They are not a perfect guide, because the fossil record is incomplete. Soft and squishy creatures do not form fossils as easily as animals with hard shells or skeletons, and we can only look at the fossils that have been found. New fossils are discovered all the time, so the evidence can change quickly.

The creature that all living things are descended from is known as the Last Universal Common Ancestor (LUCA). We do not have a fossil for this creature, but it is thought to have been a single cell that lived around 4.5 billion years ago. Around 3.5 billion years ago, the bacteria and archaea branches of the tree of life split from each other. Around 1.8 billion years ago, the first eukaryote appeared.

A history of 4.5 billion years is very hard to imagine, because our brains are so used to thinking in human timescales. We can make it easier by comparing the entire history of life on Earth to a single 12-hour day. If Earth formed at midnight on this clock, each tick of the second hand is roughly 100,000 years. The oldest fossils ever found date from around half past two. The first animals appeared around two and a half hours ago. Modern humans have only been around for the last 3 seconds!

CYANOBACTERIA
3.7–3.5 bya

RED ALGAE
1.6–1.25 bya

CNIDARIANS
680 mya

SEGMENTED WORMS
560 mya

ARTHROPODS
540 mya

BIVALVES
530 mya

CEPHALOPODS
505 mya

CARTILAGINOUS FISH
455 mya

ARACHNIDS
437 mya

INSECTS
438 mya

FERNS
354 mya

PINOPHYTES
310 mya

LISSAMPHIBIA
250 mya

FLOWERING PLANTS
164 mya

MARSUPIALS
125 mya

PRIMATES
66 mya

RODENTS
56 mya

MODERN HUMANS
300,000 years ago

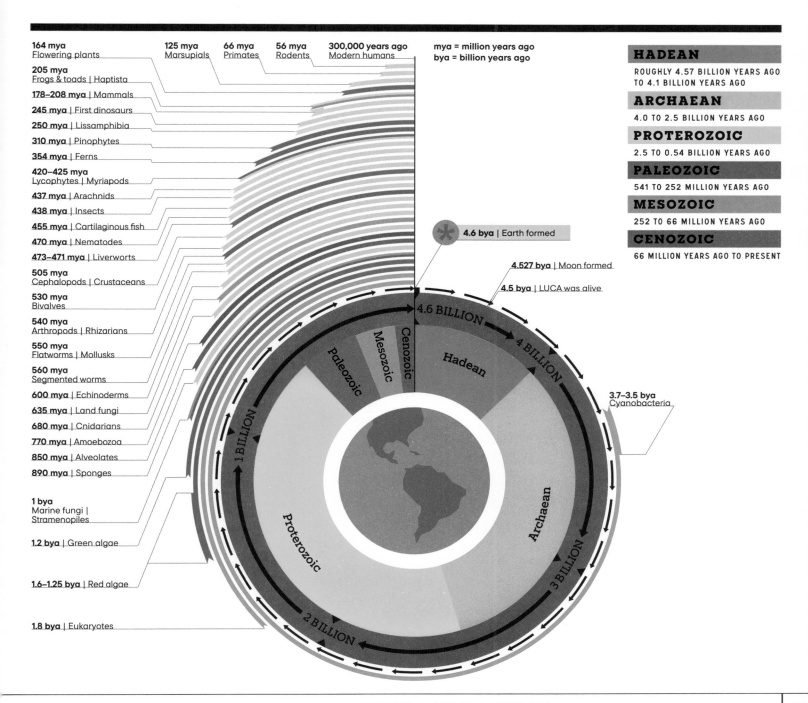

164 mya
Flowering plants

125 mya
Marsupials

66 mya
Primates

56 mya
Rodents

300,000 years ago
Modern humans

mya = million years ago
bya = billion years ago

205 mya
Frogs & toads | Haptista

178–208 mya | Mammals

245 mya | First dinosaurs

250 mya | Lissamphibia

310 mya | Pinophytes

354 mya | Ferns

420–425 mya
Lycophytes | Myriapods

437 mya | Arachnids

438 mya | Insects

455 mya | Cartilaginous fish

470 mya | Nematodes

473–471 mya | Liverworts

505 mya
Cephalopods | Crustaceans

530 mya
Bivalves

540 mya
Arthropods | Rhizarians

550 mya
Flatworms | Mollusks

560 mya
Segmented worms

600 mya | Echinoderms

635 mya | Land fungi

680 mya | Cnidarians

770 mya | Amoebozoa

850 mya | Alveolates

890 mya | Sponges

1 bya
Marine fungi |
Stramenopiles

1.2 bya | Green algae

1.6–1.25 bya | Red algae

1.8 bya | Eukaryotes

4.6 bya | Earth formed

4.527 bya | Moon formed

4.5 bya | LUCA was alive

3.7–3.5 bya
Cyanobacteria

HADEAN
ROUGHLY 4.57 BILLION YEARS AGO
TO 4.1 BILLION YEARS AGO

ARCHAEAN
4.0 TO 2.5 BILLION YEARS AGO

PROTEROZOIC
2.5 TO 0.54 BILLION YEARS AGO

PALEOZOIC
541 TO 252 MILLION YEARS AGO

MESOZOIC
252 TO 66 MILLION YEARS AGO

CENOZOIC
66 MILLION YEARS AGO TO PRESENT

GLOSSARY

acidification: Making something more acidic, such as the ocean.

alkaloid: Set of chemicals made by plants that affect the way human cells work.

antibiotic: A medicine such as penicillin, which harms or destroys bacteria.

antimicrobial: Harms or destroys microbes.

appendage: Part of an animal that sticks out from the main body, such as an arm, leg, or pincer.

bilatera: A clade of animals that have one line of symmetry.

biodiversity: The variety of life in a particular place.

biofilm: Thin but tough layer of microbes living on a surface.

bioluminescent: When a living thing makes its own light using chemical reactions.

biomass: The total mass or weight of the living things in a particular place.

carbon cycle: The process by which carbon is changed into different forms, sometimes being part of living things and sometimes part of the environment.

carbon dioxide: Gas needed by plants and algae for photosynthesis and given out by most living things during respiration.

cell: The smallest working part of a living thing.

cellulose: A tough substance found in the cell walls of plants, which does not dissolve in water.

chlorophyll: Green pigment found in all plants and algae, as well as cyanobacteria. Absorbs all colors of light except green, to power photosynthesis.

cilia: Short, hairlike structures on the surface of some cells. The cell uses them to move itself, or other objects, around.

circulatory system: Set of tissues and organs that move blood or other fluids through a creature's body.

clade: Group of living things that includes all the descendants of a common ancestor.

classification: Sorting living things into groups based on some shared feature or features.

cocci: A word used to describe bacteria and archaea that are shaped like spheres.

collagen: Protein that is an important building block of animal bodies.

colonize: Begin living and reproducing in a place.

common ancestor: An ancestor that two or more species have in common.

cuticle: The tough outer covering of a plant or animal cell, made by the cell itself.

decay: When something that was once alive breaks down, rots, or decomposes over time, in a way that returns its building blocks to the environment so they can be used by new life.

detritivore: Animal that feeds on dead plants or animals.

DNA: Stands for deoxyribonucleic acid, a chemical with large molecules that is found in almost every living cell, and which carries the coded information that tells each cell how to work.

ecosystem: A community of living things that depend on each other and their environment in many ways.

ecosystem niche: How a living thing goes about getting everything it needs to survive in a certain habitat, and the role it plays in its ecosystem as a result.

embryo: The offspring of certain plants and animals, at an early stage of their development.

enzyme: A protein that acts as a natural catalyst, starting, speeding up, or carrying out chemical reactions in living things.

epiphyte: A plant that grows on another plant, usually without harming the host.

evolution: Process by which populations of living things change over time, and new species develop from earlier ones.

excretory system: Tissues and organs involved in getting rid of waste produced by a living thing.

exoskeleton: Stiff outer body covering of certain animals.

extinct: When a species that once existed has no remaining living members.

flagella: Thin, thread-like structures sticking out from the surface of certain cells; they may look like tiny tails and can often help the cell to swim or move around. Many protozoans and some bacteria have flagella. Some sperm cells have a flagellum.

fossil fuel: Fossilized remains of ancient living things, burned to release the energy trapped inside.

genome: The complete genetic information of a living thing.

germinate: When a seed or spore begins to grow into a new living thing.

gland: Part of an animal's body that makes and releases certain substances.

Gram (negative or positive): Description of the results of a test used to quickly identify different groups of bacteria, by staining them with dyes and looking at their colour under a microscope.

habitat: Natural home of a living thing.

hummock: Small hump in a marsh or on a forest floor.

hydrothermal vent: Place where heated water escapes from Earth's crust.

hyphae: Branching thread-like filaments produced by a fungus; a bit like tiny roots.

immune system: Organs, tissues, and processes inside a living thing that help to defend it from infections and toxins.

invertebrates: Animals without vertebrae, i.e. without an inner skeleton and backbone.

larvae: Young form of an animal, which will change in significant ways as it develops into an adult. A caterpillar is the larva of a butterfly.

mammary gland: Gland found in female mammals, which produces milk.

medusa: A stage in the life cycle of cnidarians; also, another name for a jellyfish.

metabolism: The processes, such as chemical reactions, that happen inside a living thing so that it can live, such as releasing energy stored in food.

metamorphosis: The process by which a young, immature animal changes into its adult form.

microbe: A tiny living thing that can only be seen under a microscope, such as a bacterium, a single-celled fungus, or a protozoan.

microbiome: Community of microbes living in and on a larger living thing. Even microbes can have their own microbiome!

mineral: Nonliving substance found in nature, made from a particular set of elements. Living things need to absorb or ingest certain minerals to survive.

model organism: Nonhuman species that are used by scientists to help understand some aspect of human biology.

molecule: The smallest piece of a pure compound, made up of two or more atoms bonded together. For example, a molecule of carbon dioxide is made from two oxygen atoms bonded to one carbon atom. DNA has some of the most complex molecules, each made up of billions of atoms.

naturalist: Person who sets out to learn about nature, often by observing it closely.

nitrifying: Able to convert nitrogen into forms that can be used by living things.

nitrogen: A chemical element that is an essential building block of proteins, and therefore of all living things.

nodule: Small swelling on plant roots.

Northern Hemisphere: The half of the world from the Equator to the North Pole.

nutrient: A substance needed by a living thing for living and growing.

parasite: A thing living in or on another species when the parasite benefits but the host (the species it is living on) does not.

pathogen: A microbe that can cause disease in another living thing.

pH: The pH scale measures how acid or alkaline something is. An acidic substance has a pH less than 7. An alkaline substance has a pH greater than 7.

photosynthesis: The process by which plants and certain microbes convert carbon dioxide and water into food, using energy from sunlight.

phylogenetic: A word to describe evolutionary relationships between living things, which have been figured out by comparing DNA and other molecules.

pigment: A chemical that has a certain color because it absorbs other colors of light.

protein: A complex molecule made by a living thing, which does certain jobs inside that living thing.

rhizoid: A thin "hair" sticking out from on a plant's root, which may be part of a fungus living in the root or part of the plant itself. Rhizoids help to collect water and anchor the plant in the soil.

ruminant: An animal that regurgitates plant food and chews it for a second time to help with digestion.

scavenger: Living thing that mainly eats dead or rotting plants or animals, rather than eating things that are alive.

sediment: Tiny pieces of sand, silt, or another substance.

sepal: The outer part of a flower, which protects the other parts as they develop.

sexual reproduction: When a species reproduces by combining genetic information from two parents of different sexes.

Southern Hemisphere: The half of the world from the Equator to the South Pole.

species: Group of living things that are so similar, they can reproduce or share genetic information in a different way.

spores: Tiny single cells made and released by fungi, some plants, and protozoans, for reproduction.

sterilize: Kill any microbes or destroy any toxins that might be lurking.

sulfur: A chemical element that is an essential building block of all living things.

symbiosis: When two or more species live closely together, in a way that benefits both.

temperate: An area or climate that gets mild temperatures all year-round.

tissue: A certain type of material formed by an animal or plant, made up of cells that specialize in a certain job or jobs.

toxin: A substance made by a living thing, which can poison other living things.

FIND OUT MORE

Thousands of sources were consulted to write and illustrate this book. It is impossible to list them all here, but the author recommends the following books and websites to readers who would like to keep on exploring the tree of life!

BOOKS

- *Consider the Platypus: Evolution through Biology's Most Baffling Beasts* by Maggie Ryan Sandford and Rodica Prato (Black Dog & Leventhal, 2019).
- *One Million Insects* by Isabel Thomas and Lou Baker Smith (Welbeck Editions, 2021) delves into the biggest single branch of the tree of life.
- *The Tree of Life: A Phylogenetic Classification* by Guillaume Lecointre, Dominique Visset, and Hervé Le Guyader (Harvard University Press, 2007) is one of the best academic guides to modern classification.
- *What is Life? Understand Biology in Five Steps* by Paul Nurse (David Fickling Books, 2020).

WEBSITES

- The Darwin Tree of Life project plans to read the genomes of all living things in the UK, as part of the global Earth Biogenome Project. You can find out more, follow their work, and even get involved here. https://www.darwintreeoflife.org/
- The OneZoom tree of life explorer is an interactive map of the connections between all living things. You can start at the origin of life and clamber through the whole tree or zoom in to find out which branches your favorite creatures are found on. http://www.onezoom.org/
- The Linnean Society has learning resources for budding naturalists. https://www.linnean.org/learning
- The Encyclopedia of Life is an online bank of knowledge about life on Earth, with vast resources to explore. https://eol.org/
- The Natural History Museum has lots to discover online as well as in its museums. https://www.nhm.ac.uk/discover.html
- The Smithsonian National Museum of Natural History also has fantastic online resources. https://naturalhistory.si.edu/education
- Nikon's Universcale lets you compare the sizes of living things and other objects in the universe. https://www.nikon.com/about/sp/universcale/scale.htm#

INDEX

Thank you to the amazing creative and editorial team behind this book, Sara Gillingham, Maya Gartner, Meagan Bennett, and Robin Pridy, for wrangling all this information and creating a thing of beauty.

Thank you to Dr. Jack Ashby of the Museum of Zoology at the University of Cambridge, for invaluable help in the early planning stages and sage advice not to try to include everything! Thank you to our expert readers Charlotte Wright, Dr. Claudia Weber, Dr. Lewis Stevens, and Dr. Jessica Thomas Thorpe of the Wellcome Sanger Institute's Tree of Life Programme for sharing your scientific knowledge and eagle eyes. And a special thank-you to Jack Monaghan for involving me in the brilliant Darwin Tree of Life School Fly Trap project (www.darwintreeoflife.org).

I was very grateful to receive an Authors' Foundation Grant from the Society of Authors, to help fund the months of research that went into writing this book.

I am also grateful to the people who passed on to me their enthusiasm for the study of biodiversity while I was a human sciences student, in particular Dr. Joy Boyce and Dr. George McGavin. I hope that this book will do the same for its readers.

— Isabel Thomas

Special thanks to Isabel Thomas for your wise guidance on the visuals in this book, and the passion in your words, so full of life; to Maya Gartner for more kindness, support, and vision than any illustrator could ever hope for; to Meagan Bennett for the lavishly thoughtful and exquisite art direction and design, and Michelle Clement and Nora Aoyagi for your brilliant production assistance and support.

— Sara Gillingham

Phaidon Press Inc.
65 Bleecker Street
New York, NY 10012

phaidon.com

© 2022 Phaidon Press Limited
Text © 2022 Isabel Thomas
Illustrations © 2022 Sara Gillingham

Text set in TT Commons Pro, Elizeth & Signal No1 D
IBSN 978 1 83866 536 4 (US edition)
Printer code 004-0722

Designed by Meagan Bennett
Edited by Maya Gartner
Production by Rebecca Price

Printed in China